Joseph Jones, M.D.

James O. Breeden

Joseph Jones, M.D.
Scientist of the Old South

The University Press of Kentucky

Publication of this book was assisted
by the American Council of Learned Societies
under a grant from the Andrew W. Mellon Foundation.

ISBN: 0–8131–1296–6

Library of Congress Catalog Card Number: 73–80462

A statewide cooperative scholarly publishing agency
serving Berea College, Centre College of Kentucky,
Eastern Kentucky University, Georgetown College,
Kentucky Historical Society, Kentucky State University,
Morehead State University, Murray State University,
Northern Kentucky State College, Transylvania University,
University of Kentucky, University of Louisville, and
Western Kentucky University.

Editorial and Sales Offices: Lexington, Kentucky 40506

To Dr. Stanhope Bayne-Jones

Contents

Illustrations follow page 156

Preface

This book attempts to recount and to interpret the Old South career of Dr. Joseph Jones, an important member of the antebellum southern scientific community. Although he is little known in the history of American science today, Jones's interests were many and his accomplishments praiseworthy. He was, at the same time, a teacher, both a natural and a research scientist, an expert on southern diseases, and a scientific writer. His masterful studies of the Confederacy's chief medical problems were his greatest achievement. My account of Jones's career in the New South is in preparation.

There was no shortage of material for this study. Indeed, in addition to an impressive array of important secondary sources, a surprisingly large amount of material of a primary nature, both manuscript and printed, pertaining to Joseph Jones has been preserved. Five major collections of the various members of the Jones family exist: the Joseph Jones collections at Tulane University in New Orleans and at Louisiana State University at Baton Rouge; the Charles Colcock Jones Papers at Tulane University; and the Charles Colcock Jones, Jr., collections at the University of Georgia in Athens and at Duke University in Durham. Printed primary material ranges from the numerous published writings of Joseph Jones (his monumental three-volume *Medical and Surgical Memoirs* in particular) to those of his father, brother, and other family members, and to several important official government publications. These first-hand accounts, especially the manuscript material, are delightfully rich in language and content, so rich in fact that a special effort was made to allow the leading figures in this study to speak for themselves—idiosyncracies of spelling and all.

There are many people to whom I am indebted. Chief among them are Dr. John Duffy, now of the University of Maryland, and the late Dr. Stanhope Bayne-Jones, to whom this volume is dedicated. The former not only patiently guided me in the preparation of this study in its earliest stages while I was a graduate student at Tulane University but also cheerfully read the revised manuscript, offering many suggestions for improvement. The latter was responsible for putting together the Joseph Jones Collection at Tulane University, the largest and most important single source for a study of Jones's life. Dr. Bayne-Jones, a noted medical scientist in his own right, was a grandson of Joseph Jones and assembled this material in the hope of writing a biography of his eminent forebear, only to have his plans thwarted by a busy professional life. He enthusiastically endorsed my undertaking of this project and was a constant source of encouragement until his death at the age of eighty-one in 1970. The late William R. Hogan of Tulane University also deserves a large measure of gratitude both for introducing me to the study of the history of medicine and for steering me toward Joseph Jones.

Others to whom I wish to express my indebtedness include the Eugenie and Joseph Jones Family Foundation (Merrick Jones and George Denègre in particular) for its support and encouragement; the American Council of Learned Societies for underwriting the cost of publication; the editors of the *Journal of Southern History*, the *Bulletin of the History of Medicine*, the *Georgia Historical Quarterly*, and the *Magazine of Albemarle County History* for their kind permission to include in this study material which formerly appeared in their journals; and the library staffs at Tulane University, Louisiana State University at Baton Rouge, University of Georgia, Duke University, the National Archives, and the National Library of Medicine for their valuable assistance. Finally, I fondly acknowledge a special debt to Lee, my valued editorial critic and devoted wife.

Prologue

The Old South is not remembered for the pursuit of science. In the 1820s and early 1830s science had found an encouraging environment in the South, but mounting sectional tension changed this. As this section steadily broke with the rest of the nation during the three turbulent decades preceding the Civil War the southern mind was increasingly dominated by proslavery sentiments, romanticism, and religious orthodoxy, all of which severely inhibited the critical mind and intellectual curiosity vital to scientific inquiry. With the decline of free thinking there developed a cultural climate distinctly unfavorable to the pursuit of science.[1]

But scientific interests did not die out in the Old South. On the contrary the full spectrum of scientists was found here: there were amateur scientists and professional scientists, physical scientists and biological scientists, pure scientists and applied scientists. Undeniably they lagged behind their counterparts in the North, but when the adverse cultural climate in which they labored is taken into account, the antebellum southern scientists made a creditable, perhaps even an enviable, showing. Indeed a few of them—Matthew Fontaine Maury and William Barton Rogers, for example—were first-rate, and numerous others—men like John Bachman, Josiah Nott, and Joseph LeConte—were nationally and often internationally known.[2]

Yet the Old South's scientists have received little attention from historians. Joseph Jones is but one of many cases in point. Although virtually unknown outside a small circle of scholars, Jones was in reality one of the antebellum South's leading scientific investigators. In a life dedicated to research and teaching his accomplishments were many.

The descendant of a prominent family, Jones was born in Liberty County, Georgia, on September 6, 1833. The youngest son of Charles Colcock Jones, a prominent planter and one of the Old South's foremost ministers to the slaves, he was the brother of Charles Colcock Jones, Jr., a distinguished lawyer and historian. After having been graduated from Princeton in 1853,

Jones enrolled in the medical department of the University of Pennsylvania and received his M.D. degree three years later. He developed a seemingly insatiable interest in scientific research during his professional training and upon his return home decided to pursue a career in teaching, believing that it would afford him the best opportunity to continue his investigations. Subsequently Jones taught chemistry at the Savannah Medical College, natural science at the University of Georgia in Athens, and chemistry and pharmacy at the Medical College of Georgia in Augusta. By the time of the outbreak of the Civil War he had become a respected teacher, an important southern natural scientist, a leader in the movement to raise the standard of medical education, an expert on southern diseases (especially the various fevers that preyed upon the nineteenth-century South), and an accomplished scientific writer. His articles appeared in the leading medical publications of the day, including the *American Journal of the Medical Sciences,* the *Southern Medical and Surgical Journal,* and the *Transactions of the American Medical Association.*

Jones's greatest achievement was his remarkable Civil War medical investigations. At first, however, he succumbed to the emotional patriotism that characterized the South in the early days of the war and put aside his medical training to enlist as a private in the Liberty Independent Troop. He soon realized the folly of this act and at the end of his six-month enlistment accepted a Confederate commission as surgeon with the rank of major, a position he held until the end of the war. He came to view the hostilities as a giant laboratory in which to learn valuable lessons for peacetime purposes, and instead of becoming a combat surgeon he prevailed upon Surgeon General Samuel Preston Moore to allow him to visit and to conduct investigations in the armies, hospitals, and military prisons of the Confederacy. Subsequently he investigated medical problems in the armies of Northern Virginia and Tennessee; in the large hospitals at Richmond, Charlottesville, Charleston, Savannah, Augusta, Macon, and Atlanta; and in the main southern prisoner of war camp at Andersonville, Georgia.

Despite wartime conditions Jones was able to undertake detailed studies of such diseases as tetanus, gangrene, typhoid fever, malaria, smallpox, scurvy, diarrhea, dysentery, and pneumonia. An avid microscopist, he saw the bacilli of gangrene and typhoid fever but, bound to the contemporary miasmatic theory of disease, failed to see their causal relationship to these disorders. At Andersonville he instituted a series of postmortem examinations with the intention of clarifying the pathology of prevailing diseases. His knowledge of the filth and misery there qualified him in 1865 to be an important, if reluctant, witness at the trial of Captain Henry Wirz, the commandant of Andersonville.

To date only three studies of Joseph Jones have appeared and these are far from thorough. The first was written in 1942 by Joseph Krafka, Jr., for the *Journal of the Medical Association of Georgia;* the second, a 1958 study by Jones's grandson, Dr. Stanhope Bayne-Jones, was published in the *Bulletin of the Tulane University Medical Faculty;* and the latest, a 1960 article by Harris D. Riley, appeared in the *Journal of the Tennessee State Medical Association.*[3] More recently Robert Manson Myers's *Children of Pride,* a monumental edition of the Jones family correspondence on the eve of and during the Civil War, pays distressingly little attention to Joseph Jones, largely because Myers failed to make use of the two sizable collections of Jones's papers available to the scholar. Like many of his contemporaries in the southern scientific community, Joseph Jones deserves a full-scale biography. This study details and analyzes his Old South career.

Joseph Jones, M.D.

Chapter 1
Formative Years

No son could have had kinder or more indulgent
parents, or fuller opportunities for indulging
in those pastimes which a plantation life
afforded.

The diverse background of her founders has prompted E. Merton Coulter to label colonial Georgia "a sort of crossroads of the world."[1] Of the many groups who came, one of the most interesting was a band of New England Congregationalists who settled in the verdant, marshy coastal region between the Medway and and South Newport Rivers at the middle of the eighteenth century. This area has often been in the vanguard of Georgia's history. At the onset of hostilities with England, for example, the colonists here, well ahead of the rest of Georgia, enthusiastically embraced the American cause. As a reward for such exemplary courage the state legislature in 1777 combined the three small parishes of St. John, St. Andrew, and St. James to form Liberty County. Thus while the rest of the newly created counties— Wilkes, Richmond, Burke, Effingham, Chatham, Glynn, and Camden—honored the names of old friends of the colonies, Liberty proclaimed the patriotism of her citizens. From this cradle of Georgian independence have come many of the state's notable sons and daughters.[2] Joseph Jones was one of them.

Joseph Jones was descended from a prominent Georgian family founded by his great-grandfather, Major John Jones. Shortly before the Revolution John Jones left his native South Carolina for the rich coastal marshlands of Liberty County, where he soon became a prosperous planter-merchant. He wholeheartedly supported the break with England, a move which cost him dearly. During the British invasion of the Georgia coast in the winter of 1778–1779 his home, store, warehouses, and plantation were pillaged and many of his servants driven off, forcing him to move his family to the safety of South Carolina. Jones's personal loss further fired his already zealous devotion to the struggle for independence. Such unbridled patriotism did not go unnoticed, and he was soon appointed to the staff of Brigadier-General Lachlan McIntosh. Jones's military career ended tragically at Savannah on October 9, 1779, when he was struck down by cannon fire while leading an unsuccessful assault against the British lines.[3]

Despite his colorful life John Jones has been overshadowed by his grandson, Charles Colcock Jones, a wealthy planter and, paradoxically, one of the Old South's foremost ministers to the slaves. He was born December 20, 1804, to Captain John Jones and Susannah Girardeau at his father's Liberty County plantation. Young Charles, orphaned at five, was raised by his uncle, Captain Joseph Jones, "who ever sustained to him the relation of a father, and to whose influence, protection, and kindness he ever accorded the respect, obedience and affection of a son."[4]

Charles Colcock Jones began his education under the Reverend William McWhir in Liberty County's Sunbury Academy. At fourteen he entered a Savannah counting house. Six years later, a religious experience following on the heels of an almost fatal disease persuaded Jones to renounce his promising business career for an uncertain future in the Presbyterian ministry. But first he had to overcome the influence of Senator John Elliot, a family friend, who was urging Joseph Jones to send his nephew to the United States Military Academy. Young Charles, unyielding in his desire to enter the ministry, persisted and in 1825 was sent to Andover, Massachusetts, first to Phillips Academy and a year later to Andover Seminary.

Charles Colcock Jones left Andover after three and a half years in protest against what he felt was the school's antisouthern bias. He completed his theological education at Princeton, a school then noted for its indulgence toward the South. Upon graduation in September 1830 newly ordained as the Reverend Charles Colcock Jones, he returned home to marry his first cousin, Mary Sharpe Jones, and to begin his career in the ministry. He had vowed to minister solely to the slaves but found himself unable to live up to such a profound commitment when the time came to act. Subsequently he adopted a compromise position, preaching both to blacks and to whites. By the spring of 1831 Jones was devoting an ever-increasing amount of his time to slave religion.

For example, he helped organize the Association for the Religious Instruction of the Negroes in Liberty County and was designated one of its missionaries. But after serving in this capacity for only a few months he began to have renewed doubts. Still unable to commit himself to a life of ministering to the slaves, Charles Colcock Jones accepted a call from the First Presbyterian Church of Savannah.

Jones's interest in slave religion dated from his seminary days. He had come to believe that it was "unjust [and] contrary to nature & religion to hold men enslaved" but, reflecting his southern heritage, he questioned whether emancipation was in the best interests of the slaves and the South. Even if slavery was a necessary evil, it did not, he argued, relieve southerners of their responsibility for redeeming the lost souls of the slaves. By the time of his graduation Jones had fashioned what he considered to be a workable scheme—the establishment of a program of Negro religious training within the framework of the institution of slavery. He announced that upon his return to Georgia he intended "to introduce a system of religious instruction by word of mouth into our County, for our poor degraded slaves and . . . if the plan succeeds and God opens a door to me, to devote my life to missionary work among them."[5] This was the commitment which Jones had found so difficult to live up to. Eighteen months of soul-searching in Savannah convinced him that the cause of slave religion was both just and necessary. With a clear conscience at last he returned to Liberty County in December 1832 to resume his missionary activities.

There were no precedents to which the youthful missionary could look for guidance, and, finding himself confronted by suspicious and often hostile neighbors, he approached his duties with understandable caution. "This work," he later recalled, "was one of exceeding delicacy. A slight impropriety might ruin it, while on its success the spiritual welfare of multitudes might depend. The public was sensitive and tender. There were fears and there were objections. Some of them I heard expressed in no measured terms."[6] Indeed Jones's neighbors emphatically dismissed the necessity of preaching to the slaves, believing that no good would come of it and that the Negroes were doing well enough without religious training. Their concern, a product of the South's nearly paranoid fear of slave revolts, is understandable. Most feared that permitting large assemblages of slaves on the sabbath with no control other than the personal influence of the missionary would inevitably lead to rioting and insubordination, that so much attention would make the Negroes unruly and unprofitable, and that they would be constantly carrying outrageous tales of mistreatment and overwork to the missionary. Particularly disturbing to Jones was the inference that his ministry was some sort of abolitionist movement which would open the door to all manner of improper teachers and ultimately lead to the ruin of the country.

Charles Colcock Jones worked diligently to allay the fears of his neighbors. At every opportunity he stressed that he was not launching an attack on slavery. On the contrary, he argued, the gospel would do more to instill obedience in slaves and to maintain peace in the community than the use of force. Pointing to Nat Turner's Rebellion (in Southampton County, Virginia, August 13–23, 1831), Jones warned that leaving Negroes in ignorance and superstition was the surest way to breed insubordination. On the other hand, he observed, few slaves well instructed in the Christian religion and taken into the white man's churches had ever been found guilty of taking part in servile insurrections.[7] Jones's persistent pleas won him enough support to begin his ministry, but years were to pass before all prejudice and fear disappeared.

With a single two-year break Charles Colcock Jones continuously served the Negroes of Liberty County from December 1832 until December 1847. In 1837, at the repeated urging of the Synod of South Carolina and Georgia, he put aside his missionary duties to accept the chair of church history and polity in the Presbyterian Theological Seminary at Columbia, South Carolina. He was back home after two years, explaining: "I have come to the conclusion, that it is my duty to return to my old field of labour; and my sincere hope is the blessing of God may be with me in the decision."[8]

Within less than a decade, in November 1847, Jones succumbed again to the advances of his synod and accepted a second appointment to the chair of church history and polity. The missionary phase of his ministry to the slaves was at an end. He utilized his final report to the Association for the Religious Instruction of Negroes in Liberty County to assess his accomplishments. "Without overstepping the bounds either of truth or modesty," Jones asserted with obvious pride, "it may be said, that the purposes contemplated in the beginning have been, to a gratifying measure, realized." He called attention to the noticeable improvement in the conduct of the slaves—runaways were almost unheard of and the patrol system had fallen into disuse. Jones was even more pleased with the moral elevation of the blacks, pointing proudly to the large number of Negroes brought into the churches of Liberty County.[9]

Charles Colcock Jones's untiring efforts in behalf of the Negroes of Liberty County brought him wide acclaim. Many, in both North and South, considered him the leading minister to the slaves, and his advice was frequently sought. In 1845, for example, he was summoned to Charleston to share his experiences with a committee composed of such leading South Carolinians as Robert B. Rhett, Joel R. Poinsett, and Robert W. Barnwell, who were interested in establishing a system of slave religion similar to the one in Liberty County.[10]

Jones held the chair of church history and polity until 1850, when he accepted the secretaryship of the Presbyterian Church's Board of Domestic Missions, necessitating a move to Philadelphia. The slavery question had already caused the Baptists and Methodists to divide along sectional lines and was a growing divisive factor among Presbyterians. Thus the election of Jones, a dedicated southerner, to this important post reflects the general esteem with which he and his ministry to the slaves were held by the church leaders. He thoroughly enjoyed his new duties and worked hard at them, but in 1853 a debilitating and ultimately fatal disease of the central nervous system forced his resignation. Jones returned to his beloved Liberty County, where, despite failing health, he undertook limited missionary work and began writing his *History of the Church of God during the Period of Revelation*, a labor of love based on his lectures in the Columbia Theological Seminary.[11]

Charles Colcock Jones's ministry to the slaves represents only one side of his life. He was also a prominent planter and devoted father. One of Liberty County's leading landholders, he successfully operated three sizable plantations. Two of these were seasonal homes, since, like most upper-class southerners living in the malarious regions of the lower South, Jones believed it mandatory to maintain separate summer and winter residences. Monte Video, a 941-acre estate located a mile and a half below Riceboro at the head of tidewater on the North Newport River, was the winter home. It was the Jones family's favorite residence. "This precious home," Mary Jones wrote her daughter in 1863, "had always peculiar charms for me. Your beloved father often asked if I was conscious of always singing as I came in sight of the house."[12] Charles Colcock Jones had personally supervised its construction in an expansive grove of virgin oaks and had meticulously laid out its twenty- to thirty-acre lawn, "covered with live oak, magnolias, cedars, pines, and many other forest trees, arranged in groves or stretching out in lines and avenues or dotting the lawn here and there." The plantation gates lay a mile away at the end of a broad avenue which bisected this magnificent lawn.[13]

In late May or early June each year most planters residing in Georgia's coastal plain moved their families into the Piedmont to escape the heat of summer and the threat of malaria, but Maybank, the Jones family's summer home, was located on Colonel's Island, a small sea island lying between the larger St. Catherine's Island and the mainland. Colonel's Island had much to offer. Its dense vegetation, winding creeks, and salt marshes drastically limited the amount of arable land and therefore the number of inhabitants. Refreshing ocean breezes swept the island all day and far into the night. Most important, malaria, owing to the salt water marshes which did not support the disease-bearing *Anopheles* mosquito, was virtually nonexistent. Maybank consisted of 700 acres and was the smallest of Jones's plantations. The Jones family spent many happy moments here. "Some of the pleasantest recollections of youthful days," Charles Colcock Jones, Jr., reminisced in October 1857, "are connected with the first fall fires on the Island, shedding their cheerful rays around the parlor while the rude northeast wind came dashing its watery gusts against the windows."[14] Charles Colcock Jones kept his family on Colonel's Island until the first killing frost, usually about the last week in October, which was known to remove the threat of malaria.

The Jones family frequently spoke of Monte Video and Maybank—neither of which, although both were tastefully furnished, fit the stereotype of antebellum southern mansions. On the other hand not much is known about Jones's largest plantation, Arcadia, which encompassed 2,107 acres in the sparsely settled northwestern portion of Liberty County. Because of its isolated location the operation of Arcadia was left almost exclusively to an overseer. The Jones family seldom resided at Arcadia, although Charles and Mary Jones did seek refuge here during the Civil War when Union invasions of the Georgia coast seemed imminent.

Jones's plantations primarily produced staple crops. Cotton was grown at Arcadia and Maybank and cotton and rice at Monte Video. Sizable portions of each plantation, however, were reserved for the production of livestock, poultry, fruit, and vegetables for home consumption. Because of his time-consuming ministry and lengthy stays in Columbia and Philadelphia Jones was able to exercise only general supervision over his plantations. Day-to-day management was largely entrusted to hand-picked overseers and drivers.

Charles Colcock Jones's plantations were profitable, making him moderately wealthy. According to the censuses of 1850 and 1860 he was one of Liberty County's leading planters. This fact is nowhere more evident than in the size of his slave force. At the high point of his career as a planter Jones owned in excess of a hundred Negroes.[15]

These slaves were treated exceedingly well, for Jones regarded the taking advantage of slaves or the willful mistreatment of them as unconscionable. Further, he abhorred the selling of bondsmen and only engaged in this heinous practice as a last resort in cases of irrepressible misbehavior. In these rare instances he refused to break up a slave family, selling instead the entire household, no matter how large, to a handpicked buyer. During times of sickness he personally treated them or, if the case warranted it, summoned a physician. Upon learning of the death of a family favorite, he lamented: "A good servant is a blessing for which we should be thankful, as we are thankful for good children. We cannot but feel, and I have felt deeply, at their dying beds."[16] Jones's personal attachment to his slaves made him reluctant to leave them, and prior to each of his extended absences he painstakingly selected overseers who shared his liberal views on slave management. The slaves' response to such a paternalistic regime was overwhelmingly favorable, as evidenced by a lack of major disciplinary problems and few runaways.

Jones's paternalistic views on slavery were shared by his wife and children. Eager to assist him, they proved especially helpful in advancing the spiritual state of the Negroes on the Jones plantations. While Jones was making his sabbath rounds Mary

Jones and the children held Sunday school classes for the family servants. She instructed the adults, and the young Joneses taught the slave children. Play between the juvenile groups, however, was explicitly forbidden.

Charles Colcock Jones's ministry and plantations commanded the major part of his time, but not at the expense of his family. He was the proud father of three remarkable children. The eldest, Charles, Jr., who was to become a prominent lawyer and noted historian, was born in Savannah on October 28, 1831. Less than two years later, on September 6, 1833, Joseph, destined for fame as a physician, research scientist, and teacher, was born at Monte Video. The last child, and only daughter, was born at the home of relatives in Liberty County on June 6, 1835. Named Mary Sharpe after her mother, she was to become the wife of Robert Quarterman Mallard, a well-known nineteenth-century Presbyterian minister.[17]

These were fortunate children, incalculably benefitting from two indelible influences during their formative years—dedicated parents and one of the most unique societies in the Old South. Charles Colcock and Mary Jones did not pamper their children; rather they played a leading role in their development, instilling in them, through parental example, values in which they strongly believed. In social relations the young Joneses were taught the virtues of chivalrous manners, hospitality, a high sense of personal honor and duty, a sincere concern for the less fortunate, an eschewing of ostentation, and an elevated view of women. In religion they were indoctrinated with orthodox Calvinism. In politics they were imbued with the conservative philosophy of the Calhoun wing of the Democratic party, developing an unwavering support of the South on the question of slavery and the broader issue of southern rights.

This maturation process produced an extremely tight-knit family in which there was much mutual respect and an absence of internal tension. Its members thoroughly enjoyed one another's company. Family gatherings were anxiously anticipated and long savored in the recollection. As a married woman with children of her own Mary Sharpe still treasured the happy home life of her childhood. "What cold weather," she wrote her mother,

we have had for several days past! This early cold always carries me back to Maybank. *Well* do I remember the first fires that were kindled in the fall, and how we used to gather around the hearth—Father reading aloud, Mother knitting or sewing, Brother Charlie sitting upon the floor with a bunch of wire grass and ball of flax thread making mats with *Taddy* at his side (or else sinewing arrows), Brother Joe with his paint box and some megatherium skeleton model before him, and I think I used to make mittens or sew my hexagon quilt. Sometimes a hoarded stock of chinquapins would engage the attention of all the children, each one counting his store.

"We all have hearths of our own now," she concluded nostalgically, "but I do not think any of them will ever burn as brightly or possess the same attractions of that one at Maybank."[18]

Within this remarkable family Charles Colcock Jones was unquestionably viewed as the patriarch and was affectionately revered and obeyed. His advice was sought as a matter of course by his children, even into their adult lives. But it was indicative of the confiding fellowship existing between parent and child that Mary Jones was equally loved and respected. It is not surprising then that these youngsters developed a sense of appreciative indebtedness to their parents which they frequently and fondly acknowledged in later life. Joseph's parental homage as a young man is typical. "If I have any good principles," he apprised his father, "I owe them all, under Providence, to your's & mother's kind, laborious & self sacrificing efforts."[19]

Reinforcing and expanding parental example in shaping the character of the Jones youngsters was the society into which they were born. "Throughout the antebellum South," it has been pointed out in a recent study, the people of Liberty County "were justly known for their remarkable way of life. No planting community could boast of deeper religious convictions, higher intellectual cultivation, gentler social refinement, or greater material wealth."[20] The inhabitants of Liberty County also felt their society was unique. Their assessment of it was best expressed by Charles Colcock Jones, Jr., when he asserted:

> While there were few who could lay claim to large estates, the planters of this community were in comfortable circumstances. They were industrious, observant of their obligations, humane in the treatment of their servants, given to

hospitality, fond of manly exercise, and solicitous for the moral and intellectual education of their children. The traditions of the fathers gave birth to patriotic impulses and encouraged a high standard of honor, integrity, and manhood. The military spirit survived in the person of the Liberty Independent Troop; and on stated occasions contests involving rare excellence in horsemanship and in the use of the saber and pistol attracted the gaze of the public and won the approving smiles of noble women. Leisure hours were spent in hunting and fishing, and in social intercourse.

"Of litigation," he continued, "there was little. Misunderstandings, when they occurred, were usually accommodated by honorable arbitration. Personal responsibility, freely admitted, engendered mutual respect and a most commendable degree of manliness. The rules of morality and of the church were respected, acknowledged, and upheld. The community was well-ordered and prosperous, and the homes of the inhabitants were peaceful and happy. . . . Of all the political divisions of this commonwealth," he concluded, "none was more substantial, observant of law, or better instructed than the county of Liberty. Enviable was her position in the sisterhood of counties."[21] The youthful Joneses partook fully and freely of these offerings and bore their marks the rest of their lives.

An orthodox, practical, unpretending, and exalted religious faith was the cornerstone of this remarkable society.[22] This feature of Liberty County life was especially characteristic of the Jones family. Devotions were held each morning and evening and were supplemented by private meditations. In the summer the Joneses attended church at Sunbury. In winter they worshipped at Midway. Church was an all-day affair; the family left home after breakfast, taking lunch with them, and did not return home until sunset. It was a family custom in good weather to retire to the piazza after supper to enjoy the evening breeze and sing favorite hymns.

After religion, education was next in importance, Here again Charles Colcock Jones had a greater than average interest. His deep-rooted desire to ensure his children a thorough education led him to build schoolhouses at Monte Video and Maybank and to hire private tutors—always licentiates or probationers for the ministry. Other planters cooperated in the venture: at Maybank the children of Roswell King were taught with the Jones youngsters; at Monte Video there were the children of John Barnard. Jones himself determined the curriculum. It went much further than the three Rs, stressing those elements of the classical curriculum required for college entrance. He often personally supervised the instruction and in those rare instances when the tutor was absent conducted the classes himself. School hours were from eight in the morning until two in the afternoon in summer and from nine until three in winter. The school day always began with Bible reading and prayer.

Literary pursuits at home supplemented the lessons of the classroom. Books abounded in the Jones homes and, according to Robert Quarterman Mallard, who was to marry Mary Sharpe Jones, "were prized and treated as honored guests or cherished inmates." "Only the choicest," he added, "had admittance and hospitality. No second-class fiction was permitted to enfeeble the minds or pervert the morals of the household; it was kept out as one would keep out the germs of an infectious disease."[23]

Jones insisted that study be balanced with play. A variety of pets—birds, cats, dogs, and horses—provided many happy long-remembered moments. A veritable colony of cats were especially enjoyed. In addition Mary Sharpe played with her dolls and dishes and learned to sew, and Charles, Jr., and Joseph, or "Bubber Dodo" as he was fondly called, were encouraged to excel in every manly sport. The fields, forests, and streams teemed with wildlife and fish, and the boys spent many carefree hours hunting and fishing. They also learned to sail and worked hard at mastering the gentlemanly arts of riding and swordsmanship. A miniature cavalry company, formed with neighborhood youngsters, paraded weekly at their various homes. "It is easy to see how such a life," Mallard, himself a product of it, wrote, "gave the Southern youth a skill with firearms rarely attained in a shooting gallery, and a free, firm, and graceful seat in the saddle, seldom if ever acquired in the sawdust arena of a riding school; and how it developed a splendid physical manhood, unknown to the dwellers in the cities, with their billiard table exercise and theatrical diversions, and what is at best but a poor substitute for outdoor sports, the gymnasium."[24] The outdoor life of their plantation surroundings did indeed give the young Joneses vigorous health. They grew up robust and strong, with an uncommon staying power which was to prove invaluable in their demanding careers.

Few holidays were celebrated in the Old South—generally only the Fourth of July, George Washington's birthday, and Christmas—and the Jones children enjoyed them immensely. Independence Day celebrations were held under an enormous live oak tree on the lawn at Maybank. Its highlights were patriotic speeches by the youngsters and a bountiful picnic. On Washington's birthday the citizens of Liberty County gathered at the parade ground of their famed militia unit, the Liberty Independent Troop, to hear an oration, watch a parade, and witness marksmanship contests. Christmas was a quiet family holiday spent at home.

Charles Colcock Jones appreciated the broadening influence of travel and took his family with him when he filled positions in Columbia and Philadelphia. In addition the Joneses spent the summer of 1839 touring the northeastern portion of the United States and Canada. Sailing from Savannah in June, they visited New York, Massachusetts, Connecticut, New Hampshire, and eastern Canada, not returning home until November.

Thus the three young Joneses spent a happy childhood, the imprint of which they were to carry the remainder of their lives. Charles Colcock Jones, Jr., probably best summarized its virtues when describing his childhood to his own daughter. "No son," he wrote, "could have had kinder or more indulgent parents, or fuller opportunities for indulging in those pastimes which a plantation life afforded."[25]

Chapter 2
School Days

*No other science is more extensive, it embraces
Heaven, Earth & Man.*

Charles Colcock Jones's acceptance of a second appointment at the Presbyterian Theological Seminary in Columbia brought an end to his children's happy plantation childhood. But it was due in large part to his deep concern for his sons that he accepted this position. They were ready for college, and South Carolina's capital, depicted by observers as a "small, quiet, and unimposing-looking" but "rather . . . interesting little town" of six thousand at the head of navigation on the Congaree River with "an air of neatness and elegance" and "the residence of a superior class of people," was the home of South Carolina College (later the University of South Carolina).[1] Here was to be found the best education in the lower South.

With the notable exceptions of the University of Virginia and South Carolina College, antebellum southern institutions of higher learning were largely second-rate. The former owed its prominence to the careful planning and lasting spirit of Thomas Jefferson; the latter's position was primarily due to an enlightened state legislature. Proud of their school, the South Carolina legislators consistently voted it generous state support and exercised great care in appointing trustees, administrators, and faculty. The school was at the high point of its prewar eminence when the Joneses returned to Columbia in 1848, and South Carolinians were justifiably proud of its large enrollment (in excess of two hundred), ten fine buildings, first-rate library, excellent eight-man faculty, and progressive offerings in chemistry, history, and natural philosophy.[2]

The school year at South Carolina College began in January and ended in December with a summer break between semesters.

13

The 1848 school year was well under way by the time the Jones family arrived in Columbia, but Charles, Jr., owing to his age, was allowed to enter the freshman class. Joseph, having but recently turned fifteen, was asked to wait until the start of the next full session.[3] There was no question concerning the preparation of either youth, for both possessed the requisite "accurate knowledge" of English, Latin, Greek grammar, modern and ancient geography, arithmetic, and selected writings of Sallust, Virgil, Cicero, Xenophon, and Homer. A serious-minded, sensitive youth of average height and build, bent on succeeding, Joseph Jones enrolled in January 1849 along with 236 other students—the largest enrollment in the school's history and a figure not again equalled until 1905.

Charles Colcock Jones urged his sons at the beginning of their collegiate careers to use their time for serious study. They heeded his advice. Neither youth experienced any academic difficulty nor became embroiled in the levity and riotous behavior characteristic of antebellum college students. Those at South Carolina College were typical. They drank, gambled, and engaged in all manner of merrymaking to the chagrin of the faculty and administration and the annoyance of the citizens of Columbia. Rules were laid down and attempts were made to enforce them, but such endeavors met with only limited success. A code of conduct put into effect in 1848 prohibited students from keeping "any pistol, dirk, sword-cane, bowie knife, or other deadly weapon" in their rooms or in the town of Columbia. Using or bringing "any spiritous liquors, dogs or arms or ammunition" on the college grounds was forbidden. Students were warned against entertaining company in their rooms and leaving the town of Columbia without permission. Balls and "festive entertainment," except at commencement, were banned. Students were forbidden to "make any bonfire" or to "throw or use any fire-ball or lighted torch" on or in the vicinity of the college grounds. "Blowing any horn or trumpet, or beating any drum, or . . . disturbing the quiet of the institution by riding any horse or mule within or near the College enclosure, or . . . making any loud or unusual noise by any other means" was likewise prohibited. Finally the students were warned against knowingly receiving, harboring, or entertaining suspended students in their rooms.[4]

Joseph Jones's first year at South Carolina College was unusually free of student unrest. Only three students were suspended during the entire year. In fact so tranquil was this year that Maximilian LaBorde, the professor of logic, rhetoric, and belles lettres and one of the school's earliest historians, was convinced that it was "entitled to a most exalted position in the history of the College." "Never did the College," he explained, "have as large numbers; never did it have greater internal quiet, and never did it enjoy a larger measure of the public confidence." But the next year, 1850, was quite a different story, prompting LaBorde to observe that it "cannot be regarded as a bright one in the history of the College." The campus was quiet until April when the junior class revolted. This rebellion, "about a mere trifle" according to LaBorde, was sparked by Richard Brumby, the professor of chemistry. He had been forced to cancel several classes because of illness and upon learning that James H. Thornwell, the professor of religion, was to be absent a few days attempted to force the students to make up their missed work in chemistry during the time freed by Thornwell's absence. They refused. When the faculty failed to support them, the students revolted on the evening of April 10.[5] The scene was vividly described by President William C. Preston. "At twilight," he wrote,

> noises began to arise in the Campus, and large groups to be formed before the Professors' houses. In a short time the mob increased to a multitude. Shouts and riotous yells were heard; and as darkness closed, a bright flame arose from the midst of the crowd. Upon hastening to the spot with some of the Professors, I witnessed a scene of confusion, uproar and turbulence, beyond what I had ever seen. . . . The whole college apparently was assembled—one boy brandishing a sword, but with no indication of murderous intent—though its flashing in the light of the blazing fire looked fearful enough. The fire was consuming a table covered with a pile of books—the Chemical Text Books, which the members of the Junior Class had devoted as a solemn sacrifice to the flames.[6]

All attempts to restore order were in vain. In the end the entire sixty-man junior class was suspended.

Despite the fact that two new dormitories had been opened in the fall of 1848, living space was inadequate at South Carolina

College. This situation, coupled with a desire to continue personal supervision of his sons' education, prompted Charles Colcock Jones to persuade the boys to live at home, a step which accounts in large measure for their good conduct and academic success. In Joseph's case his family may have wished that he had lived on campus, for by his sophomore year he began to show a marked interest in natural history, the product of his inquisitive intellect and plantation childhood, and had started a small but rapidly growing museum in the family home.[7]

The curriculum at South Carolina College was grounded in the classical tradition with its emphasis on ancient languages and the classics. Each year the Jones brothers were subjected to a battery of required courses in Latin, Greek, mathematics, English, and history. They did exceedingly well, consistently placing near the top of their respective classes. Their exemplary performances did not go unnoticed. Joseph, for example, won one of South Carolina College's highest honors during his sophomore year when he was elected secretary of the Euphradian Society, one of the school's two debating clubs.[8]

Such organizations were the collegiate manifestations of what has been labeled "the passionate addiction of Southern people to florid and emotional oratory."[9] Campus oratorical societies, in the absence of fraternities, organized athletics, or similar diversions, were the chief outlet for coordinated extracurricular activity, serving as political, social, fraternal, and intellectual clubs. Spirited competition for college honors existed between them. More important, campus status was determined largely by participation in these organizations. Hence few students failed to join. Oratorical societies, then, played a paramount role in the student life of the Old South. Such was the case at South Carolina College, where, according to this school's most recent historian, "the story of the societies is in considerable part the story of the college."[10]

The debating clubs at South Carolina College, the Clariscopic and Euphradian societies, proudly traced their origins to the opening of the school in 1805. By the time Joseph and Charles Jones, Jr., enrolled, each organization had its own hall in which weekly meetings, usually consisting of a debate on some previously assigned topic, were held. A majority of the subjects debated were political, but occasionally philosophical, religious, or historical themes were argued. Slavery was the issue most frequently discussed, and the history of these debates parallels the transformation of the southern position on the slavery question. The early ones advocated general emancipation or at least voluntary manumission. By the early 1830s and 1840s, as the sectional conflict intensified, these collegiate oratorical societies were not only defending the institution of slavery but were demanding the reopening of the slave trade. A similar shift to a southern nationalist position is discernible in debates on other controversial topics, such as the tariff, disunion, and territorial expansion.

After two years at South Carolina College the Jones brothers transferred to Princeton. This move was not prompted by any dissatisfaction with the Columbia school but was an outgrowth of their father's acceptance of the secretaryship of the Presbyterian Church's Philadelphia-based Board of Domestic Missions. Fearful of the evils that could overcome college students left to themselves, Charles Colcock Jones was reluctant to leave his sons in Columbia. Of great importance, too, was his fondness for Princeton, his alma mater. It was only a short distance from Philadelphia and its domination by the Presbyterian Church guaranteed his sons a Christian atmosphere not found at South Carolina College.[11] There was also the long-standing tradition among upper-class southerners to send their sons north for an education. Of the northern schools Princeton was a southern favorite. "In the old days," one historian of the Old South has observed, "Princeton had been a favorite college with the South. In the arrogant spirit of the time, it was considered *aristocratic* and the best place North for the education of a gentleman's sons, and its rolls had carried generation after generation of the best families from every Southern state."[12]

The Jones family spent the summer of 1850 at Maybank. Joseph and Charles, Jr., were forced to abbreviate their vacations owing to Princeton's mid-August opening. The days preceding their departure at the end of July were filled with an air of expectancy, for not only were the youths looking forward to enrolling at Princeton but even more exciting was the anticipated thrill of their first unaccompanied journey, since their parents were not to leave for Philadelphia until October.

Charles Colcock and Mary Jones did not share this excitement. Their sons' traveling "a great distance among strangers" was a matter of utmost concern, prompting them to offer each youth "a few parting counsels" upon which he was urged to base his life and character. These admonitions were restrictive and all-encompassing. Social conduct received the greatest attention. Joseph and Charles, Jr., were explicitly forbidden to drink, smoke, gamble, attend the theater or racetrack, frequent taverns, engage in ungentlemanly behavior, or associate with *"profane, sabbath breaking, idle, intemperate, immoral* & dissipated young men."* Instead they were advised to "look upward," seeking the friendship of "young gentlemen of intelligence, integrity & piety" and welcoming opportunities for introductions into "religious, respectable and honorable families." In regard to women the youths, while urged to "enjoy the refining influence of elevated Female Society," were cautioned to "lay aside any flippancy of behavior & excesses of manner & dress and to form no connections beyond those of friendly intercourse."

Considerable emphasis was, of course, placed upon religious observance. Joseph and Charles were reminded to keep the sabbath, to pray regularly in secret, and to read the Bible twice daily, never doubting "in the least degree the Truth of GOD's Holy WORD." In school academic excellence was to be their goal. It was suggested that this be attained through conscientious study, efficient use of time, faithful attendance of recitations, lectures, and chapel, observance of all rules and regulations, and respect for authority.

Other points touched upon included health, economy, and behavior toward one another. The youngsters were urged to protect their health through a rigid system of diet, rest, and exercise. They were admonished to be *"economical in your expenditures: & never run in debt,* but meet all your pecuniary engagements *upon your word & to your word."* Finally the youths were reminded that they were brothers and should "promote each others peace, happiness, reputation, & success in life, without envy or jealousy, through every lawful & just means in your power."[13]

Joseph and Charles made the trip to Princeton by train and boat with stopovers in Washington and Philadelphia. Each utilized his free time in ways indicative of his future career. In Washington Charles, who was to become a lawyer, visited the Capitol to witness the nation's leaders at work, while his younger brother, who aspired to a career in science, passed his time examining the "unnumbered curiosities" at the patent office. Upon reaching Philadelphia, Joseph left Charles in their hotel to write home and hurried off to see the many natural wonders housed in Phineas T. Barnum's much publicized American Museum. His interest in natural history was becoming "an unconquerable passion." He had set up small museums in each of the family homes and frequently added new specimens. When departing for Princeton, for example, Joseph instructed his parents to preserve the skeletons of numerous birds and a large shark, all of which he had left in various stages of maceration.[14]

Knowing little of Princeton other than what their father had told them, the youths left Philadelphia on the last leg of their journey with mixed feelings. But any apprehensions they may have felt were quickly dissipated in the excitement of arrival and the frenzy of getting settled. Joseph and Charles were assigned a room in historic Nassau Hall (or North College as it was called), the school's oldest building. Although pleasant and well-lighted, the room was strikingly austere with its plank floor, bare plaster walls smudged with candle smoke, and cheap, plain furniture, consisting of a pair of cots, clothes press, bookcase, washstand, rocking chair, and table. Its most redeeming feature was the charming view it afforded of the tranquil New Jersey countryside, but even this could be enjoyed only in mild weather, since the small, green translucent panes obscured it when the windows were closed. These patriotic brothers treasured their east wall, which bore scars inflicted during the Revolution when George Washington's artillery had reluctantly taken the building under fire to rout a body of Hessians who had taken refuge there.[15]

Matriculation held a major disappointment. The admissions committee readily accepted the youths, but with the condition that they repeat their previous year's work. Thus Charles was admitted as a junior and Joseph as a sophomore. This unexpected setback prompted them to seek parental advice as to what they should do. Charles blamed his misfortune on a poor background in mathematics. Although upset he expressed a willingness to accept his reversal. Joseph, on the other hand, who had been found deficient not only in mathematics but in ancient languages as well, reacted quite differently. In a manner which was to become characteristic of him in times of personal adversity, he implied that foul play may have been responsible for the treatment he and his brother had received. Pointing out that South Carolina College's commencement was in December and Princeton's in June, he charged: "I think myself that one of the strong reasons why the Faculty did not admit us to those classes for which we applied, was because they did not like the idea of our graduating six months sooner than we would have done in Columbia." Charles Colcock and Mary Jones sympathized with their sons but advised them to remain at Princeton.[16]

Princeton's many advantages soon made the youths forget their initial disappointment. Indeed the school had much to offer. Although the student body was slightly smaller than South Carolina College's, Princeton could boast of a larger and better-known faculty. The library contained fewer volumes than the one in Columbia, but young Joseph Jones hardly noticed this in his enthusiasm over the school's museum of natural history containing nearly a thousand specimens. The classical curriculum was stressed here, too, but not to the exclusion of popular offerings in history, science, and modern languages.

Socially the Jones brothers' first few days at Princeton were lonely ones. Not until they put aside parental advice to select their friends with an extreme caution did they make a number of warm friendships. Then, despite their reserved behavior and steadfast refusal to drink, gamble, or participate in disruptive types of campus revelry, Joseph and Charles were happily caught up in the school's frequent unorganized diversions, ranging from swimming and walking in the woods in the summer to skating and sleigh riding in the winter. In the absence of organized athletics, they wrestled, battled with snowballs, and went on hiking expeditions. And, like their many southern comrades, they came to endure, if not enjoy, the frequent good-natured raillery aimed at their distinctive southern attire, with its "broad-brimmed hat, bobtailed coat, baggy breeches, and high-heeled boots."[17]

Joseph and Charles were especially enthusiastic about invitations to join one of the school's oratorical societies. Princeton's Cliosophic and Whig societies were much like their counterparts at South Carolina College. The only significant differences were that these northern organizations debated a wider range of topics and reached less sectional conclusions. Yet even they tended to recruit along regional lines. The Cliosophic Society, or Clio Hall as it was popularly called, was composed largely of northerners, while the Whig Society was considered to be a southern organization. But the Jones brothers, as had their father and most Georgians, ignored this sectional distinction and accepted bids from Clio Hall.[18]

The scholarship of Joseph and Charles Jones enhanced the campus status of Clio Hall. In turn the society rewarded them for their hard work. At the end of their junior year each was chosen to speak at commencement as junior orator. Joseph apparently was quite popular, for he was elected almost unanimously to this prestigious position. His proud parents attributed this honor to his conduct, scholarship, and fidelity to the duties of the society "without any disparagement" of his fellow students.[19]

He consulted his father on topics for his address, and at the Reverend Jones's urging decided to speak on the origin of the races from a purely biblical standpoint. The question as to whether there had been a single creation or a number of them was one of the most hotly contested scientific and theological issues of the day. Although this controversy had strong sectional overtones, neither North nor South could be viewed as a bulwark for either side of the argument. Joseph was one of many southerners who was shocked at the irreligious suggestion of multiple creations, and his address, entitled "Unity of the Races," struck "a manly blow for truth."[20]

Despite academic success Joseph Jones did not enjoy many of his courses. His primary complaint, like that of more than a few other Princeton students, was of the rigidity and dullness of the classical curriculum. As a sophomore and junior he was subjected to what seemed an unending round of classroom recitations, essays, and examinations on subjects that had little appeal for him—mathematics, history, philosophy, natural theology, and a legion of Greek and Roman writers. These labors were made bearable only by the fact that in his senior year he would be allowed to study science.[21]

He could not have chosen a better place than Princeton for the pursuit of science. "There was no more distinguished group of scientists in the country," according to one historian of the school, "than was embraced by the Princeton faculty in the fourth and fifth decades of the [nineteenth] century."[22] Four of them were members of the National Academy of Scientists (three of whom were original members); two belonged to the American Philosophical Society; two were members of the American Association for the Advancement of Science; and two were fellows of the American Academy of Arts and Sciences. To his regret Joseph Jones missed the opportunity to study under the greatest of them, Joseph Henry, who had resigned in 1846 to become the first director of the newly created Smithsonian Institution. Still Princeton could claim such well-known scientists as Stephen Alexander (astronomy), John Torrey (chemistry), and Henry Vethake (economics). Joseph found the study of chemistry especially enjoyable and with the encouragement of Torrey developed a lifelong love for this science. He found it of immeasurable importance in his choice of professions.

By the time of his graduation in June 1853 Joseph Jones had decided to pursue a career in medicine. His parents felt that he had chosen too demanding a profession but out of respect for his maturity and judgment said nothing to change his mind. In light of his long-standing and continually growing interest in natural history, he probably made the right choice. He spent the summer prior to entering medical school at Maybank conducting sophisticated independent physiological studies, which he was to continue during the next three summers. These experiments were performed on a variety of vertebrates—alligators, snakes, and terrapins—in an attempt to determine the chemical, physical, and microscopic character of the blood and various organs in their normal state and during thirst and starvation, the relations of the constituents of the blood of the different species and genera of animals, and the effects of gases upon the blood, secretions, and excretions.[23]

Joseph selected the University of Pennsylvania's medical department for his professional training. This was the oldest and by far the best medical school in the United States. Founded in 1765 by John Morgan as part of Benjamin Franklin's College of Philadelphia, it had successfully weathered serious internal dissension and strong competition from the rapidly proliferating proprietary schools to retain its foremost position. Joseph could have attended one of the southern proprietary schools at considerably smaller expense, both mental and monetary, but he chose to enroll at Pennsylvania for a variety of reasons: he was aware of the school's reputation; it was highly recommended by his teachers at Princeton; his parents admonished him to secure a good education; Pennsylvania was popular with southern youths in training for medical careers; and the presence of his parents in Philadelphia would allow him to economize by living at home.[24]

Joseph Jones had barely turned twenty when he faced the admissions committee of the University of Pennsylvania's medical department in the fall of 1853. This examination was largely for show. There was keen competition between schools, and the fear of losing students kept standards low. While rigid entrance requirements were solemnly intoned by the faculty, in practice little more than the proven ability to read and write was required. Although not beginning his medical training until almost a decade later, the noted surgeon John A. Wyeth, organizer of the first postgraduate medical school in the United States and president of the American Medical Association, brought this era's incredibly low prerequisites for pursuing a medical education into sharp focus when he wrote: "The medical department of the university I attended was . . . one of the oldest and deservedly the best known of medical colleges in the United States. The course of study and the standard of requirements then prevailing at this school may be taken as typical of medical education in the United States at that period. There was no preliminary or entrance examination. Any white male who could read or write and who had mastered the rudiments of English was eligible. Neither Latin nor Greek was essential."[25]

Like most of the approximately thirty-five medical schools in the United States in the middle of the nineteenth century, the University of Pennsylvania's medical department had a seven-man faculty and offered courses in the theory and practice of physic (medicine), chemistry, surgery, anatomy, materia medica (pharmaceutics), institutes of medicine (physiology), and obstetrics and diseases of women. Expenses included a three- to five-dollar matriculation fee, tuition amounting to fifteen dollars a course paid directly to the professors, and a fifteen- to twenty-dollar graduation fee. The term ran from the middle of October to the beginning of March. Two terms, the second covering the same material as the first, were required for graduation. This curious requirement was an anachronistic holdover from the early days of American medical education when an acute shortage of textbooks, equipment, and trained teachers made it impossible for the student to cover the material adequately in one term.

Schools also required three years of private study under a respectable practitioner for graduation. But like the admission standards this requirement was generally modified and sometimes waived entirely. In Joseph's case, probably owing to his total lack of any apprenticeship, it was apparently enforced, for he was assigned to Dr. Joseph Leidy, the professor of anatomy, as an office student.[26]

Leidy was a Pennsylvania graduate himself, but he had abandoned the practice of medicine shortly after taking his degree in order to devote all his time to the study of biology and the teaching of anatomy. While in his twenties he started the serious study of paleontology in America and began his well-known research on parasitology. By the time he was thirty Leidy was acclaimed at home and abroad as America's leading comparative anatomist. He joined the Pennsylvania faculty only a short time before Joseph's enrollment. As a teacher Leidy was outstanding. "His kindness and simplicity of character endeared him to his students, and at the height of his career," it has been reported, "he drew more hearers to his lectures than any of his colleagues."[27] Thus Joseph's admiration for him is understandable.

Dr. Samuel Jackson, professor of physiology and one of America's leading advocates of medical research, also became one of the youth's favorite instructors. Like Leidy, Jackson had received his medical training at the University of Pennsylvania and returned later to teach at his alma mater. He was not nearly as dynamic a teacher as Leidy but was popular nevertheless. Joseph was especially fond of him. Describing Jackson to his parents he wrote: "I think that he has, decidedly, the most pleasant & attractive personal manners, accompanied with the most fluent, impressive, & often eloquent delivery, of all the medical Professors in Philadelphia." This high opinion of Jackson was also held by many of his contemporaries, who were convinced that he possessed "the most superior & brilliant mind" of all the medical men in Philadelphia.[28]

Medical students of this era did not, for the most part, enjoy a good press. "Their education, it must be allowed," as one Philadelphia medical journal best expressed the general antagonisms felt toward them, "is (in the majority of cases) neither finished nor respectable. They will pardon us for so severe a statement, but we make it because it is true—we make it because it ought not to be true, and because we wish to do them some good. It is true. A visit to the lecture rooms of our college will prove it to be true." "What description of young men," the writer asked,

> are to be seen in these places? The roughest we ever saw in our lives. Most of them have a Texan Ranger look. Nobody in the world would pronounce them to be refined, liberally endowed young gentlemen. Hair as long as that of a savage,

moustaches as fierce as the whiskers of a tiger, a reckless expression of the eye, a long, shuffling, clumsy gait, sword canes, dirk knives, revolvers, attire very unfashionably made, hard swearing, hard drinking, coarse language, cigars, tobacco quids and pools of tobacco spittle, are too prominent barriers for the formation of so flattering a judgment.

"The picture," he insisted, "is not overdrawn. We might make it a great deal less flattering, and then we would be absolutely true."[29]

At the extreme opposite of this unflattering assessment Joseph Jones was neat in dress, well-behaved, and studious, approaching his medical training with the same dedication and diligence which had characterized his undergraduate studies. According to a plan he and his father worked out he spent nine to ten hours a day studying. At night his sleep was often occupied with dreams of "Skeletons, Bones & Muscles."[30] The murderous pace of the serious medical student was well described by a sympathetic professor. "How often," he wrote, "has the experienced student felt his head ache with the confusion of over-crowded facts and opinions; how often felt his physical powers fail under the long sittings of the day, and the long vigils of the night; how often longed for time to store away and arrange the multitude of new thoughts, and for opportunity for that mental relaxation, bodily exercise, and pure air, which are essential to keep the very instrument of thought in order.[31]

The sole significant interruption of Joseph's studies occurred in November, when, following his father's resignation as secretary of the Presbyterian Church's Board of Domestic Missions, he put aside his books long enough to supervise the shipping of his parents' furniture and clothing to Georgia and to move into a boarding house at 229 Arch Street between Seventh and Eighth. He paid seven dollars a week (later thirty dollars a month) for board, lights, washing, and fuel, remarking: "This is as cheap as can be obtained in any respectable house." Treated "as if I were a relation," Joseph roomed here during the remainder of his medical training. His social life, with the exception of church, teaching a Sunday school class, and an occasional visit to family friends, was virtually nonexistent. He did, however, conscientiously guard his health, giving up tea and coffee and finding time to exercise regularly in the college gymnasium.[32]

Joseph Jones desired good education; he had received it at South Carolina College and at Princeton, and the prospect of similar quality had been one of the main reasons he had enrolled at Pennsylvania. As an undergraduate he had repeatedly objected to the rigidity of the classical curriculum, and he had not been at Pennsylvania long before he became aware of the major flaw in nineteenth-century medical education—its didactic approach. A majority of the nation's leading medical figures had been fighting this obstacle to true learning for years, and a slow reform movement was under way. It was not to reach fruition, however, until after the Civil War.

One of the most serious faults of this approach was the failure of many medical schools to allow students to learn anatomy through dissection. A few far-seeing, perhaps opportunistic, physicians moved to remedy this evil by establishing private schools of dissection. One of the best was Dr. J. V. O'Brien Lawrence's Philadelphia School of Anatomy. Located directly behind the University of Pennsylvania's medical department, it was looked upon as a valuable auxiliary. Joseph Jones, echoing Leidy's admonition that it was "folly to hope to learn Physiology and Anatomy from text books alone," enrolled in an evening dissection course.[33]

Equipped with a variety of scalpels, knives, hooks, needles, and forceps, he spent four or five months obtaining a thorough knowledge of anatomy and gaining valuable insights into physiology. Dissection usually began with the abdomen, starting with the muscles and moving on to the organs. The student then proceeded to an examination of the muscles, bones, nerves, and arteries of the legs, head and thorax, and upper extremities. Working with cadavers was thought to be potentially dangerous, and various precautionary steps were taken. Dissection rooms were heated only enough to prevent the corpse from freezing, necessitating that students dress warmly. Street clothes were forbidden in the anatomy rooms and aprons and sleeves tightly secured with rubber wristbands were prescribed. Each part of the body was disposed of as soon as it had been dissected. And finally the student was urged to eat wholesome food and drink a moderate amount of wine to revive his spirits after such debilitating work.[34]

Engrossed in study, Joseph Jones was seemingly oblivious to the passage of time and was surprised at the rapidity with which his first year of medical school passed. In the course of this year he made two irrevocable commitments—the first to the study of medicine and the second to scientific research. He freely admitted that physicians, owing to their intimate contact with sickness and death, were frequently guilty of a disturbingly calloused view of life, but he vigorously defended medicine, asserting: "My love for Medicine increases every day as the vast range of the science is opened up. No other science is more extensive, it embraces Heaven, Earth & Man." Like Jackson he looked upon medicine as "a grand Theology."[35] This year had also convinced the youth that "careful & laborious" original research was the only way to gain recognition in the world of science. Jackson's urgings and Leidy's reputation made such a conviction virtually inevitable. Thus at the end of the school term Joseph hurried to Georgia to resume his investigations of the previous summer—only to have his plans delayed by a severe case of the mumps. Upon recovery he pressed his research in order to make up for lost time.

Added to his earlier work were several new studies designed to determine the effects of various poisons on the temperature, excretions, secretions, muscular action, and blood and organs of animals; the physical and chemical changes produced in them after death; and the conditions accompanying fevers and related inflammations. Joseph hoped that his findings would shed some light on the etiology of fevers, for, as he pointed out, many scientists felt that they were caused by the action of specific, but as yet unknown, poisons. It seemed reasonable that unidentified morbific agents might be better understood through a thorough study of the effects produced by poisons whose chemical properties were known.[36]

These investigations were abruptly terminated in mid-September by the most destructive hurricane in Jones family memory. None of the three plantations escaped unscathed. Crops were wrecked, trees uprooted, and buildings leveled. Until his departure at the end of the month, Joseph worked feverishly to help repair damage to books, furniture, and pictures at Maybank caused by the torrents of rain driven by the wind through the weatherboarding of the house.[37]

Despite this serious interruption Joseph Jones returned to Philadelphia in October 1854, satisfied with his summer's work. Arriving safely in Philadelphia, he proudly informed Jackson and Leidy of his investigations. Upon reviewing his findings they urged him to prepare a paper for presentation to the next meeting of the Philadelphia Academy of Natural Sciences. The study that resulted was remarkable considering that the youthful author had attended but one year of medical school and had received no supervised research training. Entitled "Abstract of Experiments upon the Physical Influences Exerted by Living, Organic and Inorganic Membranes upon Chemical Substances, in Solution, Passing through Them by Endosmose," it was a surprisingly sophisticated study of the transmission of substances through the mucous membranes in animals and the cell walls in plants by osmosis.

The members of the academy were pleasantly surprised at such scholarly work by so young a scientist and urged that the paper be published. Regrettably the Academy could not afford the sixty to seventy dollars in printing costs. Jackson, unwilling that the lack of such a small sum should prevent the publication of so deserving a study, offered to pay the fee. Joseph was touched by his thoughtfulness but was determined to meet the expense himself. At this point, however, Jackson showed the article to Dr. Isaac Hays, editor of the prestigious *American Journal of the Medical Sciences*, who agreed to publish it.[38] Later, in 1856, the study was included in an American edition of William B. Carpenter's *Human Physiology*. This was the most widely used textbook on the subject, and the inclusion of young Joseph Jones's research was a signal honor.[39]

His findings received further recognition when Jackson incorporated them into his lectures. Joseph was justifiably proud when this widely respected teacher and research scientist singled him out as a better authority on animal temperature than the German physiologists who had long studied the subject. Joseph Leidy, although more restrained in his praise, was equally pleased with his student. In a letter to the youthful scientist's parents, after applauding the zeal with which Joseph pursued his medical studies and the scope of his research, he wrote: "His labors of last summer have excited a good deal of interest among our physiologists."[40] Leidy urged him to return home the next summer and further this work.

Armed with the encouragement of Jackson and Leidy, Joseph returned to Georgia at the end of the term in March 1855 and resumed his investigations with renewed vigor. He continued his research of the two previous summers in a makeshift laboratory hastily set up in the cotton house at Monte Video. He worked up to the last possible moment, leaving his mother barely time to get his wardrobe ready. He did make time, however, to give medical treatment to his father and several of the family slaves and to collect a large box of skeletons of local animals for Leidy's use in his comparative anatomy studies.[41]

Pennsylvania, like most nineteenth-century medical schools, required only two years of course work for the M.D. degree. Yet Joseph Jones enrolled for a third course of lectures. There are two plausible explanations for this puzzling decision: Joseph may have been held to the requirement of three years of apprentice training; or he may have been influenced to extend his education by Leidy and Jackson, who, impressed with his unusual scientific bent, wanted him to receive an especially thorough training. Whatever the case the youth returned to Philadelphia in the fall of 1855 for another year of study.

Leidy and Jackson were once again pleased with his summer's work, and the latter continued to single him out for classroom praise. Jackson was especially impressed with Joseph's recent research on digestion, an important branch of physiology which had been much advanced by the work of William Beaumont some twenty years earlier, and encouraged him to prepare his findings for publication.[42]

Two projects dominated Joseph Jones's final year of medical school—the writing of the required thesis for graduation and, at Jackson's urging, the preparation of a paper to be submitted to the Smithsonian Institution for publication in its *Contributions to Knowledge*. Rarely were these theses regarded as original contributions to medical thought. Indeed they were generally a mere superficial rehashing of some topic from a textbook or a favorite professor's lectures. But as a parting gesture of appreciation to Leidy and Jackson, Joseph painstakingly sought perfection and originality in his. The lengthy paper, "Physical, Chemical, and Physiological Investigations upon the Vital Phenomena, Structure, and Offices of the Solids and Fluids of Animals," was based upon his research of past summers. It dealt with the comparative anatomy and physiology of the circulatory and respiratory systems of vertebrates and invertebrates indigenous to coastal Georgia. His conclusions, although quite elaborate, were largely restatements of the findings of earlier physiologists. Still the scope of this study and the original research upon which it was based are highly commendable. Joseph singled out Jackson for special praise, stating: "If these investigations possess any value, it is due as much to his brilliant instruction, kind advice, and generous assistance, as to my own exertions." Jackson, returning the favor, sent a copy of the thesis to Hays, who agreed to publish it.[43]

The long hours spent in the preparation of his thesis and memoir for the Smithsonian left Joseph little time for anything else, including preparation for his final examinations. Still he did well in his courses. In fact Leidy and Jackson passed him without an examination. With his studies behind him, Joseph Jones, along with 141 other young men, was awarded the M.D. degree on March 29, 1856. It was a happy occasion for him, although he was disappointed that an unusually harsh winter and the continuing illness of his father prevented his parents from attending the ceremony and sharing directly in his happiness.[44]

Graduation did not mean that Dr. Joseph Jones was free to return home. Unexpected difficulties encountered with his memoir for the Smithsonian were to keep him in Philadelphia six weeks longer, ending his medical training on a frustrating note. This undertaking, a further product of his research of previous summers, had strongly appealed to the youth when suggested by Jackson at the beginning of the school year. Buoyed by the recollection of the relative ease with which he had prepared his previous publications, Joseph approached the task enthusiastically. He worked diligently, often six to eight hours a day at the expense of many lectures, in order to finish the article by the beginning of 1856. It was ready at the middle of January and submitted to Jackson for approval. He praised the study so highly that Leidy, to the later regret of all parties concerned, recommended publication sight unseen. Joseph thereupon set out confidently for Washington at the end of the month where he presented the memoir to Joseph Henry, who in turn referred it to a committee for evaluation.[45]

After the elapse of almost two months without hearing from Henry the youth became anxious, writing home that this unexpected delay would probably keep him in Philadelphia for several weeks after graduation. At the same time he wrote Henry to determine the status of the study. Henry's response, dated March 20, initiated a lengthy correspondence between the two. It was a dialogue between two strong-willed individuals. On the one hand there was the venerable but overly cautious secretary of the Smithsonian; on the other there was a proud but overly sensitive novice scientist. The contents of this first letter, as the delay hinted, were upsetting. Joseph was told that upon the recommendation of the review committee his memoir had been returned to Jackson with the request that the lengthy introduction, an examination of the labors of others relating to his topic, be "abridged to a mere outline." This criticism was undoubtedly well founded, for throughout his long career Joseph Jones repeatedly lessened the value of his various works through the inclusion of a seemingly interminable number of pages filled with largely irrelevant background material. Henry, however, did not stop with that point. Noting that the youth apparently desired "to establish a reputation on a solid basis as an original investigator," he warned him against relying upon "the antecedent works of others as absolute truths," urging him instead to present his own findings to the world—"if . . . but a single fact." In an encouraging postscript he suggested tentative acceptance of the memoir when he informed Joseph that if he agreed to make the corrections suggested, he could commence supervising the preparation of the plates to illustrate it.[46]

Joseph in his reply a few days later professed an unawareness of the Smithsonian's policy of publishing simply "details & facts," pleading "you must excuse my mistake on the ground of ignorance." Be that as it may, he admitted his disappointment that the introductory chapter had convinced Henry and the committee that he wished to republish "the sentiments of others & discuss theories" instead of "candidly stating" the results of his own investigations. This was by no means his intention, he insisted. The work of others had been used "only so far as it was necessary to confirm the development of important laws & principles," and the preparation of this chapter had "consumed only *2 weeks*," he emphasized, while the remainder of the paper "was the result of *2 years* hard labor." Despite his deeply felt disappointment he expressed his willingness to conform to the regulations of the Smithsonian "in all things" and grudgingly accepted the assessment of his article. In fact, he revealed, he had already consulted Jackson and Leidy as to the best means of reworking the introduction. He had also begun visiting the various Philadelphia artists to determine the best and most economical method of printing the plates. He could not close, however, without taking issue with Henry's well-intended and innocuous remark concerning his career plans. He emphatically denied that his investigations were aimed at establishing a reputation. Instead, he asserted, they were dedicated to "the discovery of truth, & the acquirement of that practical knowledge, which would guide me in the investigation of the effects of diseases upon the blood of human beings."[47]

Sensing the great distress his communication had caused the young scientist, Henry responded the same day, March 26, that this letter was received, to clarify his position. He pointed out that it was not the intention of the Smithsonian to prohibit entirely the publication of hypotheses or germane background material, but they should be put forth "with great caution" and "as merely provisional opinions" to be changed or abandoned in the course of further investigation. In Joseph's case the remarks of a member of the review committee and a letter from Jackson convinced him that the major part of his memoir was devoted to "an exposition of known physiological principles." "Indeed Dr. Jackson," he revealed, "appeared to consider your exposition of the philosophy of vitality as the most important part of your paper."[48]

On graduation day Joseph wrote home of his misfortune. Whether the result of having had his article returned for revision or having had to attend the commencement exercises alone, the letter was not flattering to his character. He allowed his worst trait to show when he insinuated that he had received an unusually rigid examination at the hands of the review committee owing to his age and Henry's undue concern for the reputation of the Smithsonian's *Contributions to Knowledge*. The latter was, Joseph openly asserted, "very doubtful whether so young a man could add anything to the advancement of knowledge." Oddly he was unwilling to find any fault with Jackson, who was in large measure responsible for his running afoul of the Smithsonian's publication policies. Joseph vowed to put his personal feelings aside and see the project through in accordance with Henry's dictates, observing: "It is considered an honor to have a piece published in the Journal of the Smithsonian & I must endeavor by all means to sustain its reputation." Thus, although he greatly missed "the quiet comforts of home," it appeared that he would have to remain in Philadelphia about a month longer.[49]

Charles Colcock and Mary Jones hastened to console their

distressed son. They reaffirmed their faith in his ability and urged him to stay in Philadelphia until the memoir had been completed —no matter how long it took. To underscore their support his father, although "pretty drawn down" like most planters in the spring, offered to aid him financially.[50]

Joseph's attempts at shortening his introduction proved futile and he scrapped it. He tersely informed Henry of this action on March 31, writing: "You will therefore be entirely relieved . . . from the fear lest the reputation of your Journal be injured by the publication of what you consider transient hypotheses & theories."[51] If such curtness bothered Henry he did not show it, for in his courteous reply he gave his hearty approval.[52]

Joseph, through no fault of his own as it turned out, believed that the deletion of the objectionable introduction cleared the way for publication of his memoir and returned it to Henry at the beginning of April. But by the middle of the month he had heard nothing further and began to worry anew. Then, as the result of a chance meeting, he learned from Leidy that the manuscript had been sent to him for final approval. Joseph immediately wrote Henry demanding an explanation.[53] Henry's reply was a bitter blow. He was hopeful, he began, that the memoir could appear in the eighth volume of the Smithsonian's *Contributions to Knowledge* scheduled to appear in July. "It is more important," he then added, "that it should be done well than done quickly." This was the reason the paper had been sent to Leidy for final approval. His reading of it convinced him that its numerous chemico-physiological observations were of the highest value to science. He felt, however, that some of the tables were unnecessarily duplicated and the conclusions crudely drawn. The paper, he concluded, should be rewritten.[54]

To Joseph this was the last straw. Feeling complete frustration, he was unable to control his emotions any longer. On April 22 he wrote Henry that he had been led to believe that the revision of the introduction was all that stood between his article and publication. He had done everything asked of him, he charged, only to have the rules changed. He was especially upset that Leidy had been sent the manuscript and insinuated that he had made his unfavorable assessment after having read only one-fourth of it. He reacted indignantly to the criticism of unnecessarily duplicated tables and crudely drawn conclusions. He emphatically denied the former charge, claiming that not more than half-a-dozen tables were repeated and these for emphasis and clarification. Joseph pointed out that he had believed that he was about ready to leave Philadelphia, having worked on this memoir six to eight hours a day for the last six months sparing "neither time, nor expense, nor health." "Still," he concluded resignedly, "out of respect for my Preceptor, in whose candor & judgment I place implicit confidence, I will remain several weeks longer, & re-write all those portions which Dr. Leidy may think necessary, provided that the Smithsonian Institution will defray my necessary expenses for the last month & the time I may yet remain in Philadelphia."[55]

This outburst angered Henry, and he immediately sent a reply, dismantling his youthful assailant's argument. The Smithsonian did hope to publish his memoir "with the least possible delay," he reiterated, but only after it had been put in the form "best calculated to do honor to yourself and to the Institution." At no time had the manuscript been given final acceptance. The delays were the result of the initial mistake about the character of the paper and the subsequent lack of an explicit understanding between them, an understanding which he had tried to produce through his correspondence not only with Joseph but with Jackson and Leidy as well. Obviously he had failed. Therefore he now repeated that the memoir would not be sent to press until Leidy had given it final approval. He did make the concession of committing the Smithsonian to a modest contribution toward his expenses.[56]

The force of Henry's counterattack, coupled with the realization that the Smithsonian's early letter containing the requirement that the paper was to be reviewed a second time before receiving final approval had miscarried, completely unnerved the youth. He penned an apology, explaining: "The fact that I misunderstood the position of the Smithsonian Institution arose from no neglect or impatience on my part, but from the failure of the mails." He assured Henry that he was assiduously revising the manuscript and planned to have it finished by May 17, when he had booked passage for home.[57] Henry's immediate reply urged him to remain in Philadelphia until the memoir had been printed, now stressing the importance of including it in the forthcoming volume of the Smithsonian's *Contributions to Knowledge.* "To send the proofs to Georgia," he entreated, "would defeat the object of an early publication."[58] Joseph countered with an incontrovertible argument—the sickly season was beginning in his part of the country and a change from the North to southern Georgia was almost certainly to be followed by an attack of seasonal fever; he had been working steadily for the last three years without any real break and his health was at present not robust; and the printer was printing those portions of the manuscript approved by Leidy at the ridiculous rate of eight pages a week. At this pace he might be forced to remain in Philadelphia for several months—an impossibility.[59]

Henry did not attempt to detain the youth any longer. Instead he expressed his regrets for the delays that had kept him in the North and sent him a check for fifty dollars. He also used this opportunity to express his affection for Joseph, for despite their quarrelsome relationship mutual bonds of respect between the mature scientist and the novice were being formed which were to remain intact until the former's death. "I shall take a lively interest in your future course," he wrote, "not only because I am kindly disposed to you personally but because we have adopted your results and given them to the world under the sanction of the Institution." He concluded with a warm invitation to visit him on the way South.[60]

There were some unavoidable delays caused by Joseph's return to Georgia, but none of these were serious nor prevented the appearance of the memoir on time. The final editing was done by Spencer F. Baird, the well-known nineteenth-century zoologist, and Henry. Baird's greatest contribution was the compilation of the index, a service he gladly performed in return for Joseph's promise to help complete the Smithsonian's collection of the quadrupeds of North America by sending him some specimens of Georgia reptiles.[61]

The published study, "Investigations, Chemical and Physiological Relative to Certain American Vertebrata," was quite impressive in both content and appearance. Its 137-page text was further explained by 31 valuable tables and beautifully illustrated by 27 striking woodcuts. The memoir was divided into several sections: the first was a physiological discussion of the blood of animals; the second dealt with the physical and chemical changes in animals when deprived of food and drink or affected by a marked change in diet; and the remainder was a series of physiological observations upon various body organs such as the pancreas, liver, spleen, and kidneys. No new physiological discoveries were revealed, but the study was still a remarkable piece of research for so young a scientist and was testimony to his thorough training under Leidy and Jackson and to his demonstrated ability as a scientific investigator. Joseph was proud of the careful hard work that had gone into the memoir and was convinced of the validity of his conclusions. Yet he seems to have taken some of Henry's advice to heart, for in his introduction he pointed out that, owing to the complexity of the topics discussed, the results should be viewed as incomplete and should be considered solely as scientific beginnings.[62]

By the summer of 1856 Joseph Jones had concluded an excellent collegiate career. He had received his undergraduate education at two of the nation's finest colleges and was a graduate of its best medical school. He had excelled at all three institutions. His outstanding academic record and his love of scientific research won him the respect and admiration of Joseph Leidy and Samuel Jackson, two of nineteenth-century America's foremost scientists. He had also published four first-rate articles as a medical student. Three had appeared in the leading national medical journal, the *American Journal of the Medical Sciences*, and the fourth in the Smithsonian Institution's prestigious *Contributions to Knowledge*. This was an exceptional accomplishment for one so young. But brilliant as it was, Joseph Jones's collegiate career was only a foundation on which he was to build a long and successful future as a physician, teacher, scientist, and author.

Chapter 3
Young Professional

I feel it my duty & destiny, to make the attempt
at least, to determine the symptoms & cures
of disease.

Joseph Jones's penchant for scientific investigation complicated his choice of a career. The problem, simply stated, was that despite his training in medicine Jones hoped to avoid the life of a practicing physician because it would leave little time for research. He wrestled with this question during much of his last year of medical school, and at graduation the young physician's future was uncertain. He had, however, reduced his alternatives to two: he could stay in Philadelphia and continue his physiological investigations on a full-time basis or accept the chair of chemistry at the Savannah Medical College. At the outset Jones's eagerness to become a research scientist coupled with his fondness for Leidy and Jackson and his desire for their continued encouragement caused him to incline strongly toward the former alternative. It was not until May 14, some six weeks after his graduation, that he finally reached a decision to go to Savannah. The determining factor was the mental and physical strain of his last year of medical school, which convinced Jones of the health hazard in undertaking anything so demanding as full-time research at this time.[1]

The Savannah Medical College was one of four or five medical schools in Georgia. It had been founded in 1838 but did not admit its first class until 1853. Like most medical schools this one was privately owned. The stock was evenly divided among seven trustees, most of whom were not members of the faculty. A notable exception was Dr. Richard D. Arnold, one of the Old South's foremost physicians, who served as a trustee and as professor of the theory and practice of medicine.[2]

37

Dr. Charles W. West, the professor of chemistry, was related to the Jones family. Advancing age and failing health had led him as early as 1853 to urge his young kinsman to prepare to replace him. In January 1856 he made a formal proposal through the youth's father. West offered the chair of chemistry in return for Jones's assumption of his three-thousand-dollar share of the school's debt.[3] In relaying the offer to his son Charles Colcock Jones counseled against it. He first noted the impossibility of raising the initial investment. Then he pointed out that to assure the seven-man faculty one thousand dollars a year each the school would have to attract at least 120 students. The enrollment then stood between 40 and 50, and owing to competition from the state's other medical schools the possibility of improving upon this figure did not look encouraging. What would happen, he asked, should the school fail? Its professors were in "easy circumstances" with lucrative private practices and could survive the loss, but what would be the effect on a "young man just entering life?" "Position is much—and honorable appointments are much," he concluded, "but we may pay too dear for them."[4]

Apparently Joseph Jones did not act on the proposal nor did West inform his colleagues of it, for on April 2, without reference to an earlier offer, Dr. J. G. Howard, the dean of the faculty, wrote the young scientist of the soon-to-be-vacant chair of chemistry, urging him to apply for it. No terms were specified, so Jones naturally assumed them to be the same as West's earlier ones. He therefore declined to seek the position, explaining that he was heavily indebted for his medical training and research projects and had no means of raising the several thousand dollars required of him. Besides such a sizable sum could be better invested in books, apparatus for experiments, or a trip to Europe. An investment of this magnitude might also preclude the acceptance of a more favorable future offering.[5]

Although puzzled by Jones's letter, Howard seems to have preferred him over several other candidates and chose not to regard his decision as final. He learned that Charles Colcock Jones was to be in Savannah in early May on business and requested a meeting. During its course he was told of West's proposal. Its rigid terms surprised him, for there were, he revealed, two other ways in which the youth could become affiliated with the school without assuming West's share of its debt: he could be employed as a lecturer in chemistry without full faculty status at a salary of one hundred dollars a month, or he could become a full-time faculty member and receive a portion of the school's revenue after expenses.[6]

As a result of this meeting Howard again approached Joseph Jones, this time offering him the chair of chemistry. His offer was supported by the youth's father. Strangely ignoring the school's low enrollment, a problem which was soon to plague his son, he now made as strong a case for accepting the position as he had earlier made for rejecting it. Charles Colcock Jones enumerated for his son its many advantages: he would be teaching an important branch of medicine in which few men were well-qualified; he would be occupying an important place within the state medical profession; he would be a colleague of Savannah's leading medical figures; he would be free to accept a better offer at any time; and he would be near his parents and friends and could minimize expenses by living with his brother, now an attorney in Savannah.[7] Fearful of his health should he stay in Philadelphia and seeing the major obstacle to his acceptance of the Savannah position removed, Jones was swayed by his father's argument. On May 14, four days before leaving for home, he informed Howard of his decision to join the school's faculty as "a Professor . . . ready to bear my full proportion of all the expenses & liabilities, & not as a hired lecturer."[8]

Jones's last year of medical school had left him "much worn down," and he decided to spend the summer regaining his strength at Maybank before embarking upon his arduous duties at the Savannah Medical College. He rested there, visited friends and relatives, took long walks, hunted and fished, and engaged in some light research. These investigations were conducted in a small office which Jones set up under the southeast end of the piazza and furnished with "quite an array of medicines, chemicals, apparatus, and instruments." Parental permission to conduct research in the family home was obtained only after he promised "to put in no explosive substance to blow us all up!"[9] This incident amused Charles, Jr. "I should have exacted from him," he quipped, "a written obligation to the effect that not only explosives but also combustibles, gases of an unpleasant character, and also all remnants of birds of the air, fish of the sea, and all creeping things should be positively excluded from this new sanctum and the vicinage. Otherwise the summer air may perchance be robbed of its sweet perfume."[10]

Joseph Jones moved to Savannah in early October of 1856. Situated on a high bluff overlooking the southeastern bank of the Savannah River some eighteen miles from the ocean, Savannah was the commercial center of Georgia and its largest city, with over 15,000 inhabitants. It had been settled in 1733 by General James Oglethorpe, the chief proponent of Georgia colonization. Laid out in the form of a large rectangle encompassing twenty-four square wards which were bisected by streets and through-fares, Savannah was one of America's most carefully planned and prettiest cities. "Of all the cities in America," Charles Mackay, an English traveler, wrote, "none impresses itself more vividly upon the imagination and the memory than this little green bowery city of the South. It stands upon a terrace about forty feet higher than the river, and presents the appearance of an agglomeration of rural hamlets and small towns. If four-and-twenty villages," he continued, "had resolved to hold a meeting, and had assembled at this place, each with its pump, its country church, its common, and its avenue of trees, the result would have been a fac simile of Savannah."[11]

In Savannah Joseph and his brother rented a small house, christened "Castle Dismal" by a female acquaintance, and set up housekeeping. Once settled, he turned his attention to establishing a part-time medical practice and preparing his introductory lectures. Private practice, he felt, was an economic necessity, since he feared that his salary would be inadequate for his support. The series of public lectures presented for the ten days preceding registration was designed to generate interest in the school.[12]

All faculty members were required to take part in the program, and Jones was assigned to speak on comparative anatomy. Despite his thorough training in the field under Joseph Leidy, he was apprehensive of his reception. By the start of the series in mid-October he was sick with worry. His fears proved groundless. The large audience listened attentively and responded warmly. Of far greater import was Dr. Richard D. Arnold's great pleasure with his youthful colleague's competence; he ebulliently communicated to one of the city's newspapers: "Young as he is, he has, at one bound, attained a high position in the world of science . . . and when time shall have matured his experience, we trust the South may point favorably to him as a worthy son, vindicating her claim to have representatives in purely scientific walks."[13] The youth's father took a more conservative stance. "The notices of Joe and his lectures are such as to encourage him," he observed, "but I hope he will have the good sense modestly to pursue the even tenor of his way, and to remember that his success as a lecturer remains to be proved, and that his reputation as a professor must be based upon solid and progressive learning and improvement in his department."[14]

Jones's financial fears soon became stark reality. The introductory lectures, although heavily attended, failed miserably as a means of attracting students. Only twelve enrolled at the opening of the session on November 3, not enough to pay the school's operating expenses. Even in his most pessimistic moments Jones had not envisioned a situation this depressing. Dismayed, he wrote home: "I may have to pay for the privilege of working hard, day & night, for 4 months."[15] Jones's distress was aggravated by the failure of his medical practice. By the middle of November he could report only three patients—two poor Irishmen and one free Negro.

The prospects of the Savannah Medical College soon began to improve. During the first month of classes enrollment doubled, guaranteeing at least temporary solvency. Yet this development did little to ease Jones's financial plight, since his share of the school's revenue amounted to only a few hundred dollars, far short of the thousand necessary for his support. Moreover his private practice did not improve and was apparently beyond hope. Something more promising was urgently needed. Then fate seemed to intervene in his behalf. Several prominent citizens, who had been impressed with his introductory lectures, asked him to deliver a course of popular lectures in chemistry. Jones readily agreed, planning to offer an evening course beginning in January 1857. He envisioned twenty lectures and set a five-dollar fee for the series or twenty-five cents for individual lectures.[16] The first audiences were large, promising success. "The Doctor," his brother happily reported to their parents, "is succeeding capitally with his lectures. His audience at the medical college in attendance upon his first two lectures numbered about one hundred and fifty . . . of the most intelligent ladies and gentlemen in the city, and I hope the interest will continue."[17] But such was not to be the case and any hopes of financial gain were short-lived, for as the early enthusiasm waned attendance steadily declined.

Jones was at his wit's end, having exhausted every means in

his power to bolster his sagging finances. Reluctantly he concluded that his career in Savannah was doomed to financial failure, and he began making preparations to seek the University of Georgia's less desirable but better paying vacant chair of natural sciences. These plans had not advanced far when Arnold learned of them. He asked his youthful friend if he would remain in Savannah if the faculty guaranteed him one thousand dollars a year. Jones gave an unqualified affirmative response, and Arnold, eager to keep him in Savannah, offered him this sum "on his own responsibility."[18] Jones had such a strong faith in this friend that he unwisely considered his financial woes at an end. In fact so confident was he that he terminated his plans to pursue the opening at the University of Georgia, busying himself instead with professional studies, making a collection of the reptiles of tidewater Georgia for the college museum, and planning a much-needed vacation in Charleston.[19]

Optimism gave way to despair at the beginning of July when Jones learned that Arnold's efforts in his behalf had failed. It is not clear why Jones's colleagues refused his request. It was certainly not personal, since he enjoyed the friendliest of relations with the other faculty members. They may simply have refused to show one of their number any favoritism, holding Jones instead to the terms of his contract in which he had agreed to settle for one-seventh of the school's revenue after expenses. It is also possible that they did not understand, or at least did not appreciate, his situation, since they were successful physicians with lucrative practices and taught mainly for prestige. Thus they may have believed that Jones too could succeed in this way if he but tried harder. None of them, however, seemed willing to accord him a share of their medical monopoly among Savannah's leading families. Outraged at their reaction, Jones immediately announced his candidacy for the opening in Athens and let it be known that he was doing so solely for financial reasons, caustically asserting: "The faculty of the Savannah Medical College do not seem to set much value upon my services, & expect to receive them without remuneration."[20]

Had it not been for this financial crisis, Joseph Jones probably would have stayed at the Savannah Medical College for an indefinite period, for otherwise his position was ideal. Indeed, despite the fact that on the days he lectured he spent seven hours at the school, the short session (only four months) and the facilities offered by Savannah's large combination marine hospital and poorhouse provided the young scientist with an enviable research opportunity. He exploited it fully as he made clear at the time of his departure from the city, avowing: "I have never spent in my life a more profitable season."[21]

The Savannah Marine Hospital and Poor House was a veritable gold mine for Jones in terms of his current research interest —the fevers of the nineteenth-century South. This institution, established to provide medical care for transient seamen and certain charity cases, often admitted over a hundred patients monthly, many of whom were fever victims. Jones's friend and benefactor, Dr. Richard D. Arnold, was the hospital's chief administrator. He was interested in his enterprising colleague's work and sought to facilitate it through assigning patients to him for treatment and allowing him free access to any patient and to all hospital records. Jones was elated and worked hard compiling detailed histories of the most interesting cases, recording their symptoms, course, and outcome.

The amount of research Joseph Jones launched during his single year at the Savannah Medical College was truly prodigious and went far beyond the preparation of case histories of fever victims. He began an in-depth study of malaria, a project which carried him not only into the wards of the Savannah Marine Hospital and Poor House but to Georgia's swampy malaria-ridden coastal plain. This constant exposure inevitably led to his contracting the disease. Jones's interest in febrile poisons, moreover, caused him to undertake a preliminary examination of yellow fever, a disease which soon captivated his interest as thoroughly as did malaria. He also began an inquiry into the climate, topography, and diseases of Georgia's rice and cotton plantations, which he was to continue intermittently until the outbreak of the Civil War. Finally Jones launched a statistical study of Savannah's most prevalent diseases. Hoping to achieve historical perspective, he spent many hours poring over mortuary records for the previous half-century, identifying diseases and determining the ages of those who had died from them. He planned similar studies for the state's other urban centers— Athens and Augusta.[22]

Jones approached these diverse projects with a characteristic self-assurance which often bordered on brashness, smugly proclaiming that his past investigation of the blood of various animals had well prepared him to study the diseases of man. Still these were important investigations worthy of notice and compared quite favorably with much of the research under way in the American medical profession at this time; moreover, despite Jones's arrogant self-confidence these undertakings clearly reveal his love of and capacity for original research.[23]

Although harboring all the while his lingering reluctance to leave Savannah with its "golden opportunities for advancement," Jones vigorously sought the University of Georgia's chair of natural sciences. His candidacy was impressively strong: it rested not only on solid personal credentials but also on the laudatory recommendations of Leidy, Jackson, and Henry. At the local level his brother and uncles Henry and John Jones lent their support. The latter uncle, an alumnus of the University of Georgia, presented his nephew's case to the board of trustees when it met in August to fill the vacant chair. Jones's qualifications were so obviously superior to those of the only other candidate, N. A. Pratt, Jr., that he was unanimously elected to the position.[24]

Charles Colcock Jones was far more excited than his son about the outcome of the election. He extolled the position's advantages —sufficient pecuniary support (in excess of one thousand dollars), a three-month summer vacation, good social connections, and abundant religious opportunities. He also warned of its responsibilities and in so doing bared the reason for the young scientist's lack of excitement. "And now," the Reverend Jones counseled, "your *Physiological Investigations must be suspended for a while:* and your attention be given to a thorough preparation on the different branches of natural sciences, which you are required to teach in the College. . . . It is essential to your success & good standing & to your character that you be a good Professor."[25]

Joseph Jones was indeed less than enthusiastic about his victory. His feelings are understandable in light of the professional sacrifice he had to make in accepting his prize. He had long since resigned himself to the fact, however, that in this instance finances must take precedence over research, and in early September he formally severed his ties with the Savannah Medical College. In an unusually warm letter of resignation he expressed a deep regret to his colleagues at the necessity of so drastic a step, praised the school for its "high and honorable stand upon Medical Education," and vowed that he would "ever cherish a lively remembrance of the courteous and gentlemanly treatment which

I have uniformly received" and "promote the interest of your noble Institution by any means, however feeble, in my power."[26]

Jones's new appointment did not start until the beginning of the spring quarter in January 1858. He planned to spend the interim in Savannah winding up his various investigations and making preparations to move. Upon learning this, his former colleagues, recalling the spirit of his letter of resignation, asked him to remain on the faculty until December 23, arguing that the lateness of his action left too little time to obtain a suitable replacement. Jones was inclined to do them this favor but decided to consult his father before committing himself. Charles Colcock Jones saw the matter in a different light. "Had the faculty earnestly desired your continuance & deemed it of vital importance to their enterprize," he asserted, "they would have done more to retain you than they have done, and I do not see that you are called upon to do more than you have done."[27] This advice caused Jones to turn down the request, pleading the importance of his research and the necessity of a vacation before undertaking his new duties. Jones's rebuff caught the faculty of the Savannah Medical College by surprise. Disappointed in him, they launched a frantic search for a successor.[28]

Coming on the heels of his trying financial crisis was a critical review of Jones's Smithsonian article in the *North American Medico-Chirurgical Review*, an important Philadelphia medical journal. The reviewer quickly recognized and came down hard on the youthful author's most glaring shortcoming as a scientific writer, which even Joseph Henry had not been able to overcome entirely in the end. Calling attention to the many pages devoted to an account of "how this and that man's method is in fault," the critic remarked: "Let us hope that the next book from this source may be really and simply 'contributions to knowledge,' and not to such an extent as this one, a réchauffé of the views of others." Jones was further criticized for confusing his readers by failing to distinguish between new and outmoded ideas within this body of literature. He was also taken to task for several misleading statements, some questionable laboratory practices, the "most astonishing" accuracy of his blood analysis tables (with the implication that Jones may have aided his results by fudging), and a number of minor errors.

The review was not entirely adverse. In fact the reviewer found much in the study to commend. He praised Jones's observations upon the habits of animals, his analyses of the effects of thirst and starvation of both warm- and cold-blooded animals, his tables of the length of the intestinal canal and the weights of the pancreas, spleen, and other vital organs, and his charts on the relative size of the heart and the rapidity of circulation. This type of physiological investigation, he noted, "is rarely procured without the utmost difficulty, and . . . we think our author deserves the thanks of physiologists." The young scientist's industry and perseverance were also the subject of special notice. So impressed was his critic by them that he asserted that the work's defects "are almost atoned for by an industry and perseverance, which in time will, no doubt, attain to more perfect and more accurate results."[29]

The only other review which Jones had seen he considered favorable and this one enraged him. He still had not learned to accept criticism. Samuel D. Gross, one of the journal's editors, was the major recipient of his ire. Jones had known Gross in Philadelphia, and considering him a friend, he was shocked that the editor would publish a derogatory notice of his study. Charles Colcock Jones also expressed surprise at Gross's action, labeling the review "brief, dogmatical & rather testy." Then, not so much to stem his son's anger as to use this situation to teach him a valuable lesson, he advised: "you must . . . learn to stand fire. He who writes for the public must expect the public to notice him publically. If our work cannot stand examination & criticism, & even unjust dealing they are feeble."[30]

Gross sensed that the review would upset Jones and in a lengthy letter explained his role in its history. He liked the article personally, but owing to his lack of expertise on the subject he had sent it out for review. Gross regretted that "the reviewer should have found fault with the work." At the same time he informed Jones that his critic was a competent scholar and that editorial integrity precluded the alteration of a review except in case of obvious personal attack. The explanation, coupled with Gross's profession of fondness for his young friend and prediction of a bright future for him, abated the youth's anger, and in the frenzy of activity surrounding his move to Athens the affair was soon forgotten.[31]

Jones took up residence in the "very pleasant arrangements" he had found in Athens shortly after the beginning of the new year. Although considerably smaller than Savannah, Athens was looked upon by many as the social center of Georgia and a leader in cultural offerings among all the towns of the Old South. "The social graces and amenities," it has been reported, "were well and consciously developed here. Its educational background, as well as the prominence of its citizens and visitors, was equaled in few of the Southern towns."[32] The presence of the University of Georgia accounts in large measure for this preeminent position. Founded in 1785 the University of Georgia, or Franklin College as it was generally called before the Civil War, had eighty students, an endowment of approximately $100,000 and consisted of two dormitories, a science building, a chapel, a library, the president's house, and three houses for professors on a forty-four-acre tract at the time of Jones's arrival. The library had nearly 13,000 volumes, a figure exceeded in the South only by the University of Virginia and South Carolina College. Especially appealing to Jones was the school's collection of scientific equipment, one of the most extensive and complete in the country, and its well-stocked botanical garden.

Jones's students were juniors and seniors; he instructed the former in physics and botany and the latter in natural philosophy. Like most college students in the Old South those at the University of Georgia, according to this school's leading historian, "held firmly to the belief that the professors were the chief obstacle to their thorough enjoyment of life, and that, therefore, they were objects of ridicule, scorn, and attacks." "The attitude of students toward professors," he continued, "found a wide variety of ways in which to express itself from mild dislike to malignant hatred, ranging from prankish indifference to deadly intent."[33] Jones was fortunate, for he encountered no ill will from his students, and instead he praised them for their attentiveness. Much of his success is attributable to his concern for good teaching. Apparently because many lectures were of low quality, teaching by this means was held in low esteem at the University of Georgia. An excellent lecturer, Jones vowed to revitalize this method of instruction, which he viewed as essential in imparting the weighty content of his subjects. So dedicated was he to the lecture system that he favored measuring a student's performance not only on the usual daily recitations and final examinations but also on "the style, manner, & execution" of his class notes.[34]

Joseph Jones had been at the University of Georgia less than two months when James A. Sledge, editor of the *Athens Banner*, called upon him. His visit, Sledge explained, was at the behest of a relative, a faculty member at the Medical College in Augusta, who wished to have Jones informed that the school's chair of medical chemistry and pharmacy had been recently vacated and to obtain his candid views on seeking it. Jones, caught by surprise and unsure what his course of action should be, stalled for time, telling Sledge that he was too indebted to the University of Georgia to seek the position but would give a formal offer "a most respectful & careful consideration."

He immediately sought his father's advice, making no attempt to hide his longing for the vacant chair in Augusta. The advantages of the Medical College of Georgia over the state university, he argued, were overwhelming. A professorship at the former was "probably the most desirable situation for a physician in the state of Georgia," and while his brief stay at the latter had been "pleasant & commanding," his duties involved "the expenditure of a vast amount of labor and time." His time, he complained, was so completely monopolized by lectures, recitations, and care of the school's laboratory equipment that he had little opportunity to pursue his own research "with any success or vigor." Should he move to Augusta, he would have to work only four months a year instead of eight for the same salary. Having presented his case, Jones wistfully sought his father's approval to change schools, querying: "If the professorship in the Augusta College was offered, do you not think it would be my duty to accept?"[35]

Charles Colcock Jones did not share his son's excitement. Until the position could be thoroughly investigated, he advised, *"Do not commit yourself in any way or degree."*[36] His advice came too late, for by the time it arrived Jones had committed himself. On March 3, two days after Sledge's visit, he was contacted by Dr. Henry F. Campbell, professor of anatomy at the Medical College of Georgia and secretary of the board of trustees. Campbell informed Jones that he was the first choice of the faculty and trustees for the vacant chair but that it would not be offered to him unless his acceptance was assured. Should he refuse to give his assurance, it would be offered to either John or Joseph Le-Conte of Columbia, South Carolina. Jones had not yet heard from his father and Campbell was pressing him for an immediate answer. Afraid to procrastinate any longer for fear of losing this golden opportunity, he gave in to Campbell's tactics, firmly convinced, however, that he had made the right decision.[37]

Two days later Jones was formally invited to join the faculty of the Medical College of Georgia. Although honor-bound to accept, he sat on the invitation for a week in order that he might review and reassess the events of the previous five days. On March 12, after "many anxious thoughts," he wrote Campbell that he was honoring his commitment. On this same day Jones submitted his resignation to the trustees of the University of Georgia, giving six months notice. In both communications he enumerated a single determining factor for his decision—research opportunities. "The only motive which has induced me to accept the Professorship of Chemistry & Pharmacy in the Medical College of Georgia," he maintained, "is a desire to assist in elevating the standard of medical education & establish medicine upon a firm scientific basis, by careful chemical, physical, physiological & pathological investigations." Nothing less was acceptable, for Jones was convinced that such was his destiny, asserting: "Whether I shall be successful or unsuccessful, whether or not I am deceived in supposing that I have the ability to do this; nevertheless I have the desire, & would conceive that I was not pursusing my destiny if occupying any possition however exalted or profitable in which I would be debarred from the successful prosecution of original investigations." So, while the decision may have been a tortuous one, the basic issue was quite simple: the University of Georgia inhibited research while the Medical College of Georgia encouraged it. Jones insisted that this was the entire story and that there had been no deceit on his part.[38]

Charles Colcock Jones was not convinced that his son's action or motives were above reproach. His reaction may have been prejudiced, however, since the youth had acted entirely on his own without waiting for parental advice. In any case to the Reverend Jones the decision was not only "unexpected & sudden" but was "carried through so expeditiously that we have had no opportunity of offering any special opinion in the matter." He further felt that his son had left himself open to charges of treating the University of Georgia inconsiderately, cast himself as an opportunist, and embarrassed his brother and friends who had helped him gain his present position. "We ought not," he moralized, "to make highly responsible & honorable appointments & appointments of public trust matters of personal convenience & necessity; nor so to seek & use them as to carry the appearance of so doing."[39]

This unexpectedly strong criticism surprised Jones but did not change his mind. He was still unwavering in the belief that he had made the right choice and rushed to his own defense. In a lengthy letter he discussed again his grounds for leaving the University of Georgia. "If I remained in Athens, " he began, "I must determine to be a teacher & nothing more for the rest of my life." One had only to look at his duties to realize this: "Prayers at sunrise— recitations before breakfast—recitations & lectures at 11 A.M. & 4 P.M. & Prayers again during study hours—attendance upon the examinations of all the other officers, of the regular students, & of all applicants, even for the Freshman class." It was physically impossible, he contended, to fulfill these duties conscientiously and make any significant contribution to science. Jones ruled out any hopes for improvement, since older and wiser men than he had tried to plant seeds of change only to reap criticism and disillusionment. In fact, instead of improving, conditions seemed to be deteriorating. A shortage of funds prevented the hiring of additional faculty, precluding a better division of labor; a general reduction of faculty salaries at the end of the year was a real threat; and of equal seriousness was the fact that the school had "bitter enemies in all parts of the State" who were actively seeking to bring about its failure by blocking appropriations and exploiting "any circumstance which affords an opportunity for vituperation." In light of its almost insurmountable problems he feared that the school was on the verge of becoming a second-rate institution.

The true state of affairs, Jones implied, was unknown to him until his arrival in Athens. Now, fully aware of conditions at the University of Georgia, he felt that he must choose one of three alternatives. First, he could "settle down as a mere teacher & go round & round year after year in the same beaten track." This choice, although conducive to "personal ease & comfort," his sense of destiny would not allow. Jones's logic smacks heavily of pretentiousness, but he sincerely believed that it was his "duty & destiny, to make the attempt at least, to determine the causes symptoms & cures of disease." Second, he could neglect a portion of his duties in order to make time for his scientific studies. Jones flatly rejected this alternative, asserting that it could "never enter into the calculations of an honest minded man." Third, he could "resign promptly & honorably, & allow the place to be filled by a man who expected to make teaching the business of his life." He believed this to be the only practical course of action, arguing that "a resignation at no time is dishonorable," that he would "violate no obligation, by allowing others more distinguished & learned to fill the responsible station," and that he would "accomplish much more for the good of the College by a prompt resignation, & candid statement of . . . reasons, than by any number of protests or complaints, or recommendations to the Board of Trustees."

Jones envisioned only two valid objections to his resignation— that he had treated lightly his unanimous election to the faculty and that his leaving so soon after joining the faculty would aid the school's enemies. He dismissed the first with the revelation that he had intended to resign before receiving "any intimation of a call to Augusta." He further believed that this objection would not be raised for he had "taken special pains to ascertain the opinion of all the Professors, & of several of the Trustees & Citizens of Athens" and not one of them had viewed his actions in this light. He contended that the second objection could not with justice be used against him, since it was not his fault that the University of Georgia had been allowed to deteriorate to a point where it could be injured "by the resignation of a young man with little or no reputation."

At the conclusion of his defense Jones looked back over the whole affair one last time. He was even more convinced that his actions were correct and justified. He hoped that his father would now think so too. But in case he still objected, Jones made his personal position clear. "I have," he wrote, "endeavored to act in this matter conscientiously, & in such a manner as to throw the entire responsibility upon no one but myself. I believe it to be the duty of every honest minded man to take the whole responsibility in all the important steps of life. Then if he fails the fault is entrely his, & relatives & friends are relieved."[40]

Charles Colcock Jones had obviously reacted too strongly, since public opinion indicated approval of his son's move. The trustees of the University of Georgia accepted his resignation with understanding. His brother was elated, predicting: "The change from Athens to Augusta will be in every respect favorable for him. He will be there in the regular line of professional engagements, and occupations well suited to his natural tastes."[41] The medical press of the state also enthusiastically endorsed the move. Juriah Harriss, editor of the *Savannah Journal of Medicine* and one of Jones's former colleagues at the Savannah Medical College, reported: "We not only congratulate the members of the Faculty of the Medical College of Georgia, upon so valuable an acquisition to their number, but also the profession upon his more immediate connection with it, than has been the case for months past."[42]

Jones's next major decision was as much a source of pleasure to his parents as his previous one had been reason for concern. In late April of 1858 he wrote home of his intention of joining the Presbyterian church, asserting: "I feel it to be my duty to halt no longer between two opinions, & rely no longer upon my own efforts, but to accept of the Savior as my only hope of salvation."[43] He had become increasingly interested in religion since his arrival in Athens, a development largely attributable to the Sunday school class of young adults which he had been asked to teach. His actual conversion, however, was sparked by a revival which saw thirty-seven others, including his manservant Titus, take the same step. Charles Colcock and Mary Jones had long worried about their sons' souls, warning on one occasion: "A death bed, my dear Sons, is no place for you to prepare to meet your God!"[44] They were so overjoyed at the news of Joseph's conversion that they "knelt down & returned thanks to our gracious covenant keeping God & Redeemer who had bestowed such mercy."[45]

Jones's religious commitment was genuine, but he was apprehensive about living up to it. Specifically he feared a "coldness and careless-mindedness" stemming from his personal nature and "continued application to purely literary and scientific pursuits."[46] To counteract this tendency Jones felt that he must find a way to keep his Christian duties constantly before him. Teaching Sunday school and participating in the religious life of the University of Georgia was not enough: something more spiritually challenging was needed. He soon hit upon an idea—to follow his father's earlier example and establish a slave Sunday school in Athens. The amateur missionary found this experience so rewarding that he continued it upon moving to Augusta. Here he personally founded one slave Sunday school with the approval of the Presbyterians and assisted in the establishment of another in conjunction with the Reverend Samuel S. Davis, his future father-in-law, at one of the local Baptist churches. In each case Jones began his missionary work "in a quiet way," taking extreme caution to "offend no one, & avoid all officiousness." He did most of the teaching himself at first, putting his father's techniques and catechism to good use. In addition he encouraged the formation of Negro choirs. He also adopted the habit of presenting the children on each sabbath a portion of scriptural history. In every instance Jones's efforts succeeded handsomely, and within a short time each of the slave Sunday schools in which he had a hand came to have over a hundred members of all ages and a sizable number of dedicated assistants.[47]

Joseph Jones's appointment at the Medical College of Georgia did not begin until the opening of the 1858–1859 session on November 1, but as early as May, Campbell began publicizing the school's new faculty member in the *Southern Medical and Surgical Journal.* This journal, which he edited, was one of the Old South's leading medical periodicals and the school's official organ. Upon Jones's acceptance of the chair of medical chemistry and pharmacy in March, Campbell had pressed him for a contribution, being "particularly anxious that it should appear with the announcement of your appointment."[48] Jones, ever eager to share the results of his research, submitted two studies, both based on material he had collected at the Savannah Marine Hospital and Poor House.

The first appeared in May. In it he attempted to use blood analyses as a basis for drawing comparisons between diabetes and malaria. His findings showed more dissimilarities than similarities, but more important this study revealed that Jones, like most of his contemporaries, was aware of the nature of diabetes, but could offer little in the way of controlling it.[49] The second article was a lengthy examination of malaria, so long that nine installments were needed to complete it. The first appeared in June, and by the time the series was finished the following March it had described 53 cases of malaria in 235 pages of agonizing repetitiousness punctuated with a plethora of findings compiled from 16 autopsies, 66 urine analyses, and 9 elaborate blood analyses.[50]

Jones seemed to realize that his study was liable to criticism for its length, detail, and repetition, for in the fourth installment he moved to quiet potential critics by explaining his methodology. "Our knowledge of Malarial fever, and in fact, of all fevers," he began, "is imperfect." This situation existed because many of the phenomena of malaria had never been analyzed or had escaped observation, largely as a result of inadequate instruments, crude research techniques, and the complicated nature of the phenomena. A true understanding of this dread killer could be established, Jones argued, if scientists would patiently proceed upon "the strict principles of induction." He was unwavering in the belief that through observation, experiment, and reason, in which facts were recorded and compared, complex phenomena observed and analyzed, and "errors of the senses" corrected, fundamental laws could be discovered. Such laws were invaluable to the scientist, for they enabled him "to predict with absolute certainty the future course of events." The physician, therefore, should strive "to discover the fixed relations or laws of the animal economy, and the definite action . . . and relations of morbific and remedial agents" so that he would be prepared "to predict the results of the actions of these agents, and also to control and direct their action." "This is our object," Jones proclaimed, "and this is our method."[51]

Despite such lofty goals there is little new in this study. It reveals Jones as a typical figure of nineteenth-century American medicine. He accepted unquestioningly the miasmatic patho-genesis of malaria and sought to combat it through the standard heroic principles of treatment—bleeding, blistering, purging, and the administering of excessive doses of dangerous drugs, especially calomel. In the case of malaria quinine was used as a specific in conjunction with these usual therapeutic measures. But bound as he was to the tenets of traditional medicine, Jones did exhibit a refreshingly modern side. His detailed investigation of malaria had led him to doubt the value of copious bloodletting in con-trolling the fever and to favor the substitution of diet in its place.

The article's most rewarding points are found, paradoxically, in its introduction: paradoxically because this was a typical Jo-seph Jones introduction—lengthy, discursive, and largely super-fluous—and a sad testimony to the fact that he had not learned from past criticism of his writing. By way of an abstract philo-sophical examination "of the relations of animated beings to ex-terior inorganic bodies, to each other, and to the physical and chemical forces," he hoped that these "preliminary investiga-tions" would show that "in the present state of Medical Science, the complete investigation of all the effects and phenomena of disease, is impossible." On the whole this argument can be dis-missed as extraneous to the rest of the paper, but from it can be gleaned important information concerning Jones's attitudes toward the study of disease. In general he adopted an unrealistic approach to medical research, arguing that man was a microcosm of the universe and to understand him in sickness or health it was necessary first to understand the mutual relations of all animate and inanimate bodies, both terrestrial and celestial. Disease involved simply abnormal changes in the body, the result either of a derangement of the blood or organs or of the invasion of foreign morbific agents. The intensity of the attack depended upon the individual's constitution and the interaction of the organs and tissues of the body. Therefore, if scientists were to investigate properly the origin, treatment, and effects of disease, man must be studied in health as well as in sickness. The magnitude of the task ruled out the possibility of any individual studying all the phenomena of disease. The solution—cooperation among investigators—was obvious, and he suggested potential research areas: analysis of the urine and the blood; determination of animal temperature; functions of skin and lungs; meteorologic, geologic, and topographical investigations, and records of symptoms and treatment and of mortuary statistics; and detailed postmortem examinations.

Jones was highly optimistic about the dividends attainable from such a division of labor and predicted: "If a corps of intelligent, generous-minded observers would act with zeal and unity, the results for medicine would be of the most momentous character. It would, in time, rank amongst the exact sciences and the physician would become a true prophet; and instead of the frequent disagreement between theory and practice, and between rival schools, we would have harmony; instead of distrust in the public, and even in the minds of physicians, themselves, we would have confidence."[52] Jones was far beyond his time in such hopes, perhaps even visionary, and much of his scheme was impractical. Yet he revealed an awareness of traditional medicine's problems —its empirical and unscientific nature, factional feuds, the mediocrity of medical research, and the loss of public confidence—and pointed a way toward reform.

Joseph Jones did not move to Augusta until late September of 1858, but he paid several visits there beginning in April (in this instance while recuperating from a severe attack of malaria) to become acquainted with the professors of the Medical College of Georgia, to inquire into the condition of the school, and to find a place to live. He was received with "marked attention and kindness" and found a small brick house to rent near the college next door to Dr. Joseph A. Eve, the professor of obstetrics and diseases of women. The renting of a house was a costly undertaking for one already financially strapped, but Jones felt that his position demanded such a move, remarking that "the social qualities deteriorate very much in hotels & boarding houses."[53] He found Augusta quite appealing, as did most persons who visited there. "Augusta," Fredrika Bremer wrote, "is a little city of the same style as Savannah, but less great, less beautiful in every way; but very pretty nevertheless, and situated in a broad bend of the Savannah. Around it are many charming country-houses with their gardens."[54]

Jones was delighted with the Medical College of Georgia. It was the first and by far the best medical school in the state. Founded in the 1820s, it had already compiled an enviable record of solid achievement when he joined the faculty. Much of its success can be traced to enlightened leadership and generous state and municipal support. Appointments were highly sought after, and the faculty included some of the best medical minds in the South. Clinical instruction, either absent from the curriculum of most antebellum medical schools or consisting of "a walk through the wards," was first-rate and free; and it was conducted in Augusta's City Hospital, which was under the charge of the faculty. The school boasted of a library of over five thousand volumes of the leading works in medical science. New volumes were added at the rate of two hundred annually. The museum of anatomical and physiological specimens, a valuable teaching aid in nineteenth-century medical schools, was said to be one of the best in the United States and was undergoing constant improvement with the addition of new contributions.[55] The important position occupied by this medical school was best summed up by William F. Norwood, the leading historian of medical education in antebellum America. "It is worthy of record," he wrote, "that Georgia's first medical college filled a long felt need in the state and also served the South at large. Its chief contributions were its sincere efforts, without encouragement, to elevate educational standards, and its most successful recognition and provisions of practical instruction in the clinical subjects of medicine. Hundreds of Georgians and Southerners benefitted by its existence."[56]

Jones excitedly looked forward to the opening of the Medical College of Georgia because he had been selected to deliver the introductory address which formally marked the beginning of the four-month school year. It was considered an honor to be designated the inaugural speaker, and Jones was moved by such a warm gesture of welcome from his new colleagues. Determined to merit their confidence, he took great care in selecting a topic, spending most of the summer preparing it. He decided to speak on the ideal in medical education with the thesis that "to be a good physician, a man must study all knowledge whether relating to matter or mind." In doing so he hoped to show the "extent & dignity" of medicine and "excite the students to pursue it as a noble science & not as a mere trade." Alas, on the day of his address Jones was too ill with a cold to deliver it. Campbell substituted for him.[57]

Despite this inauspicious beginning Jones's first year at the Medical College of Georgia was rewarding. He became genuinely fond of his colleagues and was pleased with the school's enrollment, the largest in the state, of 150 students. His class in medical chemistry, consisting of lectures in physics, "chemical affinity," organic and inorganic chemistry, physiological and pathological chemistry of the blood and urine, and toxicology, drew especially well, prompting him to write home: "My lecture room is at the present time crowded with students & visitors."[58] He was also favorably impressed with his sixty students. "Whatever their short comings may be," he remarked, "I am persuaded that they are errors of the head rather than of the heart."[59]

With the close of the school term on March 1, 1859, Joseph Jones looked forward to renewing his original investigations. For a brief period he was undecided whether to work in Augusta or at Maybank. This question was quickly resolved when he learned that $1,000 of his $2,400 salary was to be withheld as his share of the costs of renovating the school's laboratory. Finances dictated, therefore, that he return home, for should he stay in Augusta he would be forced to practice medicine part-time to offset this loss of income. Jones planned to use his time to expand his study of southern diseases and plantation hygiene. In anticipation of this undertaking he had enlisted the aid of his students. During their examinations he had exacted a promise that they would collect and send him all the facts of interest in their sections of the country bearing upon these subjects. In a rare moment of humor he quipped: "I knew that it was the right time to exact promises."[60]

Jones was forced to delay his research for over a month in order to perform several duties for the Medical College of Georgia which carried over into the eight-month recess between sessions. Despite his eagerness to begin his investigations he willingly performed this work, remarking that "the great competition between medical schools, demands the most active & energetic conduct on the part of professors."[61] In the middle of April he helped represent the school at the annual meeting of the Medical Association of Georgia in Atlanta. Delegates from the host Atlanta Medical College were in a majority, but the Medical College of Georgia dominated the program, its representatives reading seven of the ten papers presented. Jones was not on the program and, upon noticing the many distinguished members of the audience, wished that he was. He lamented that "it was a favorable opportunity to make an impression." But all was not lost, for to his surprise and pleasure he was asked to comment upon his study of southern diseases. He talked extemporaneously for an hour and a half. His remarks were vigorously applauded, and at the annual banquet the first and last toasts were offered in honor of them.[62]

A week later Jones was in Athens to act as the spokesman for the Medical College of Georgia in a meeting with representatives of the state university aimed at exploring ways to unite the schools. The idea had originated in Athens, where the trustees of the University of Georgia were anxious to add medicine to the curriculum. Jones and his colleagues favored the proposal, and he was empowered to report their feelings. Nothing of importance, however, was accomplished.[63] Jones was disappointed with the results of the session but was otherwise pleased with his stay in Athens. He visited with faculty and student friends at the University of Georgia and spoke at the Negro Sunday school he had helped found. It now had nearly 300 members and 25 "excellent, pious & intelligent teachers." Jones was thrilled, boasting: "It is one of the best organized, & conducted schools that I have ever seen. It gave me great pleasure to see such large results from my feeble efforts."[64]

At the end of April, Jones, on the spur of the moment, accepted an invitation from Campbell to accompany him to Louisville, Kentucky, to attend the twelfth annual meeting of the American Medical Association, further postponing his research. The trip, made by train to a point shortly beyond Nashville and by stagecoach the remainder of the way, was long and tiring. "Nine of us," as Jones reported it, "were packed in a close stage—the weather was rainy and the roads in shocking condition. Packed closely together, jolting and rocking was not so pleasant. We were 28 hours in travelling 90 miles."[65] The young teacher-research scientist willingly sacrificed valuable research time and underwent the discomforts of mid-nineteenth-century travel because of a "firm conviction that the interests of the Medical College of Georgia are at stake." To him the forthcoming session was unquestionably "the most important one that the National Medical Association has ever had," since a convention of medical school teachers preceding it was to tackle the sensitive problem of medical education.[66]

American medical education was in an appalling state, primarily as a result of the evils arising from the proliferation of proprietary medical schools after 1820. Competition between schools was fierce and blatantly commercial; degree requirements varied widely (in most cases, two four-month terms in which the same courses were repeated each year); medical education frequently presented a curious blend of a formal collegiate program and the older apprenticeship system; and few schools offered clinical instruction. The desire to standardize the training of physicians had been one of the principal reasons for the formation of the A.M.A. in 1847, but all attempts at reform had been thwarted by the proprietary schools, their conservative graduates who feared the consequences of change, the A.M.A.'s lack of any real power to regulate medical education, and, to a lesser degree, the doctrine of states' rights and sectionalism. In 1858, however, the advocates of reform succeeded in calling a convention of the teachers of medicine to meet the day before the next annual convention to examine the entire subject of medical education.[67]

The high hopes of the reformers were quickly dashed since the meeting was a colossal failure. It was doomed from the start: the nation's leading medical schools, in Philadelphia and New York, were not represented; discord was rampant among the delegates of the twenty-one schools which did participate; and the one day allotted to the session was grossly inadequate to deal with such a complex problem. The proceedings rapidly degenerated into a fruitless discussion of the old question of whether the A.M.A. had the authority to regulate medical education. "After organization, & the delivery of several windy speeches," as Jones aptly put it, "the convention was adjourned." He vehemently opposed adjournment, because he was painfully aware of the crisis facing the nation's medical schools and was eager to do his share to ease it. "It was provoking," he deplored, "to travel more than one thousand miles with an honest desire to advance the interest of medical education or at least hear it discussed & then have the whole matter terminate in smoke."[68]

Jones hoped that the A.M.A. session would be more rewarding. His keen interest in the proceedings of the convention was to a considerable extent, however, a matter of self-interest, since he had submitted a 600-page manuscript (entitled "Observations on Some of the Changes of the Solids and Fluids in Malarial Fever") to the committee on prize essays. These investigations were an elaboration, shortcomings included, of his work on malaria recently published in the *Southern Medical and Surgical Journal*. Like its predecessor this study, although the cases of malaria cited and the illustrative tables had been greatly increased, contained little that was new. The best that can be said for it is that perhaps for the first time the medical profession had at its disposal a systematic study of the changes of the temperature, pulse, respiration, blood, urine, and vital organs in the various forms of malaria.[69]

Jones had submitted his manuscript to the prize essay committee only two days before the opening of the convention, and the committee members were obviously irritated at the lateness of the entry. Noting its inordinate length, they promptly excluded the study from the competition "on account of the absolute impossibility of reading [it] with a critical purpose and effect." Rebuffed in his quest for a prize, Jones laid his findings before the committee on voluntary contributions. Here they were received in a much different vein. The committee was surprised at such thorough work by one so new in the profession and obtained permission for him to present a verbal abstract of his paper and an exposition of his theory to the full convention. The delegates also greeted Jones's research with enthusiasm, and on the motion of Dr. D. W. Yandell of Louisville his manuscript was referred to the committee on publications for inclusion in the next volume of the association's *Transactions*.[70] The young scientist's presentation also impressed the Louisville press. "Dr. Jones though a young man," the *Louisville Courier* reported, "was listened to with profound attention by the large number of gentlemen present. He is an eloquent & forcible speaker & his happy mode of simplifying a subject would indicate his superior fitness as a lecturer & teacher."[71]

The committee on publications must have suggested that Jones revise his manuscript, for at the adjournment of the convention he hurried home and commenced extensive revisions. This task so fully monopolized his time that he was forced to postpone indefinitely his summer research plans and, with but one short interruption, he worked steadily at editing the study throughout the remainder of May and during all of June and July. At the beginning of August Jones announced his satisfaction with the manuscript and sent it to the printer in Philadelphia. As proud as he was of this study he considered it no more than "a beginning in the right direction" and vowed to continue these investigations "with vigor."[72]

Three months still remained before the beginning of school, ample time for Jones to make considerable headway in his research, take a well-earned vacation, or prepare for the opening of school. In characteristic fashion he tried to combine the three. Jones showed no inclination to pursue his study of southern diseases this late in the summer. Instead he investigated the therapeutic qualities of electricity. Charles Colcock Jones, suffering from a debilitating disease of the central nervous system, served as his son's subject. The younger Jones's findings yielded material for several fresh lectures and an article.[73]

Jones divided his leisure time between two projects. He prepared a collection of coastal Georgia invertebrates for the Medical College of Georgia's museum. In the war between schools for students, a first-class collection of anatomical and physiological specimens was a distinct advantage. Jones vowed "to make the museum in Augusta one of the best in the United States." He amassed almost three hundred specimens which made a welcome addition to the school's already sizable collection. He also helped his brother excavate a local Indian mound. Both young men were fascinated by Indian relics and were to build up impressive collections.[74]

Jones's major task in preparing for the opening of school was the drafting of the introductory lecture. Illness had prevented him from delivering the previous year's address, so his colleagues asked him to inaugurate the 1859–1860 session. Jones again planned to speak on the ideal in medical education, but owing to his disappointment about the outcome of the convention of medical school teachers, he completely rewrote his lecture. While he had previously stressed generalities, he now concentrated on specific recommendations. His goal was to suggest a model program of the type which he thought should have been drafted in Louisville.[75]

Jones delivered his address on November 7. He began with a charge. Calling attention to the solemn responsibility inherent in the practice of medicine, he urged the students to seek the best possible training in order to perform the duties of the lofty profession to which they aspired. His concept of the ideal in medical education revealed the paradoxical dichotomy of vision and impracticality characteristic of his attitude toward scientific research. On the one hand he wisely advocated the replacement of abstract reasoning and theorizing in the training of physicians with experimentation and observation, but on the other he made the abstruse assertion that the duty of education was "to enable us to realize the true nature of the human race." Jones's "philosophical pursuit of medical education," as he called his proposed program, consisted of at least two prerequisites and six fundamental branches of medical science. This plan had been derived from his study of the past, since any "true theory of education," he held, "can be obtained only by the study of all history."

A thorough grounding in languages and the physical sciences were the prerequisites. Jones was convinced that languages developed "all the faculties of the mind" and should be "the starting point of all education." He was distressed that they were "too often neglected as a waste of time in this utilitarian age." As for the physical sciences, Jones believed that they should be studied in order of their generality, beginning with logic and then moving to the mathematical sciences.

Once he had mastered these prerequisites the prospective physician was ready to tackle the six fundamental branches of medical science. Like the physical sciences they were to be pursued in order of "least complex phenomena." The first—astronomy, physics, and chemistry—provided an extensive knowledge of "the physical and chemical elements of man, plants, animals, and inorganic bodies." Anatomy comprised the second branch. It familiarized the student with "the organs and tissues and systems of organs and apparatus of the human body, in their general and minute structure, and in their relations with each other, and with the structures of vegetables and animals." Physiology, the third division, revealed "the material structures in action." Then came the study of pathology which explained the "nature, relations, and causes of the abnormal, physical, chemical, nervous, vital and intellectual actions of the organism." Materia medica and therapeutics, with their valuable lessons on the "physical, chemical, anatomical, physiological, and pathological relations of remedial agents," made up the fifth category. A sixth division was necessary, Jones lamented, because of many physicians' greater concern for profit than for the welfare of mankind. This shameful situation could be overcome, he felt, only if future practitioners understood that the medical profession demanded the "highest moral training and the purest religious beliefs." Accordingly he proposed "Moral Training" as a "fundamental branch of medical science."

Jones was proud of his plan and believed that, if fully implemented, it would lead to a true understanding of the art of medicine. Indeed there is much in this program to commend, but it has an air of unreality too. This shortcoming is primarily a product of Jones's unattainable goals for education and research —the contention that education should reveal "the true nature of man" and that the "great end" of all scientific investigation was the determination of "the fixed relations or laws of the universe; so that the precise condition of things at any future time may be predicted with absolute certainty; and so that the human mind may appreciate its relations with the universe, and with the great Creator of the Universe."[76] He realized, of course, that everyone would not agree with his interpretation of the ideal in medical education and, as the title of his lecture—"Suggestions on Medical Education"—suggests, encouraged the drafting of other plans. The validity of Jones's scheme is not important; what is important is that he was painfully aware of the glaring shortcomings of American medical education and was deeply interested in reforming it, a goal he was to pursue zealously for the remainder of his life.

Owing to a significantly smaller enrollment the Medical College of Georgia's prospects were considerably less encouraging in November 1859 than they had been a year earlier. The faculty optimistically hoped to increase the student body of 110 by 20 or 30 before the end of the session, but the likelihood of doing so

was not great. The source of the problem—the rapid proliferation of medical schools—was apparent to Jones and his colleagues. Georgia already had five, and a sixth was soon to be
opened in Griffin. It was also probable that a seventh, a summer
school, would be established soon in Athens. The real threat to
the Medical College of Georgia came, however, not from its
own state but from Alabama, a state from which the school had
heretofore drawn heavily. Now, a first-class institution with 50
students had been opened in Mobile. Jones was frightened by the
proliferation of medical schools, not because of the increased
competition for student fees but because of the ensuing erosion
of the standards of medical education. "This strife for publick
favor . . . ," he warned, "inevitably lowers the standard of medical education."[77]

Jones's aversion to the further creation of medical schools
played a dominant role in his declining of a promising summer
post. In the fall of 1859 Dr. Austin Flint, one of the nation's most
respected medical writers and teachers, offered him the chair of
physiology and chemistry in an experimental summer school to
be established in Brooklyn, New York. The position was very
attractive: it would in no way interfere with his present one and
would be both financially and professionally rewarding. Jones,
however, refused to compromise his principles. His primary reason for declining the offer was his opposition to the creation of
additional medical schools, summer schools in particular. Other
reasons given included the health hazard of two courses of lectures a year, the distance between the schools, and the fear of
prejudice on the part of friends at older institutions such as the
University of Pennsylvania. Jones's parents supported his decision, but his brother, with notable insight, cautioned against
peremptorily denouncing all summer schools, pointing out that
if properly managed they might become valuable auxiliaries of
the regular medical schools.[78]

What made the fall of 1859 most memorable for Joseph Jones
was not his introductory lecture, the plight of the Medical College of Georgia, or even finances: it was his marriage. Shortly
after moving to Augusta, he had met Caroline Smelt Davis while
assisting her father, a Baptist minister, in the establishment of a
slave Sunday school. She was an attractive, charming young lady
with long blonde hair. For Jones it was love at first sight, and he
set out to win this beauty's heart and hand. He was an ardent

suitor and launched a determined campaign consisting of frequent visits to the Davis home and a flood of letters and poetry. The letters are of importance, not because they are unique, but because they portray a side of Joseph Jones seldom seen. Since entering college he had become increasingly intense, hard driving, and success-oriented with little time or apparent concern for anything that did not advance his career. His letters to his beloved Carrie, however, reveal a tender and sentimental side.

They let us see a young romantic hopelessly in love. "Whether I am writing or reading, sitting or walking, talking or keeping silence," he wrote in February 1859, "your image is always before me—now it smiles—now it encourages—now it inspires." "I will turn over a new leaf," he promised, "& not study so hard—& will walk more erect, & strive to look better. I have some one now to care for."[79] A month later in a remarkable effusion, the love smitten youth poured out his heart beginning with the following salutation: "My Dearest! my Precious One! my Love! my Guardian Angel! my Pearl of Great Price! my Spirit of Light, Love & Truth! my Bright Star of Happiness! my Morning Star of Hope! my Evening Star of Comfort & Peace! my own dear, dear Love! my own dear, dear Heart! my own dear precious Carrie!" *"You shall,"* he pledged, *"have my love—the fires of love shall burn brighter & brighter upon the altar of the innermost chamber of my heart, by day & by night, at all times & in all places, & under all circumstances—in the hour of prayer, of calm meditation—in the hour of temptation when the soul is tempest tossed—in the hour of joy & in the hour of sorrow—in the hours of life & in the hour of death.*[80]

This romance, as might be expected, had heavy religious and moral overtones as shown by frequent exchanges of favorite Bible verses and portions of scripture. In April, when attending the annual meeting of the Medical Association of Georgia, Jones discovered upon retiring that he had forgotten to pack his Bible. Reporting this incident to his sweetheart, he wrote: "What do you think I did? I read your dear letter over, then repeated one of *our* chapters in the Bible."[81] But the high point of this side of Jones's courtship was reached when he wrote that "the *first act* of our lives after we are married & when we are *alone with God & ourselves* will be to set up *our Family Altar, & consecrate ourselves* to his service & *ask his blessing upon our union.* And after this will not our hearts & lives be mingled in the *sacred union of true love,* like the waters of two rivers, which have united into one.

They will flow harmoniously together, to the great ocean of eternity."[82]

Joseph Jones and Caroline Davis announced their engagement in February 1859. In a letter to his parents seeking their blessing Jones built a prodigious case for this union. He assured them that he had "too high a conception of the solemnity, & importance of such a step as to be led by any exterior motives, or influences, however subtle, however strong." There was no doubt in his mind about the sincerity of his own feelings or "the worthiness, intelligence, piety & sincerity of Miss Davis." He was confident that she would encourage him "in every noble & generous undertaking," "advocate the right & repress the wrong," and "prove a loving daughter to you my dear Parents." His fiancee, he proudly pointed out, was the "idol of her family, & every one who knows her, loves her." Her parents were "persons of undoubted piety, & refinement," and her sisters had "few equals, & no superiors in intelligence & refinement." He moved to thwart any charges that this might be a precipitate action. "I think," he pointed out, "that I can say with truth that I have acted from high & holy motives, & have earnestly sought guidance & council from a source far higher & purer than any on earth." Asking his parents' approval at last, he implored: "The happiest hours of my life were spent with you. Your approval will always give my heart joy, your disapproval will always give deep & lasting sorrow."[83] Charles Colcock and Mary Jones were elated and gave the happy couple their warmest blessing.

The couple had originally planned a May wedding, but the date was changed when Jones persuaded his fiancee to honeymoon on Colonel's Island instead of at Lookout Mountain in northern Georgia. This move dictated a fall wedding because Caroline Davis had never lived outside the relatively salubrious Piedmont and was not acclimated to the malarious coastal lowlands. Fearful for her health Jones rescheduled the wedding for late October, well after the usual onset of the area's first hard frosts.

The wedding vows were exchanged at the bride's home on Wednesday evening, October 26, 1859. It was a happy occasion. The bride's father officiated and the groom's offered the benediction. The only unpleasant note was another change of honeymoon plans, for, despite the postponement of the wedding, unusually late frosts prevented the newlyweds from honeymooning on Colonel's Island. They were forced to fall back on their original plans to visit Lookout Mountain. Jones was disappointed and lamented: "I wished so much for you to go to my Island home."[84]

The newlyweds returned to Augusta after a two-week trip, and expecting to spend many fruitful years at the Medical College of Georgia, Jones moved his bride into a large house he had recently rented at 90 Green Street. It was ideally located on a site "as retired & as quiet as a county seat" only "one & a half squares from the Medical College, two squares from the Presbyterian Church, & two squares from the market." He eagerly resumed his teaching and spent the remainder of his time entertaining bridal company, poring over an unusual number of important new works from Europe bearing upon his lectures, and correcting the proofs of his A.M.A. article. His free moments were filled planning for the future.[85]

Joseph Jones had no way of knowing that his dream of a happy future in Augusta was sheer fantasy. During the sixth decade of the nineteenth century uncontrolled forces were at work which were to change his life and the lives of countless other Americans. Misunderstanding and hatred loomed on the horizon, and the air was heavy with sectional hostility. By 1860 a serious impasse, resulting from two divergent views as to the nature of the Union, had developed, and cries of "states' rights" and "secession" were on the lips of many southerners. This deadlock was to be resolved only by the force of arms as the nation was torn apart by a bloody fratricidal war. Joseph Jones was to become deeply involved in this cataclysm.

Chapter 4
Secession

I hope that a kind Providence will over-rule all
for good—all signs forbode evil & only evil.

Joseph Jones was painfully aware of the growing sectional hostility. Although his wholehearted defense of the South and of southern institutions bordered on extremism, he sincerely hoped that disunion could be averted, and he followed the steadily deteriorating relations between the sections with visible apprehension. But at the opening of 1860 Jones, as a newlywed, was more immediately concerned with his career.

Finances continued to concern him. The Medical College of Georgia had suffered a severe setback at the opening of the 1859–1860 session when only 110 students were enrolled instead of the anticipated 150. Attempts to increase this figure were uniformly unsuccessful. Even the secession in December 1859 of nearly 300 medical students from Philadelphia's Jefferson Medical College and the University of Pennsylvania in protest of the parading of John Brown's remains through the city's streets by his supporters failed to help, for only a handful enrolled at the Medical College of Georgia. As a result faculty salaries declined. It was imperative, especially with the added responsibility of a wife, that Jones recover this lost income. A search for a solution produced three alternatives—a part-time practice, a course of popular lectures, and private laboratory instruction for medical students between school sessions. Jealously guarding his research time, he refused to consider a limited practice, possibly the most feasible solution, and adopted both of the other alternatives.[1]

Jones spent much of the remainder of the school year planning and popularizing these ventures. Following the commencement ceremonies on March 2, he and his bride vacationed for several weeks with his parents at Monte Video. By the end of the month the couple was back in Augusta, where Jones excitedly opened his private laboratory and delivered his first popular lecture. Both ventures centered around practical instruction in physics, chemistry, toxicology, microscopy, experimental physiology, and comparative anatomy. The main difference seems to have been in the level of instruction and the time of offering. The more intensive private instruction for medical students was conducted during the day, and the popular lectures, aimed at the general public, were presented in the evening. The facilities of the Medical College of Georgia, for which Jones paid a fee, were used in each instance.[2]

This was a noteworthy undertaking, for the youthful scientist was well ahead of his time in the utilization of such modern medical instruments as the microscope and the clinical thermometer. Although few American scientists were using the microscope in their research, Joseph Jones could boast of hundreds of microscopic specimens. His use of the clinical thermometer is even more commendable. This instrument had been in existence for some two centuries but had been used only sparingly by physicians and scientists. Historians of medicine generally credit Carl Wunderlich, the eminent German physiologist, with developing the systematic study of temperature change in disease during the 1860s. Yet Joseph Jones had been meticulously recording temperature variations in his research since 1855 and possibly as early as 1854.[3]

This rare and exciting opportunity for study did not go unnoticed. The editor of the *Southern Medical and Surgical Journal* urged medical students to exploit it, remarking: "We know of no more improving way of spending the interval between the courses of lectures than in devoting the time to a thorough attainment of these important and most difficult departments."[4] A Philadelphia medical editor, impressed by Jones as well as his endeavor, wrote: "Dr. Jones although a very young man, has already distinguished himself by his attainments in these branches of medical sciences and we trust that his course will meet with support."[5] The strongest endorsement came from Dr. Daniel Lee. Although trained as a physician, Lee devoted his life to agricultural reform. He had distinguished himself in his native New York as editor of the *Genesee Farmer* and in the U.S. Patent Office, where he had been a strong advocate of congressional aid to agriculture, before moving to Georgia in 1847 to edit the *Southern Cultivator*, a leading southern agricultural journal. In 1859 he became agricultural editor of the *Southern Field and Fireside*, a weekly journal of "agriculture and polite literature." It was in this capacity that he endorsed Jones's laboratory. Lee confidently predicted that students "will enjoy rare advantages for acquiring a knowledge of the Microscope, the Balance, and of Chemicals, which will enable them to make valuable researches in other departments of natural science." He singled out the youthful scientist's reputation as a fine teacher for special praise, commending him to the attention "of all who would, like the *Field and Fireside*, foster Southern talent, genius and enterprise."[6]

Despite such high acclaim Jones's financial ventures were in trouble from the beginning. His private laboratory drew but one student, and the response to his popular lectures was equally disappointing. He had planned to deliver 100 lectures, at a fee of $130, spread over the course of a year. The first night's attendance was discouragingly small, but the second night brought a heartening increase. Any hopes of remuneration that Jones may have entertained quickly dimmed thereafter. The lecture series soon became so poorly attended that he discontinued it in dismay after only seven had been presented. His efforts netted him $200.[7]

Jones was discouraged. His carefully laid plans to supplement his meager income had met with complete failure. The future looked bleak indeed. Then at the end of April, just when he seemed resigned to sacrificing his research for the practice of medicine, Jones had a stroke of good luck: he learned that the Cotton Planters' Convention of Georgia had an opening for a chemist. This organization, part of the broader sectional movement in the slave states, was founded in 1858. It was composed primarily of planters who were concerned about the declining state of agriculture in Georgia and who were particularly distressed by the state's loss of its once dominant position in cotton production. The most cursory examination revealed that they were the cause of their own woes. Motivated solely by the desire to achieve quick profits they had intentionally ignored the vital question of soil exhaustion, and large areas of "one of the finest countries in the world" had been ruined. The members of the Cotton Planters' Convention pledged themselves to bold action in the hope of restoring Georgia's agricultural superiority. Their primary objective was to improve the soil of the older portions of the state and to conserve the fertility of the newer areas just coming under the plow. A vital part of their plan was the employment of a chemist, who was to be commissioned to conduct a comprehensive survey of the state's agricultural resources and to help protect the planters from fraud by carefully analyzing the chemical content of the various commercial fertilizers.[8]

Joseph Jones sought and won the position. He did so with the full realization that it would be laborious and confining and that it would certainly dictate some curtailment of his own research. Its strong points, however, carried the day: these duties would infringe less on his investigations than the practice of medicine, and the remuneration was far more promising; aware of the movement to appoint a full-time state chemist, Jones felt that if he performed well for the influential Cotton Planters' Convention, which was spearheading the campaign, he stood an excellent chance of securing the appointment; there was also the plight of the planters—his own class—and the possibility of helping ease it; in addition there were the gloomy prospects of the Medical College of Georgia on one hand and an opportunity to combat them, at least indirectly, on the other, since the cut-throat competition between schools dictated that every professor attract as much personal attention as possible in the hope of persuading students to come study under him; and, finally, if all else failed, he could use his research on the agricultural resources of the state to advantage in his study of southern diseases.[9]

Jones, with instructions to "protect the Agricultural interests of the state of Georgia, by all the means in his power," began his new duties immediately. He divided his time between gathering information on the agricultural resources of the state and analyzing the commercial fertilizers sold there. The former duty necessitated several field trips to representative geological areas of the state, and on these occasions he was forced to leave his bride of a few months alone. As Jones dutifully waded the swamps of the coastal plain and climbed the hills of the interior, he was accompanied by his faithful manservant Titus, whose assistance greatly expedited his labors. "It would have amused you," he wrote his wife, "to have seen me riding as occasion required through the mud 'a la Titus,' on the back of an Ethiopian."[10]

There were twelve brands of fertilizer to be examined and Jones was to receive fifty dollars for each analysis, prompting him to write his father that "the office promises to pay something during the summer."[11] In making these analyses he demanded that the vendors of commercial manures throw open their entire stock to inspection, threatening that "those who offer fertilizers to the planters of Georgia and *will not* submit to this examination will receive no notice from me as Chemist of the Cotton Planters' Convention." Working with notable diligence, he completed his first analysis, an examination of Rhodes' Super Phosphate of Lime, by the middle of May. Howell Cobb, the president of this organization, enthusiastically endorsed Jones's work in a letter to the Georgia press. "Planters *may* by observing the Reports of Dr. Jones," he remarked, "save themselves from loss and disappointment."[12] Jones continued his investigations for the Cotton Planters' Convention throughout the remainder of the spring and summer and into the fall of 1860. He still found time, however, to advance his study of southern diseases and to earn almost seven hundred dollars in his laboratory by conducting several private soil analyses and toxicological examinations of evidence in three cases of poisoning.[13]

The summer of 1860 also brought the last of some dozen reviews of Jones's malaria study written for the American Medical Association's *Transactions*. The critiques, which had begun appearing in January shortly after publication, were mixed: a few were laudatory; several, critical; most, lukewarm. The most favorable notice appeared in the *American Medical Monthly*, a New York City publication. Convinced that Jones's contribution was "the feature of the volume," the reviewer asserted: "This is one of the most valuable papers that has yet been presented to the Association, and alone makes this volume one of the best of the series."[14] In a similar vein the *Nashville Journal of Medicine and Surgery* insisted that Jones had "opened up a wide field for observation and investigation, which if properly cultivated will clear up many dark places in pathology and practice, and physiology." It further predicted that his work would "long stand a land mark to all future investigators of kindred subjects, and an evidence of the learning, talents, industry and perseverance of the author."[15]

The remainder of the reviewers also praised Jones's industry and ability. "Whether correct or not," one of them wrote, "no one can take up a single article which his prolific pen has put forth, without being impressed with the earnestness, activity and ingenuity of the writer." They agreed that he had made a valuable contribution. "Should no follower have the boldness and persistence to follow in his footsteps," it was reported, "he will enjoy the high satisfaction and praise of having materially advanced our acquaintance with the pathological changes characteristic of malarial fever; shed new light upon our appreciation of its lesions, their character, symptoms and products, and consequently inaugurated a more rational and successful therapeutic than we have heretofore inaugurated."[16]

The majority of these reviewers, however, felt compelled to call attention to certain shortcomings in Jones's scholarship—his verbosity, his fondness for extraneous material, and his unrealistic approach to research—which by now, unfortunately, had become habitual. All of them criticized the study's extraordinary length—some four hundred pages. The reviewer for the *Louisville Medical Journal* accused Jones of discussing "everything in the heavens, on the earth, and in the waters beneath the earth!" and skillfully allowed the work to indict itself by quoting the first sentence of the first chapter. It read:

> The object of this chapter is to sketch in the mutual relations of celestial and terrestrial bodies and animated beings, and demonstrate—that the existence of man is absolutely dependent upon the relations of the component members of the universe—that a single alteration in the chain of phenomena would destroy the conditions necessary for the existence and manifestation of the phenomena of man—that the forces of man are all resultants of the forces of the sun and fixed stars, which keep up a never ending circulation and change of matter upon the surface of our globe—that man cannot create or annihilate force any more than he can create or annihilate matter—that the great law of the Indestructibility of Force, of Action, and Reaction, applies to all the Phenomena of man—that man is a type of the Universe, and comprehends within himself all phenomena, astronomical, physical, chemical, physiological, and psychological—that the knowledge of the structure, phenomena, and relations of man includes a knowledge of all science, whether relating to matter or mind.

"And so he goes on," the exasperated critic asserted, "for more than forty mortal pages writing sentences forty and fifty lines in length, and heaping quotation upon quotation until 'the mount makes Ossa like a wart!' "[17]

The *Charleston Medical Journal and Review* seized upon Jones's impractical approach to scientific investigation. The only serious blemish on the youthful author's past works, the reviewer stated, was "a lofty and assured dogmatism, a confidence never shaken, an affected nicety of analysis, and great ambitiousness of method." He had not only failed to benefit from past criticism but had compounded these shortcomings, for "in the present essay they are obtruded most prominently into notice, and sadly disfigure what is otherwise an interesting, laborious and useful work." This critic, too, found ample material in the first chapter to illustrate his criticisms. He strongly resented Jones's virtual wasting of it on a discussion of the relations of man to the entire universe "with the avowed object of deducing therefrom the character and extent of physiological and pathological researches." This chapter appeared "to have been written," he asserted, "simply as a show bill for the astounding foot notes which load its pages—a cheap and vulgar erudition, whose display might well have been forgone, even at the expense of the truisms so pompously enunciated." The reviewer was especially angered at what he called the "novel and striking conclusion" that: "*Man is a type of universe; and to understand the phenomena of man in health and disease, and his relations to the universe, we must comprehend the phenomena and mutual relations of all animate and inanimate bodies, terrestrial and celestial.*" This was one of Jones's pet theories, but his critic reduced it to ridicule with one sweep of the pen. "That is to say," he snapped, "no physician is competent to appreciate and relieve an attack of simple diarrhoea or colic, who is not prepared to demonstrate the correlation of the physical forces, and explain the precession of the equinoxes and the cause of the tides." Despite his obvious dissatisfaction with much of the work, this reviewer, as had several others, attributed its shortcomings to Jones's lack of experience, explaining: "His faults are those which naturally spring from his youth and temperament; serious and lamentable, doubtless but not irremediable, and which will probably be eradicated by the attainment of the very object to whose zealous pursuit is indirectly attributable much of their display."[18]

Two of Jones's preliminary reports to the Cotton Planters' Convention, which appeared in August 1860, were better received. Both dealt with the agricultural value of the marls and shell limestone of Georgia and certain commercial manures. These investigations were replete with detailed tables of complicated chemical analyses which lent an air of thoroughness. Generally Jones concluded that Georgia's indigenous lime resources were capable of supplying the state's needs for an indefinite period and that if the planters would but utilize this home product, they would "have no need whatever, to purchase a single pound of phosphate of lime, in whatever form it be present in the market." The application of commercial phosphatic guanos and superphosphates to soils which had been dressed with Georgia marls and shell limestone was therefore wholly unnecessary, he pointed out, and would produce no noticeable advantage; moreover the high price of Peruvian guano, although admittedly a superior natural fertilizer, was a serious obstacle to its extensive use.[19]

Jones's findings enjoyed a wide circulation, increasing interest in the activities of the Cotton Planters' Convention. Daniel Lee promptly publicized them in the *Southern Field and Fireside*, commending the Cotton Planters' Convention for its "promotion of southern industry and enterprise" and Jones for his competence "to give the great agricultural interest of the country reliable facts in all that relates to the analysis of soils, rocks, marls, swamp muck, and other fertilizing substances." He pledged his columns to a true reporting of the future labors of each. At the same time he felt compelled to advise Jones against generalizing his findings prematurely, warning that "in the warmth of our agricultural enthusiasm" it was tempting to draw unreliable and often invalid inferences and deductions from known facts.[20]

Toward the end of the summer of 1860 Jones felt that he had sufficiently investigated Georgia's agricultural resources to begin the writing of his main report for the Cotton Planters' Convention. He had conducted a truly prodigious amount of research in a very short period, an accomplishment which had not been achieved without a heavy physical toll. His appearance frightened his brother, who visited him in early September. "The Doctor," he reported, "is looking thin, and rather badly. He has been taxing himself severely in the preparation of his report."[21] This news disturbed Jones's parents, and in an impassioned appeal Mary Jones urged him to "reform & not devote yourself so entirely to labor." Labeling his pace as almost suicidal, she warned: "If you continue it you will shorten your days or bring on premature old age—*body & mind* must give way under such pressure." The likelihood of such a development seemed all the greater considering that without his having taken any rest or relaxation it was almost time for Jones to resume the demanding duties of his professorship. After apprising her son of her fears for his well-being Mary Jones asserted: "I will not say commands to you about this reckless destruction of your health & constitution. As a Christian you ought not to do so. As a husband & child you ought not."[22] All warnings were to no avail, for Jones continued to ignore his health in his haste to commit his findings to paper, a task he completed at the end of the month.

This manuscript was a typical Joseph Jones product, a curious amalgam of his industry and ability on the one hand and his characteristic shortcomings on the other. The 312-page report began with a statement of the problems confronting the planters of Georgia and a strong admonishment that the future of agriculture in the state depended on how they were solved. Jones warned his readers to prepare for a long struggle, since it would take years of concerted action to restore Georgia's agricultural superiority. There followed an extensive examination of the state's agricultural resources, a defense of home products, the results of Jones's analyses of commercial fertilizers, and the dosages of fertilizer he felt necessary to restore the fertility of the state's exhausted lands. These findings were supported by sixty elaborate tables of original analyses and another one thousand compiled by "reliable" chemists and agrologists.

At the end of this report, in a section which appeared to be an afterthought, Jones discussed the threat of malaria in Georgia's coastal plain and suggested certain preventive measures. Like most of his contemporaries he felt this disease was caused by noxious odors or miasms arising from the decomposition of animal and vegetable matter. Suitable prophylactic steps, according to Jones, were the substitution of cistern water for well and spring water (with the purification of the latter with alum in the event it had to be used), the prohibition of work in rice fields and low grounds before sunrise and of any work on an empty stomach, the avoidance of dews, the prompt changing of wet clothes, the clothing of the feeble during the fall and winter with red flannel undergarments, and the treatment of diseases of the rice plantations and low lying areas upon the stimulant plan through the liberal use of quinine and the avoidance of depletive measures.

Jones envisioned this report as a mere beginning, labeling it a first report. He planned at least eight others dealing with a variety of related topics, including Georgia's soils, mineral resources, plants and animals, diseases, and aboriginal remains. The outbreak of war in 1861 abruptly ended these ambitious plans.[23]

Jones did not wait until the convening of the Cotton Planters' Convention, scheduled for early December, to reveal the contents of his report. Instead, immediately upon its completion, he had one thousand copies printed and distributed at his own expense. He did so at the urging of Howell Cobb and J. V. Jones, the chief officials of the Cotton Planters' Convention, who were fearful for the success of the organization's memorial calling for the appointment of a state chemist. Now in the final stages of preparation, the memorial was to be presented to the Georgia legislature when it convened on November 7. Anticipated opposition pointed to a heated debate and a close decision. The leaders of the Cotton Planters' Convention decided, therefore, to seize the initiative and steal a march on its opponents by publishing Jones's impressive report before the legislature met. According to Jones they looked upon his report as "the only means of inaugurating the agricultural survey of the state." He was pleased that he was personally able to increase the memorial's chances of success, since in doing so he enhanced his own prospects of winning an appointment as state chemist. Thus a satisfactory solution to Jones's recurrent financial problem seemed to be tied up with the fate of this memorial, and he was anxious to do all he could to help it succeed.[24]

It appeared to Charles Colcock Jones that in his enthusiasm to aid the Cotton Planters' Convention his son had acted imprudently—to the point in fact of humiliating himself and his family. Specifically he was upset because of a letter the younger Jones had written Howell Cobb, who had immediately released it to the Georgia press. In this letter Jones, in the course of praising the efforts of the Cotton Planters' Convention and urging their continuation at the state level, revealed that he was three thousand dollars in debt for the investigations he had conducted for this organization. Charles Colcock Jones registered his strong disapproval of such indiscreet revelations.

Jones quickly apologized for any "unpleasant anxiety" his letter may have caused his family. It had been written at the request of J. V. Jones, the vice president of the Cotton Planters'

Convention, and was "intended for no other eyes than those of
the President of the association." "I had no more idea that it
would ever be published," he exclaimed, "than I now have that
the letter which I am now writing will be published." Jones confirmed that his investigations had indeed cost $3,000 but vigor-
ously denied that this was an insurmountable or pressing debt.
And, while making no attempt to hide his shaky finances, he hastened to point out that in addition to his salary from the Medical
College of Georgia, fifteen hundred to two thousand dollars, he
had made another eleven hundred dollars from his labors since the
close of the school session.

There was a positive side of the letter to be considered too,
Jones contended, for as humiliating as its unexpected publication may have been, in conjunction with his recently published report it had already had "one good & most important effect." This
was the memorial to the state legislature with its promise of an appointment as state chemist. On the whole, then, as much as he
regretted that his attempts "to develope the native resources of
the state should occasion . . . any anxiety," considering that
"there are six medical colleges in Georgia & that I must look
elsewhere than to my professorship for a support" and "the increased influence & usefulness which this field opened to me,"
the good, Jones insisted, far outweighed the bad. "He who risks
nothing under such circumstances," he concluded, "will certainly win nothing."[25]

The Reverend Jones was not fully satisfied with this explanation but chose to pursue the matter no further. His true feelings
were perhaps best expressed in a letter to his eldest son. "The
letter of your brother to Mr. Cobb, President of the Cotton
Planters' Convention," he wrote, "was a *private* one and never
intended for any other eyes than Mr. Cobb's. He should not have
published it; and some things your brother ought not to have put
in it."[26]

The completed memorial was a striking example of simplicity
and persuasiveness. It began by starkly depicting the grim situation confronting Georgia's agricultural interests through the use
of informative tables. It did not try to hide or shift the blame for
this situation but placed it squarely on the shoulders of those
responsible—the planters themselves. The memorialists pledged
a total commitment to reform, but their efforts, it was professed,
would fall short of success without legislative aid in the form of

the appointment of a state chemist. An attached copy of Jones's report was held up as an example of what could be accomplished. Comparing his work to that of Edmund Ruffin in Virginia, the memorialists predicted that "the *continuation* of these efforts, will result in the *permanent Agricultural improvement of the State of Georgia*."[27]

Jones was uncertain about the memorial's chances of success. At times the realization of the considerable influence of the Cotton Planters' Convention encouraged him; at other times he despaired, worried by alleged attempts "from various quarters to discredit my labors."[28] His fears seemed justified in November when Daniel Lee gave his report an unfavorable review in the *Southern Field and Fireside*. Lee's critique, to which he devoted two of his weekly columns, was by no means a personal attack, since he was sympathetic to Jones, characterizing him as talented and indefatigable. Instead there is a readily discernible feeling of disappointment pervading this critical notice. Lee had looked to the youthful scientist for valuable assistance in the movement to reform Southern agriculture. His contribution, however, was judged marginal at best.

Lee focused his initial attention on Jones's sixty original tables. Although considering them the most valuable part of the work, he sharply attacked them as unnecessarily complicated extraneous calculations. An obvious pragmatist, he was unyielding in the belief that scientific knowledge should be made "intelligent and attractive to common people" so that it would be read and embraced. "Authors full of book learning and the pride of authorship," Lee contended, "are apt to load their guns so heavily as to fire over the heads of their readers." The implication was clear: Jones in showing off his scholarship had lost his readers. "Having disposed of nine-tenths of the figures in these original researches," Lee continued, "let us see if the other tenth is all wheat or partly chaff." During this subsequent examination he levied one of his most damaging charges, asserting that much of the information in Jones's tables appeared to have been "simply copied from a chemical textbook."[29]

The report's primary thesis, holding that the abundance of marl and lime supplies in Georgia should persuade planters to curtail their use of expensive commercial fertilizers, was also scrutinized. Lee questioned its validity in terms of economics, arguing that Jones had not given sufficient consideration to the cost of using local soil dressings. "Sound farm economy is what Southern agriculture most needs at this time," he insisted, "and economy cannot be extracted from marl or lime by any chemist." He suggested that it was far cheaper to rest the soil in crops of plants and weeds scientifically selected for their ability to draw fertilizing elements from the atmosphere and subsoil.

The review's final indictment concerned Jones's use of his data. "Baron [Justus] Liebig," Lee argued, "generalized his agricultural facts prematurely; and Prof. Jones has done likewise."[30] He had warned Jones of this danger as early as August, but the warning had gone unheeded. "We are confident that he has overtasked his energies in this effort, and prepared in extreme haste an elaborate report of more than 300 pages," Lee wrote in summary, "when, had he consulted his reputation as a man of science, and the public interests, he would have limited his task to fifty pages, and thus saved five-sixths of the expense of printing his report."[31]

Lee's criticisms infuriated Jones. In his usual response to criticism he interpreted the review as a personal attack and replied in kind. The occasion for his assault was a supplementary report to the Cotton Planters' Convention on two more commercial fertilizers. Using his sense of duty to this organization and to the distributors of the commercial fertilizers he had analyzed as a vehicle, Jones condemned Lee's strictures as "unprovoked, unjust and utterly false." He did not stop there but upbraided his assailant. "This assertion," Jones criticized, "is publicly made by an individual with whom I have never had any personal acquaintance whatever, and whom I should not know even by sight, and who has never been within the walls of my laboratory during the prosecution of these investigations, and who has, therefore, no more knowledge of the processes employed in my analyses than if he were still a resident of the Northern section of the United States where he originated."[32]

Lee's reasoned dispassionate rebuttal was in striking contrast to Jones's emotional outburst. His youthful adversary's latest report was reprinted in its entirety, "not only on account of its intrinsic merits as a contribution to southern agricultural literature," Lee explained, "but to give the writer an opportunity of being heard in reply to our friendly criticism on *the form* in which he states the results of his analytical researches in his voluminous Report to the Cotton Planters' Convention." He sought to remove the personal element which Jones had injected into the affair and admirably chose to ignore the allusion to his northern background. Lee could not resist reminding Jones, however, of "the unsolicited, warm and earnest commendation" extended to his private laboratory several months earlier. He also readily withdrew the intimation that the report's tables had been copied only to replace it with an equally unacceptable one. "Our error," Lee apologized, "lies in the assumption that Dr. Jones has sufficient knowledge of chemistry not to waste his professional skill, his valuable time, and valuable chemicals in determining . . . quantities named in our text books." While on the subject of chemical analyses Lee availed himself of the opportunity to comment on the other one thousand included in the report. He pointed out that they extended back at least thirty years and asserted that "we trust Dr. Jones will not regard it as an 'attack' on him if we show, hereafter, how unworthy of public confidence are the statements of some men whom he endorses as 'reliable chemists.' "

Lee was concerned first and foremost with agricultural progress. It was this concern, not personalities, which was at the root of his displeasure. Lee's approach was brutally pragmatic, and when able scientists failed to measure up to his standards he spoke out. "Agricultural chemistry," he asserted:

> presents to planters a great deal of chaff with its wheat that requires winnowing out. This chaff has been ground up with the grain long enough; it makes bad flour and bad bread. It is time to discriminate between truth and error in agricultural science; and until this is faithfully done, chemistry can do very little for the advancement of sound principles in tillage and husbandry. Analysis so obscurely stated as to be unintelligible to plain farmers and planters mean just *nothing* for their benefit, and often lead astray.[33]

The controversy soon spread to the pages of the *Southern Cultivator* and the *Savannah Journal of Medicine*, raging until the spring of 1861. The affair was introduced into the former through the intervention of "Agricola," an anonymous correspondent who, as a self-professed "lover of justice and fair play," successfully sought to have Jones's charge of an "unprovoked, unjust and utterly false" attack reprinted there.[34] Lee, the former editor of this journal, felt compelled to defend himself to his old readers "inasmuch as . . . not one word of my explanation of the 'statement' complained of by Prof. Jones . . . is published." His defense was a more pointed, less patient criticism of Jones's report. He reiterated that agricultural science was "too important not to command . . . the most critical investigation and review." "I respectfully ask you, Messrs. Editors, and the readers of the Cultivator," he queried, "how a conscientious agricultural student can commend a work in which errors . . . abound from beginning to end?" Appealing to the public's sense of fair play, Lee pleaded that both sides of the controversy should be impartially reviewed and everything that he had said about Jones "should be taken together in common justice to both parties, if I am to be arraigned before my old friends, the readers of your paper, as one who has made a statement that is 'unprovoked, unjust and utterly false.' " "Any one who will take the trouble to refer to my remarks, as cited by Prof. Jones," he entreated, "will see that I did not assert the *one-half* of what he says I did 'assert.' "

Lee sought an end to the controversy. "If Dr. Jones can forgive me for having chosen the wrong place to be born, I trust we may be friends," he entreated, "for if I have committed a mistake . . . it arose from the high opinion I had of his attainments . . . and from a wish to see his second Report free from the defects of his first, as well as his benefit as for that of the agricultural interest of the South."[35]

The nadir of the entire unfortunate affair, and a sad testimonial to the parties involved, was reached in the *Savannah Journal of Medicine*. Here two reputable members of Georgia's scientific community became embroiled in blatant character assassination. The exchange was initiated by Dr. A. B. Tucker in a review of Jones's report. Critical notices, as Jones was still to learn, were to be expected and tolerated; scurrilous ones were another matter. Tucker made his intentions explicitly clear from the outset. To him there were two types of chemists. On the one hand there were eminent chemists from whom "the march of improvement and so much benefit has been derived"; on the other hand there was a second group, honest of purpose and proficient in theoretical knowledge, yet "who, from careless habits contracted in their studies, or from a want of practical knowledge, publish to the world results which cannot stand the test of scientific scrutiny, and which, though they may be true, are unreliable from the palpable evidences of carelessness upon their face." "Without hesitation," Tucker asserted, "we class Dr. J. among the latter class of chemists." This low estimate of Jones's ability prompted him to boast: "We think we can show ground to excite at least a suspicion of the correctness of this elaborate report."

Having established his ground rules, Tucker turned his attention to the contents of the work. His findings were not surprising. Many of his criticisms were valid and well-taken, but his intention and the force of his attack were deplorable. Tucker criticized Jones's analyses on the grounds of the obvious rapidity with which they had been made, the complexity of the tables, the alleged contradictions in them, and the unwarranted inferences which he charged had been drawn from them. He contended that these shortcomings were sufficiently serious "to render his report unreliable." Tucker's most damaging charge was that Jones had conducted all but one of his analyses on two plantations in Burke County while professing "to tell us the composition of *Georgian* limestones; not those of Burke county, but of Georgia, and parades them side by side with careful and scientific and thorough investigations of distinguished men in this country and Europe." "We confess we have never seen so little regard paid to what is due not to his own reputation only," Tucker exclaimed, "but to the care and precision which science has a right to demand of its votaries." Professing an overwhelming exasperation which would not allow him to continue, he sneered: "There possibly is much that is good in the report, but we confess an unwillingness to sift the sand for the grains of gold."[36]

This vitriolic notice infuriated Dr. L. D. Ford, one of Jones's colleagues at the Medical College of Georgia. He sent a lengthy rebuttal to Dr. Juriah H. Harriss, the editor, in which he scolded him for printing such a blatant personal attack, demanding that his reply be included in the next issue. Harriss vigorously denied that Tucker's strictures constituted a personal assault on Jones but grudgingly assented to Ford's demand.

The rebuttal was a detailed defense of both Jones and his report. Most of it was a saccharine exalting of the youthful scientist's worth and a vituperative denunciation of Tucker. "Have you not, in common with the citizens of this State," he asked, "felt a glowing pride in that young man—a native of Georgia— Dr. Joseph Jones, now Professor of Chemistry in the Medical

College of Georgia?" He averred that Jones was "working with martyr-like devotion." Yet this "young Giant" was forced to tolerate, on the publication of each of his works, a "pack of little critics letting themselves loose for hot pursuit; barking loudly and snapping with harmless malignity" at his heels. Ford especially resented the labeling of Jones as an inferior chemist. His "perfect system, extreme cleanliness, and Lion-hearted industry" made mockery of such a charge as did the fact that "already in his young life" he had "made more chemical analyses of animal, vegetable and mineral matters, than have been made within the limits of Georgia, from its colonial time until now," analyses which foreign journalists had quoted in their works and "endorsed [as] valuable."

Ford considered his task finished. "My object," he avowed, "is accomplished—it was to expose this act of gross injustice to Professor Joseph Jones, my friend, whom I intensely admire." "The Reviewer," he ridiculed, "I know not: him I admire not, in any of the varted characters *in which he has presented himself in his own article*—neither as the magisterial, unhesitating classifier, nor the scientific scrutinizer, nor the fallacy-shower, nor the Justice-doer, nor the table-maker, nor the title-clipper, nor the self-styled reviewer. Let his friends admire him."[37]

Two events of great import for Jones's future occurred during the controversy over his report. These were the election of 1860 and the convening of the Cotton Planters' Convention. Jones looked to the former with great anxiety. On the day of the contest he wrote his father: "The election has passed off quietly this day. I hope that a kind Providence will over-rule all for good—all signs forbode evil & only evil."[38] Like his parents and brother he was a Calhoun Democrat and an ardent states' rightist, preferring union but ready to support secession if southern rights could not be guaranteed. The results of the election had an unsettling effect on the Jones family. What they had feared most had happened—the "Black Republicans" had come to power. Charles Colcock Jones, Jr., who had taken office as mayor of Savannah a month earlier, exclaimed: "We are on the verge of Heaven only knows what."[39] His parents and brother were equally disturbed. "The future of our country," Charles Colcock and Mary Jones were convinced, "seems involved in darkness."[40] They felt that the South was endangered and called for immediate secession, asserting: " 'Forebearance has ceased to be a virtue'—and [we] believe we could meet with no evils out of the union that would compare to those we will finally suffer if we continue in it, for we can no longer doubt that the settled policy of the North is to crush the South."[41] Joseph Jones, as the events of the next weeks would prove, wholeheartedly concurred.

By the time the first annual fair of the Cotton Planters' Convention opened in Macon, a town of slightly over six thousand persons selected because of its location at the geographic center of the state and its superior transportation facilities, the pressing issues of states' rights and secession had reached such a feverish state that they dominated this popular effort to promote southern agriculture and industry. The fair began on December 5 and ran for three weeks; the first week was devoted to the exhibition and sale of southern and foreign manufactures; the second featured plantation products; and the last was highlighted by an elaborate livestock show. Interspersed throughout these three weeks were several highly publicized addresses. Those scheduled to speak were Justice George W. Stone of the Alabama Supreme Court, John W. Williams, secretary of the State Agricultural Bureau of Mississippi, Professor R. M. Johnson of the University of Georgia, Howell Cobb, and Joseph Jones. The last two speeches were awaited with especial anticipation. Cobb spoke first, reflecting on the question of promoting southern agriculture and industry and examining the explosive state of national affairs. He suggested the sending of a commission in early 1861 to each European government to promote direct trade, the formation of an association of the producers of southern products, and the suspension of commercial relations with the North until the general welfare of the South was secured.[42]

A "very thin" but "very hearty" Joseph Jones delivered his address on December 13. The performance was witnessed by his proud mother, who had attended the fair to exhibit the products of the Jones family plantation. Jones was expected to summarize his report on the agricultural resources of Georgia, but in the midst of his presentation he shifted his attention to national politics and launched into a fiery appeal for immediate secession. He interpreted the current political situation as one which should stir every loyal southerner to action. In the recent national election a sectional party dedicated to the subversion of southern institutions and the inciting of the slaves to rebellion had triumphed "which would not merely make us dream of fire, poison, and murder in our sleep, but would surround us with a wall of fire, and apply the torch of the incendiary to our cities, our farmhouses and our dwellings." In the past, he contended, the South had not only generously furnished a disproportionate share of the nation's revenue but had given in to northern domination of the government, commerce, and industry. The North had not appreciated the South's generosity but instead had become "inflamed, drunk and maddened by her success." Even worse, he continued, the North, owing to her population advantage, felt secure and had set out on a policy characterized by "cowardice and fiendishness and base ingratitude" aimed at destroying "her generous and confiding twin sister."

Jones saw two courses open to the South. The first—submission to the will of the North—he flatly rejected. He vehemently opposed yielding to the section which he openly accused of prostituting the Constitution in a Machiavellian attempt to deprive the South of her political rights and rightful position in the national government and territories. Second, the South could boldly assert her rights, peaceably if possible but at "the point of the sword and the mouth of the cannon if necessary." In an attempt to thwart Unionist opposition, which was strong in parts of Georgia, he warned: "The cry of Union at this time is the cry of submission . . . submission to what? Submission to the tyrannical rule of a purely sectional party who would degrade you to a level lower than that of an African."

Jones boasted that secession would allow the South to regain her political and economic independence, to free herself of the multitude of disruptive transient schoolteachers and preachers, to rid herself of the innumerable bothersome northern merchants and peddlers, and, most important, to purge herself of the baneful influence of the abolitionists. After secession he envisioned a truly independent South, a new nation which would lead the world in agricultural, industrial, and educational progress. Swayed by his own fiery rhetoric, Jones ended on an emotional note, urging Georgia, if necessary, to secede alone. "Georgia," he passionately proclaimed, "has been and will ever continue to be, if she improves aright the blessings of providence, the EMPIRE STATE of the South—Georgia is not only the Empire State of the South, but she has the resources and the power to maintain her independence with or without the South, and to form by herself an EMPIRE."[43]

This fervent appeal for southern independence, coming just as the campaign to elect delegates to Georgia's secession convention was getting under way, excited considerable attention. The Augusta *Daily Chronicle & Sentinel* printed the address in its entirety. The Macon *Daily Telegraph* considered it in every way "worthy of one who, though yet young, has achieved for himself, by his talents and learning, a world-wide reputation."[44] In Milledgeville, where the state legislature was winding up its session, the news of Jones's address was greeted with the Senate's passage of the bill, which had been passed by the House on December 14, creating the office of state chemist and his appointment to it at an annual salary of six thousand dollars.

Senator T. J. Smith informed the youthful scientist of his good fortune, reporting: "The Bill was almost unanimous and I am pleased to inform you your name gave it much weight. It is a very laborious task but that gives it no pangs for you as your reputation for industry is unsurpassed." "Excuse me," he added, "for personal compliments as I do it most cheerfully, and can do it in truth." Jones was jubilant and hurried to Milledgeville to claim his prize. Arriving on Christmas Day he received one of the worst disappointments of his life—the bill had been accidently lost or mislaid and had not reached Governor Joseph E. Brown for signing. Brown had left for the holidays and, although unintentional, his lack of action had the effect of a veto. Jones was grief-stricken. "This is a sore disappointment—I have done all in my power to meet my liabilities," he grieved, "& when a commanding position was placed in my hands by the almost unanimous voice of the Representatives of Georgia—through the neglect & carelessness of the officers of the Legislature all is lost."[45] With assistance from the Cotton Planters' Convention, and his brother, a political friend of Brown's, he tried to regain this lost opportunity. These efforts were futile, however, for with the secession of Georgia in early 1861, the legislature devoted its energies to preparing the state for the eventuality of war.[46]

Jones's failure to secure the lucrative post of state chemist dealt his shaky finances a severe blow, especially coming as it did on the heels of an earlier setback suffered during the Cotton Planters' Convention when the organization's executive committee indefinitely delayed paying him the considerable sum, amounting to over three thousand dollars, for the work that he had done for it.[47]

A further complicating factor was the eagerly awaited birth of his first child, a son, on December 16.[48] So for Joseph Jones 1860 had begun on a distressing financial note and had ended on a nearly disastrous one.

The opening of 1861 brought little to hearten him: his campaign to be reappointed state chemist was going badly, and his finances showed no signs of improving. Jones sought to ease his anxieties by losing himself in his teaching and research.[49] The only cheerful note was the movement of Georgia toward secession. In November 1860, after it had become clear that South Carolina was going to secede, Governor Brown, a champion of states' rights and a secessionist, had persuaded the legislature to call a convention to meet in January 1861 and determine the state's future course. When the convention met on January 16, the secessionists had more than a 30-seat majority in the 301-member body. One of the secessionist delegates, Jones happily noted, was Dr. I. P. Garvin, the professor of materia medica and dean of the faculty at the Medical College of Georgia.[50]

Many of Jones's contemporaries in the southern medical profession did not share his enthusiasm for secession. Instead, reflecting the divisions in the southern mind following the election of Lincoln, some were rabid secessionists while others were staunch unionists. All could agree, however, that southern rights had to be protected. Indeed, as the result of their own southernism, the South's physicians played as important a role as the politicians and the preachers in creating the climate of opinion which made secession possible. Although the scientists of both North and South had a gentleman's agreement that science and politics did not mix and worked with noteworthy success to keep the latter out of journals and meetings, the physicians of the South nurtured southern sectionalism in two important ways. First, they tried to promote the South's medical independence from the North by arguing the distinctiveness of southern medicine and the subsequent necessity of southern medical students pursuing their studies at home. Second, they added fuel to the proslavery argument by maintaining that the anatomical and physiological "peculiarities" of the Negro made him suitable only for the life of a slave.[51] Yet, despite its crucial involvement in the sectional struggle, the secession crisis deeply divided the southern medical profession. The actions of two physician members of the Mississippi secession convention well illustrate this division. Dr.

Alfred C. Holt of Woodville was one of the convention's most outspoken secessionists, while Dr. John J. Thornton of Brandon, elected as a unionist, was the only delegate who refused to sign the ordinance of secession.

This division of opinion was present in the Georgia convention, but there was little doubt as to what the outcome of the deliberations would be, for the secessionists were in control from the beginning. Thus after a short debate the convention voted by a margin of 208 to 89 to withdraw Georgia from the Union. Governor Brown officially signed the ordinance of secession on January 21, and Georgia became the fifth state of the lower South to secede, having been preceded by South Carolina, Mississippi, Florida, and Alabama. Joseph Jones was delighted and looked to the future with renewed hope.[52]

Chapter 5
Private Jones

*If we expect to hand down to our children the
glorious inheritance of true freedom and honorable
peace, we must cheerfully endure the sacrifices
to secure them.*

Secession had an electrifying effect on Georgians. The decision
in itself came as no surprise, since many had long felt that the
state's only choice was to join her rebellious sister states of the
lower South. Now the suspense and uncertainty were over: Georgia had taken her stand no matter what followed, and a wave of
optimism swept over much of the state. This feeling was clearly
reflected by the students of the Medical College of Georgia, who
sought and won the closing of the school on February 15, 1861,
a month early.

Joseph Jones was also anxious for the school year to end but
for quite different reasons. The past twelve months had been a
financial nightmare for him. He had failed to profit from his popular lectures and private laboratory; he had received no compensation from his work for the Cotton Planters' Convention, but
on the contrary had incurred a sizable debt in the course of these
investigations; he had lost the much-desired appointment as
state chemist; and the enrollment of the Medical College of
Georgia declined precipitously for the second year in a row. Only
seventy students had enrolled for the 1860–1861 session, causing
faculty salaries to plummet even lower and clouding the school's
future. In view of the low enrollment the faculty voted to cancel
the customary public commencement, a decision Jones endorsed.
"All things considered," he observed, "it will be a politic move."[1]
The early closing well served Jones's needs—time to rest and
reflect upon his finances. So precarious was his financial state, in
fact, that at the beginning of the year his mother had had his

brother send him sixty-five dollars "to be considered as a Christmas gift." At the same time she urged: "Do write your father candidly about your pecuniary situation."[2]

At his parents' invitation Jones and his family left Augusta as soon as the commencement exercises were over for an extended vacation at Monte Video. Jones's first concern was rest. His demanding duties and breakneck pace of the past year had weakened his health, and at the repeated warnings of becoming "prematurely old and broken down" from family and friends alike he devoted his first days in Liberty County to relaxation. But Jones was one of those individuals whose personalities do not tolerate inactivity, and he soon busied himself with his study of southern diseases. He periodically left his wife and son at Monte Video to make trips into neighboring areas of eastern Georgia to examine mortuary statistics and hospital records. He pursued these investigations with his usual vigor. "I am now just as busily employed," he reported to his wife in early April, "as it is possible for [a] mortal to be—turning over old dusty records, calculating births & deaths, tabulating diseases, examining old hospital records, &c."[3]

A major part of Jones's time was devoted to an intensive analysis of his financial condition and an evaluation of ways to improve it. After much soul-searching he recognized the inevitable —that his only real hope lay in the practice of medicine, full-time during the spring and summer and part-time while the Medical College of Georgia was in session. This was hard for Jones to accept when he realized that it would mean a drastic curtailment of his research. But there was no other acceptable alternative: only this held any promise of financial stability. His father probably put it best: "Although the times are deranged, yet sickness comes in all seasons."[4] Carrie also supported her husband's decision, stating: "I am very sanguine of his getting into practice though I know it must be gradual."[5]

Jones gave serious consideration to joining the Confederate army. Its promise of financial solvency and his emotional patriotism made this possibility especially inviting, but he declined for two reasons. He was unwilling, at least at this time, to risk an extended separation from his wife and young son; and there was his resolution of a question of divided loyalties. Jones was torn between duty at the front and the defense of his native Liberty County. In the end, following the example of Georgia's governor

Joseph E. Brown, who preached state preparedness, he chose the latter, volunteering for service with the Liberty Independent Troop. Founded in the early 1790s this militia unit was second only to the famed Chatham Artillery in age and prestige. It had not yet been activated and integrated into the state's defenses, but whenever it was Jones vowed: "I will come down & serve."[6]

Jones and his family returned to Augusta in late May after an absence of over three months. It had been a profitable respite. He was more rested than at any time in the past several years; he had made appreciable headway in his study of southern diseases; and he believed that he had found a way to put his financial affairs in order. Charles Colcock and Mary Jones were sorry to see them leave, for they had enjoyed their visit immensely. Not only did they relish the company, but Jones's medical knowledge had been a godsend in controlling a severe epidemic of colds among the family slaves. Jones was happy that he could be of assistance to his parents. In fact, worried about their safety so near the exposed Georgia coast, he offered to remain with them indefinitely. Although flattered and highly appreciative of such a generous gesture, they turned it down, explaining to their eldest son: "Carrie is not acclimated; her family are at a distance, and we know how circumscribed are our associations. . . . And your brother at home with his library and laboratory would no doubt do more in a professional way than with us."[7]

Back in Augusta, despite a heavy cold contracted while treating the slaves at Monte Video, Jones busied himself with preparations to launch his practice. He began to put out feelers for potential patients and moved his large natural history collection from his study at home to his office at the college, replacing it with his small stock of medicines. These preparations were slowed down by two time-consuming duties he was called upon to perform for the Medical College of Georgia. He was asked to prepare the annual announcement, including a list of the more than one thousand previous graduates, for the forthcoming session. He was forced to give this task his immediate and undivided attention, since, as he explained, "the season is now far advanced & our announcement should have been printed & distributed before this." Jones was also appointed to a building committee charged with the expenditure of an appropriation voted the school by the state legislature during its recent session.[8]

Jones's efforts to establish a private practice were further interrupted in late June when tragedy struck his brother's family. On June 25 Charles Colcock Jones, Jr., wrote that his wife, Ruth, had just given birth to a second daughter. The child was in perfect health, but the mother was in an undetermined state as the result of protracted hemorrhaging following parturition. To make matters worse, the eldest child, twenty-month old Julia, was critically ill, having been stricken with scarlet fever a week earlier. Fearing for the safety of his sister-in-law and niece, Jones felt impelled to go to their side. Only the health of his wife and son, who like himself were just recovering from persistent colds, persuaded him to await a further report. Two days later a second letter informed him that Ruth had contracted an undiagnosed fever. Jones believed that he could not hesitate and rushed to Savannah, asserting that "if only by relieving some of the rest as a nurse" he could be useful.

A sad spectacle greeted him. Julia was very ill, and he entertained little hope for her recovery. "For eleven days," he wrote his wife, "her fever has been very high, throat much swollen, unable to sleep, resless, continually tossing from side to side, & even throwing herself with violence against the sides of her little crib." "I sat up with her last night," he added, "& expect to do so again tonight—will do all in my power for her." He found Ruth in a critical condition and Charles, Jr., in bed with a severe attack of tonsillitis. Every effort was being made in this afflicted family's behalf. Mary Jones was there, "aiding with all her strength, energy & motherly tenderness," and three of the best physicians in Savannah, including Jones's old friend Richard D. Arnold, were in attendance.

Little Julia steadily worsened and died on July 2. Although "much worn by nursing and anxiety" Jones stayed by her side until the end. He immediately sought to comfort his grief-stricken brother and assumed a major role in arranging the dead child's funeral. On July 4 Ruth's ailment was diagnosed as puerperal fever, a leading cause of parturient mortality in the nineteenth century. Her condition, Jones believed, was complicated by phlegmasia dolens, an inflammation of the coats of the veins "induced by the absorption of the disorganized matters of the uterus." He attributed the puerperal fever to fate and the complication to the peculiar state of Savannah's summer atmosphere and the presence of scarlet fever in her own house. He held little hope for her. She lingered for three days longer before expiring on the morning of July 7. Jones was greatly moved by the drama of her death, describing it as "happy & triumphant." In an emotional deathbed scene, Ruth dictated farewell messages to her family and friends, bid the servants a personal good-bye, left instructions that her newborn infant was to be entrusted to Mary Jones, thanked her husband for a happy marriage, and commanded him, since he had not been converted, to "seek the Savior . . . right early."

Joseph Jones sorely regretted the events which had befallen his brother, but as a devout Calvinist he interpreted them as God's will and therefore "right & just." "The hand of God," he observed, "has indeed been very heavy upon us—my poor Brother is indeed afflicted—his wife & child are taken & his home left desolate." "He has," Jones added, "been a devoted husband & father, & his afflictions are correspondingly great—we must pray that they may be sanctified to his eternal salvation."[9]

Following the burial of his sister-in-law Jones hurried to Augusta to resume his efforts to establish a medical practice. He diligently pursued this goal. The only relaxation he allowed himself was greeting soldiers on their way to the Virginia front. Augusta was situated at the junction of the Georgia and Carolina railroads, vital arteries in the railroad network linking the upper and lower South. Every evening at seven the depots were "crowded with citizens anxious to welcome & cheer the troops arriving & departing." Their enthusiasm and variegated uniforms were captivating. Jones was spellbound one June evening by a 600-man battalion of Louisiana Zouaves. "They were," he reported to his parents, "composed of french & spanish desperadoes, and were a most formidable & remarkable looking set of men, with their red Turkish trousers, blue jackets with various devices, & bright red caps, singing, dancing, shouting & cutting various curious antics." Such sights further fired Jones's already blazing patriotism, but on every occasion the sobering recollection of his commitment to the Liberty Independent Troop overcame the temptation to join.[10]

Jones devoted most of what little leisure time he had to his research and the writing of three articles. He viewed the latter as practical articles which he hoped might prove of some use. "Whether or not they possess any value," he remarked, "they embody an effort & desire to contribute something to the cause of Southern Independence."[11] The first, dealing with the prevention and control of malaria, was published in the *Southern Medical and Surgical Journal* in August 1861. Basing his opinion on the experiences of the British navy on the African coast and his own research in Georgia's coastal plain, Jones contended that quinine taken during exposure in miasmatic areas would, in most cases, ward off malaria. Even if this fever should attack those to whom prophylactic doses had been administered, its severity and duration would be greatly reduced. He recommended 3 to 5 grains for those in good health and 5 to 15 for patients already showing febrile symptoms. Although sound advice the prescribed dosage was too small to be effective, according to modern medical opinion, which holds that the daily prophylactic and therapeutic doses are 10 and 30 grains respectively.[12]

The second study, an extensive examination of what Jones felt were potentially effective substitutes for quinine, appeared in the same journal beginning in September. He realized that if southern physicians were to control the ravages of malaria a substitute for quinine would have to be found, since the Union blockade was seriously threatening the foreign supply of this valuable specific. In this article he discussed the alleged antipyretic properties of some thirty-six herbs, plants, and trees, including Georgia bark, dogwood, cucumber tree, persimmon, Virginia snake root, ague weed, wild horehound, black willow, thorough wart, milkweed, and catalpa. Jones emphasized, however, that these were not the only substitutes and urged all southern physicians to engage in similar searches.[13]

In the midst of preparing these articles Jones learned of the South's great victory at Manassas on July 21. He was ecstatic, exclaiming: "I think that we can ascribe the wonderful & sudden panic, & the disastrous retreat in which far more was lost than in the battle itself, only to the direct interposition of Providence in our behalf." He was convinced that the southern forces should fully exploit this triumph. "As far as I am able to form any opinion," he remarked, "it seems to me that this great victory should be followed up by an immediate advance upon Washington—if this is taken, our cause must receive . . . respectful support, & we must be acknoweleged by all nations of Europe."[14]

Jones's summons to active duty arrived on October 2, preventing the completion of a projected third study in which he had planned to discuss his views on treating the different forms of malaria. The revelation of his enlistment as a private surprised most of his family and friends, for they had assumed that he would either seek a deferment as a physician or accept a commission in the Confederate medical service. His wife had vowed at the time of his enlistment that she would "never detain Joe when he thinks his duty calls him into service," but now that his departure was imminent she was visibly distressed. She called his attention to the reaction of a close family friend, who, upon learning of his plan, emphatically exclaimed: "No, No, never, tell Dr. Jones if he wants to serve his country go and give the wounded & sick fellow soldiers the benefit of his skill & science in putting them together & healing them but do not expose all that skill & science which he has acquired with such study & research to be a mark for the sharpshooters."[15] His brother attempted to persuade him to reassess his decision, urging him to seek their parents' "judgment of the propriety" of it.[16]

Such pleas were in vain, for Jones drowned out all opposition with patriotic platitudes. He professed that his conscience would not permit him "to remain quietly in professional pursuits" when his country was imperiled; that "the reflection in the future would be disagreeable, when all would be over . . . never to have borne any part in so good a cause"; that he "could not call upon up-country men" to defend his own home and property and remain behind; that "every true patriot should be willing to make sacrifices"; and that while he was "not a military man" and did not seek "position or fame," he wanted the "opportunity to testify devotion to his country and to aid in achieving her independence."

This stand is even more revealing of Jones's staunch patriotism when viewed in light of the fact that he was probably not liable to military service at all owing to a permanent weakness of his left arm as the result of a childhood accident. Thus, since he could not carry a musket for any time conveniently, a cavalry unit was his only choice. This being the case, the Liberty Independent Troop was ideal "for convenience, for acquaintance, [and] for character." The tour of duty was only six months initially, and he would be, in a sense, serving at home. Jones had thoroughly explored each of these points with his father before volunteering for duty in May, and believing that they were well taken, the Reverend Jones did not "feel at liberty to interpose any objection."[17] Joseph Jones was elated with this understanding and support of his controversial decision and profusely thanked his parents for the "unqualified approbation" with which they had reacted to "the motives which have led me to make these changes & sacrifices . . . in the defence of my country."[18]

Jones's attitude was not unique. Many of his colleagues in the medical profession of the South rallied to the colors at the opening of the war as officers and enlisted men in line companies, hampering the efforts of the Confederacy to establish a medical department. Although admirable in some respects such actions were short-sighted. Had these physicians calmly and rationally studied the situation confronting their beloved South, as many of them (including Jones) were to do later, they would have realized that their contributions could have been best made treating the sick and wounded southern soldiers.

Jones's call to active duty found him prepared to go. Some months earlier he had chanced upon a piece of exceptionally fine gray cloth at a bargain price. Carrie took it to a local seamstress who made it into two uniforms at a cost of three dollars apiece. She had done a first-rate job, even lining the coats and pants for warmth. Carrie made him three flannel shirts, which Jones especially prized. He completed his uniform with the purchase of an oilcloth overcoat and pants. Realizing that his buggy horse was not suited for cavalry duty, he bought one of the finest saddle horses available in Augusta. His mother and sister had aided his preparations by devoting much of their leisure time over the summer to molding and preparing several hundred bullets and cartridges for his carbine.[19]

Taking leave of his patients posed no great problem. Jones later asserted that he had left a large practice and as fine a chance to enlarge it "as could possibly be presented to a physician in the commencement of his practice in a new city" to serve as a private in the ranks "with no other purpose than to defend my state from the pollution of our enemies." But his brother's observation that he had "not secured much practice, except among the poorer class where professional services are to be regarded as a matter of love and charity" seemed to be closer to the truth.[20] Nor did Jones's professorship at the Medical College of Georgia cause any difficulty, for like almost every other southern medical school it remained closed for the duration of the war, serving as a Confederate hospital.[21]

Planning for the care and safety of his wife and young son was a considerably more complicated matter. At first there had been some question as to whether they would accompany him to Liberty County and spend his six-months enlistment with his parents or remain in Augusta. After much agonizing over the decision Jones chose the latter alternative. "It may be a little lonely," he observed, "but there are reasons which in comfort & independence alone, will counterbalance the loneliness a thousand fold." He stressed to Carrie that she would be "far more comfortable & independent" in her own home; that she would have "unlimited control, & the convenience & arrangement of no one to consult"; and that she would "be enjoying that perfect independence which has been secured for you entirely & solely by your husband's personal exertions & means." Carrie preferred to be near her husband but dutifully assented to his wishes. For company and convenience Jones arranged for Mrs. Cuthbert, a local widow, to move in with her.[22]

Jones was ordered to report to the Liberty Independent Troop's encampment at Sunbury on Monday, October 7. Allowing himself ample time, he left Augusta astride Lewis, his new horse, two days after receiving his orders. He broke his two-day journey in Savannah, where he stayed overnight with his brother, who was soon to report for active duty as an officer with the Chatham Artillery. Arriving in Liberty County on October 5, he spent the weekend with his parents at Maybank. There he busied himself with last-minute preparations.[23]

On Monday morning Jones excitedly rode the short distance to Sunbury. To his surprise and dismay, he learned upon reporting that a mistake had been made in his orders. He was sent home and told to return on October 14. His disappointment was short-lived, and he wisely used the week's delay to rest, to accustom his horse to the sound of gunfire and the rattle of the scabbard, to improve his horsemanship, and to practice with his weapons—carbine, sabre, and pistol.[24] He had not taken time to get his hair cut before leaving Savannah and allowed his mother to trim it for him. She later sent Carrie a lock of his hair, writing: "Herewith I send you one of his locks—shorne for the Confederate service & by a little coincidence on the anniversary of the day on which his great grandfather Major John Jones was killed at the siege of Savannah in our *first* struggle for independance—October 9, 1779. I cut Joe's hair on October 9, 1861 in our *second* struggle."[25] Jones devoted much of his time to writing his wife. He missed her and their son constantly, but still exuding patriotic zeal, he exclaimed: "If our separations are painful, and if our privations and hardships are great, we must remember that they are the price of liberty and justice, without which life is not worthy of a moment's consideration." "If we expect to hand down to our children the glorious inheritance of true freedom & honorable peace," he added, "we must cheerfully endure the sacrifices necessary to secure them."[26]

Upon reporting a second time, Jones, in a simple ceremony, was mustered into service. Fully armed the troopers mounted their horses and formed two ranks. The mustering officer then read the articles of war and called the roll. All those answering were viewed as subscribing to the articles, and by this act became soldiers of the southern Confederacy for six months. One young man had a change of heart and rode out of camp just as the ceremony was "about to begin, prompting three relatives to leave with him." "It was with difficulty," Jones asserted, "that the officers could prevent a general [out]burst of indignation."[27]

Jones's letters to his wife detailed life in the Liberty Independent Troop.[28] The encampment, consisting of rows of tents arranged in the shape of a parallelogram, was strategically situated on a high bluff where the Medway River empties into the Atlantic Ocean and overlooked "the beautiful sound & soft blue islands in the distance, and the green marsh, looking like a luxuriant meadow." It was a picture-book setting. The area circumscribed by the tents was used as a parade ground. In its center stood the flagpole from which the Confederate flag was proudly displayed. The flag had been made from a Union one. "Had I not been told that this was formerly a United States flag," Jones remarked, "I would not have suspected it, so well had the work been executed. The idea is we think a good one—it represents the new republic arising from the old."

An initial shortage of tents led to overcrowded sleeping conditions. Jones was forced to share a tent designed for four with his uncle and five other troopers, prompting him to protest: "Although our tent is a good large one, & we have in addition an awning spread in front, still seven men are just *three* too many." It was hoped that the anticipated arrival of Confederate stores from Savannah would alleviate the overcrowding. Jones's mother had presented him with a small couch bed. At the head of it he kept his saddle, on which he rested his weapons. Between the saddle and the tent wall he stored his extra clothing covered with a waterproof blanket ready to be strapped on behind his saddle. "So you can see my dearest," he boasted to his wife, "I can be ready at a moment's warning."

Duty began immediately after the induction ceremony, and Jones's first assignment was to stand guard from midnight until 2 A.M. At guard mount he stood out from the rest of the troopers, for the uniforms which his wife had had made for him were the envy of the entire camp. The gray cloth was a shade darker and was considered finer than that of the other troopers' uniforms. His pistols and holsters (a gift from his brother) and his horse also attracted considerable attention. "No man," his father observed upon visiting the camp, "is better supplied than he. And you don't know what a fine trooper he makes."[29]

Describing a typical day to Carrie, Jones wrote that reveille was at 6 A.M., followed by roll call a half-hour later and breakfast at 7. The meals were prepared and served by slaves. Although Titus, Jones's man-servant, had accompanied his master to Liberty County, he was not taken to camp. Instead he was sent back to Carrie with the instructions that she hire him out for at least a dollar a day in order to provide a little extra income. In his place Jones had brought Prime, an elderly Jones family servant, to camp. "You would be greatly amused," he jested, "to see the old man's attempts at spryness & activity." Jones considered the cooking excellent and the food nutritious and abundant. For the first few days, owing to the late arrival of Confederate rations, the troopers had to fall back on their own private stores. When the troop was at last supplied, there was "good fat fresh beef, coffee, sugar, corn meal & rice." The troopers supplemented this diet with fish and oysters from the river and delicacies from their nearby homes.

The day's duties began at 8 A.M. with two hours of mounted drill. The hour between 10 and 11 was devoted to maintenance of weapons, equipment, and horses. It was followed by two hours of bullet-molding and cartridge-making. The midday meal was served at 1 P.M. The high point of the afternoon was a dress parade held between 4 and 6. At 7 the evening roll call was held, followed by supper at 7:30. Lights out at 9 signalled the end of the day. These duties, coupled with guard and stable duty, left "little spare time for any thing but rest." Jones assured his wife, however, that camp life was agreeing with him. As proof he cited his hearty appetite, good spirits, and improving health. He was especially proud of his high state of health and sought to impress this development upon his worried wife's mind, insisting that it was "as good if not better than it ever was, & improving every day." "You must therefore dear wife," he entreated, "think of your husband as improving every day—the six months . . . will soon glide by & he will, if a kind & merciful Providence prospers, be restored to his most precious wife & son in improved health & strength, & be able to do more for them than ever."[30]

Joseph Jones's career as a common soldier lasted but one week. The Liberty Independent Troop was without a surgeon, and numerous of his comrades expressed great gratification at his presence and announced their intentions of seeking his professional advice. "This I shall cheerfully render *gratuitously*," he remarked, "feeling that I am thus doing all that I can to promote the welfare of my brothers in arms; & the establishment of the independence of the Southern Confederacy." Among the first to seek him out was Captain Abdiel Winn, his commanding officer. Winn's daughter had been sick for six weeks, and at her father's request Jones nursed the child back to health, sitting up with her for three nights. In addition to his genuine humanitarian impulses Jones had an ulterior motive in his treatment of Winn's daughter. "I perform these services for our good captain with great pleasure on many accounts," he explained to his wife, "but especially upon *your* account my dearest." "Perhaps this last reason will surprise you," he continued, "but you will readily understand when you reflect that these services will give me, I think, great boldness in asking leave of absence, whenever you or my precious little Stanhope are sick & even to see you several times."[31]

Winn's appreciation far surpassed Jones's expectations: on October 21 he appointed him surgeon of the Liberty Independent Troop. This honor elated Jones, and he excitedly reported it to his wife. He went to inordinate lengths, however, to make it clear that he had in no way solicited the position. "This is not the time for men to seek office," he maintained; instead, "in this time of great distress, all private considerations should be thrust aside & every man should be willing to serve his country in any capacity, even the most humble." He had certainly tried to make this his guiding principle. "In leaving Augusta," he avowed, "I determined to ask no favors & seek no appointment; but to discharge all my duties & confer as many favors upon others as possible." Therefore this honor had been totally unexpected, coming, he liked to believe, "as a testimonial of the respect and confidence of the men."

Jones's extreme sensitivity as to how his appointment as surgeon of the Liberty Independent Troop was viewed seems to have been a product of his bitter contempt for the rampant office-seeking which, he felt, characterized Georgia in the opening days of the Civil War. "Our state," he complained to his wife, "has especially suffered by the brazen hunt for office (and in some instances those seeking office were scarcely one removed from traitors and abolitionists) and by the appointment by those high in office of their own kin, regardless of every qualification." He was particularly enraged at the effect he felt this practice had had on Georgia's defenses, accusing the state's highest-ranking military officer with appointing his relatives "to the most eligible situations." So flagrant had been his nepotism, Jones insisted, that it had "excited universal comment & the question is asked what other relative has _____? Have all the appointments filled? Or have all the relatives received comfortable births?" The results of this policy were potentially fatal for Georgia. "It is the belief of almost every citizen in this section of the country," Jones fumed, "that if an attempt had been made by the enemy to invade our soil it would have proved disastrous to us in the worst degree, so inefficient, incompetent & selfish are certain officials believed to have been."[32]

Jones's new position was not a soft one. In fact he worked harder in it than he would have had he remained a trooper, for in addition to most of his regular duties he was required to treat not only the 80 men and slaves making up the command but the troopers' families and slaves in the surrounding countryside as well. The only special attention he received was relief from guard duty. During a typical day he held surgeon's call after breakfast where he inspected the sick and prescribed for them. Two hours of mounted drill followed. After a half-hour break, which he was seldom able to take because of demands on his time by the sick, there followed two hours of maintenance and inspection of arms and horses. In the afternoon he made calls in the nearby countryside. He hurried back to camp in time for afternoon surgeon's call. This was followed by a two-hour dress mounted parade. After supper he made his more distant rounds in Liberty County. These various duties kept him busy from dawn to midnight, and on an average day he rode sixteen miles on horseback and another twelve in his buggy, making calls throughout southeastern Liberty County. No wonder he was prompted to exclaim: "My work is never done."[33] His parents were proud of his devotion and determination. "Joe," Mary Jones wrote her daughter-in-law, "has been doing as usual noble duty—as private, surgeon & county physician—has calls by day & night & never thinks of himself—but I am glad to see him stand it so well."[34] Carrie, in turn, praised him too, remarking: "You ought to receive a series of silver medals inscribed with legends to the effect that this is a man who thinks of everybody else always—of himself never." She feared, however, that he was not getting that undisturbed rest of which he had boasted previously and urged him to protect his health.[35]

In the little free time that he could muster Jones outfitted a small hospital. Although little more than two whitewashed rooms upstairs in a house which the Liberty Independent Troop used for military stores, it was an improvement over an open tent and provided him with a place where he could study, write, or rest when time permitted. He also launched a campaign to collect the articles he needed to furnish and supply his hospital. His sister proved to be an able lieutenant in this operation.[36]

Jones's new duties did indeed make great demands upon him. He looked upon them, however, as far more than the providing of medical services for the troopers and their families and slaves. He further saw them as a valuable opportunity to advance his study of southern diseases. The chance for research had played an important role in his taking the position as surgeon in the first place and helps to explain his intense devotion to his duties. "This body of men serving on their own sod," Jones later pointed out, "furnished a good field for the investigation of the diseases of an isolated Command, subjected to no new conditions of climate, water or soil." "My opportunities for observing the diseases incident to the Climate," he added, "were farther increased by a practice amongst the families & servants of the Soldiers.[37]

During his six-months enlistment, October 1861 to March 1862, he treated 420 cases of disease. Of these 116 occurred among members of the command, 47 among the camp slaves, 90 among the troopers' families, and 167 among their slaves.[38] The latter two groups are of little value in comparing the relative health of the four types of patients, since there is no way of determining the total number of whites and blacks in Liberty County who were dependents of the troopers. The only comparison that can be made is between the soldiers and the camp slaves.

Jones estimated the mean strength of the Liberty Independent Troop at 80 and that of the camp slaves at 40. Comparing cases of sickness to mean strength, it is learned that each trooper had an average of 1.3 periods of illness during this six-months period and each camp slave 1.2. No deaths occurred among either group. Additional information for the Liberty Independent Troop, shown in table 1, reveals that an average of 19.3 soldiers, approximately 25 percent of the command was treated each month with a high of 25 cases in October and a low of 16 in January and March. It is obvious, therefore, that the disease rate for this command was relatively low, especially when it is taken into consideration that its members were largely unseasoned planters or planters' sons and that the first month of their service was still the sickly season with its potentially rampant malaria. The camp slaves fared equally well. Such a judgment must be made with caution, however, for, judging by the extensiveness of Jones's practice and the standards of the times, the slaves, in all probability, did not receive the same quality of medical attention accorded to the troopers and their families.

No one was more aware than Jones of the relationship between environment and disease. This awareness, a product of his coastal Georgia background and extensive study of southern diseases, played an important role in his diagnosis and treatment of the disorders of the Liberty Independent Troop. According to Jones, Liberty County consisted of two geographic divisions. The first, a zone with a tropical climate, encompassed the county's offshore islands and the coastal plain to a point some thirty miles inland. This area was covered with dense vegetation, intersected by numerous creeks and streams, and dotted with marshes. The soil, composed of vegetable matter, sand, clay, and the silt washed down from upper Georgia, was very rich. The western portion of the county was geographically quite different. The terrain was more elevated; the soil, mainly sand and clay, was drier; and the vegetation, long leaf pines and scrub oaks for the most part, was noticeably sparser.

The first division was settled well ahead of the second. Here, in the late eighteenth and early nineteenth centuries, large rice and cotton plantations were carved out of the fertile alluvial

TABLE 1

Cases of Sickness among the Liberty Independent Troop,
October 1861–March 1862

October	25
November	24
December	18
January	16
February	17
March	16
TOTAL	116

plain. In a short time, however, the planters learned that this was an unhealthy region. Waves of devastating fevers attributed to miasmatic or noxious odors arising from decaying vegetable and animal matter, as their usual name malaria or "bad air" implies, plagued the settlers during the hot humid months of late spring, summer, and early fall. The belief soon grew up that "no race but the African can ever stand the burning heat and fatal miasms of the Rice fields, and of the Cotton fields" during this so-called sickly season.[39] Subsequently the planters built summer retreats to which they fled from early May until the first killing frost, usually in late October. Some went only as far as Sunbury; a few retreated to the banks of the Cannouchee River, the county's northern-most boundary; others fled to the interior, taking refuge in towns such as Hinesville, Flemington, and Walthourville; and still others sought the safety of Colonel's Island.[40]

The Liberty Independent Troop's encampment at Sunbury occupied one of the healthiest sites in Liberty County. Founded in 1758, this town had been the county's leading seaport until shortly after the Revolution, when it was superseded in importance by Riceboro, a small village lying at the head of tidewater on the North Newport River. Accompanying the loss in importance came an inevitable decline in population until by the outbreak of the Civil War Sunbury had become a virtual ghost town. The Liberty Independent Troop's camp site, a grassy spot near the southeastern boundary of the old town, thoroughly pleased Jones, who observed: "The cool refreshing sea-breezes & the perfect ventilation which they produced were highly conducive to health. The fine bold salt river flowing within a stones throw of the Camp & opening into a wide sound afforded abundant supplies of fine oysters, crabs & fish."[41]

Unfortunately the command's stay at Sunbury was shortlived, lasting less than a month. In early November the Union navy occupied Port Royal Sound, a strategic harbor, lying near South Carolina's southern border and the mouth of the Savannah River. Sunbury was now believed to be untenable, and the Liberty Independent Troop withdrew further inland to Riceboro, where it was to remain as a home guard. This assignment apparently was a concession by state authorities to the citizens of Liberty County, who adamantly demanded protection against potential slave insurrections and Union invasions from the sea.[42]

Jones was as dissatisfied with the new camp site as he had been pleased with the old one. He was especially disturbed by Riceboro's unhealthy medical topography. The town, which straddled a small sand hill 200 yards south of the North Newport River, was surrounded on all sides except the east by marshes, ponds, and swamps. Solid ground was so scarce that the Liberty Independent Troop was forced to camp on poorly drained, marshy terrain flanked by ponds. To complicate matters further, the fall frosts were late and, although the unit did not arrive in Riceboro until November 8, the first freeze was still two weeks away. The troopers, Jones lamented, were faced with a frightful situation— the weather was hot and humid, vegetation was still rank, and at night the air was full of the "offensive vapors of the swamps." The effect of such conditions upon the health of the command soon became evident, as the troopers took on an exhausted and sallow appearance and numerous cases of climate fever were reported. Their health improved noticeably after the first frost, so much so that Jones pointed out later that they were in better physical condition at the end of their enlistment than they had been at the onset of it six months earlier.[43]

In terms of the number of cases and the percentage of the mean strength disabled by the various diseases, the medical statistics for the Liberty Independent Troop's first six months of service teach no important medical lessons. Such a contribution was precluded by the unit's size, its inactivity, and the brevity of the test period. Yet these figures, shown in table 2, are not without value. The health problems these statistics depict typify those faced by numerous other volunteer units serving on the southern coastal plain in the opening days of the war. They also afford the

TABLE 2

Causes of Disability among the Liberty Independent Troop and their Camp Slaves, October 1861–March 1862

	Liberty Independent Troop	Camp slaves
Malaria	27	4
Diarrhea and dysentery	6	0
Measles	21	20
Respiratory ailments	31	18
Rheumatism	0	2
Neuralgia	5	0
Injuries	5	3
Miscellaneous	21	0
TOTALS	116	47

unique opportunity to compare the health of whites and blacks living and working together under the same general conditions. Most important the figures frequently reveal striking parallels with those for the large northern and southern armies.

The Civil War's leading fatal diseases were typhoid fever, malaria, and diarrhea and dysentery.[44] Typhoid fever, produced by a bacillus found in infected excrement and spread by flies or human carriers, was especially prevalent in the early months of the war. The Liberty Independent Troop, however, escaped its ravages. This fortunate occurrence is attributable to the command's size and composition; its eighty members were planters' sons who, unlike the uneducated rustic youths making up the greater part of the Confederate armies, had a knowledge of and an appreciation for camp sanitation.

Malaria, endemic and often epidemic in the antebellum South, was a persistent medical problem in Civil War armies, especially those operating in the South. Its mysterious appearance was readily explained by a wide range of contradicting theories that put the blame on such factors as sudden climatic changes, poisoned camp air, and sleeping in damp blankets. The most widely accepted explanation, as we have seen, attributed malaria to miasms or vapors arising from the decomposition of animal and vegetable matter. Not until the advent of the age of bacteriology in the latter part of the nineteenth century was the infected *Anopheles* mosquito found to be the true culprit. It is not surprising, then, that malaria was the most prevalent of the Liberty Independent Troop's disorders, accounting for nearly one-fourth of the total cases. Its greatest incidence was in November when 12 of the 27 cases were reported. Jones was correct in believing that this outbreak was caused by the removal of the command from its salubrious encampment at Sunbury to a swampy, unhealthy site at Riceboro prior to the first killing frost.[45] The reduced morbidity of malaria after the first major freeze bears out the soundness of his judgment: only 4 cases were recorded in December, 2 in January, 1 in February, and 5 in March. Malaria posed no threat to the unit's camp servants (a total of 4 cases were reported), bolstering Jones's traditional southern belief that the Negro was "capable of bearing with impunity, and in fact thriving better in our hot and sickly climate than in the most healthy climates to the white races."[46]

Diarrhea and dysentery were the great enervating ailments of the Civil War. Jones later wrote: "Chronic diarrhea and dysentery were the most abundant and most difficult to cure amongst army diseases; and whilst the more fatal diseases, as typhoid fever, progressively diminished, chronic diarrhea and dysentery progressively increased, and not only destroyed more soldiers than gunshot wounds, but more soldiers were permanently disabled and lost to the services from these diseases than from the disability following the accidents of battle."[47] Despite their almost epidemic proportions there was no consensus about the cause of intestinal disorders, although numerous likely explanations, such as exposure and inadequate rations, were advocated. The incidence of diarrhea and dysentery in the Liberty Independent Troop was negligible. Six cases were reported among the troopers and none among the camp servants. This virtual absence of bowel disorders can be traced to three things. First, the Confederate ration was dietetically sound at the outset of the war. Second, and of even greater importance, these soldiers were bivouacked quite near their families and, as Jones pointed out, frequently supplemented the standard army diet with food from home. Finally the command's meals were prepared by servants, who, in all probability, had had cooking experience on the plantations. This was an improvement over the mess arrangement in most units, where each soldier cooked his own meals which too often resulted in death from the frying pan.[48]

Ranking close behind typhoid fever, malaria, and intestinal

disorders as a leading cause of casualty in Civil War armies were the so-called children's diseases such as measles, mumps, chicken pox, scarlet fever, and diphtheria. Their widespread morbidity can be traced to the overwhelmingly rural background of the soldiers. The protection that isolation had accorded vanished upon induction, leaving them easy prey for almost any contagious disorder. Consequently children's diseases were especially prevalent early in the war, often putting entire regiments out of action. In September 1861, for example, Howell Cobb's 16th Regiment of Georgia infantry was so badly ravaged by mumps and measles in its Richmond encampment that the unit was delayed for five weeks in moving to the Peninsula.[49]

Of the main forms of children's diseases persistent during the Civil War only measles is found in the medical statistics for the Liberty Independent Troop. This disorder was the second leading cause of casualty among the troopers and the leading one among the camp servants. First appearing in December, it attacked 21 whites and 20 blacks over the succeeding four months. Despite the equality in the number of cases, however, the ratio of the incidence of measles was twice as great among the camp servants as among the troopers, since the former group outnumbered the latter two to one. Highly contagious, this disease quickly spread from the troopers to their families and slaves in the surrounding countryside. The ensuing epidemic occupied much of Jones's time during the winter of 1861–1862. His treatment of measles was, in contrast to the heroic medicine of the day, quite simple. Convinced that the disease had a definite course to run, he placed uncomplicated cases in a warm, dry room and left them to the healing powers of nature. Serious cases received greater attention, since Jones felt that the body—the kidneys and skin in particular—needed assistance to overcome the poison's effect. He advocated doses of sage and flax teas, which were thought to have diuretic and diaphoretic properties.[50]

Rheumatic conditions, neuralgia, and respiratory ailments, caused in part and severely aggravated by frequent exposure to cold and rain, were common complaints in Civil War armies and were particularly prevalent during the cool, wet months of the fall and winter. Rheumatic conditions and neuralgia were minor problems in the Liberty Independent Troop, attacking a total of five troopers and two camp servants. Respiratory ailments, however, ranging from asthma to pneumonia, were the leading cause of casualty among the soldiers and the second leading one among the camp slaves. The most widespread of these disorders among the former group was bronchitis with 15 cases (10 acute and 5 chronic); among the slaves, it was catarrh or colds with 9 cases. Pneumonia was the universally feared fatal respiratory ailment, and not surprisingly this pneumococcal inflammation of the lungs became one of the Civil War's greatest medical problems. During the winter of 1861–1862, however, its incidence in the Liberty Independent Troop was negligible: three cases were reported—all among the troopers.

Fully expecting to need them, Jones had his wife send him his surgery textbooks immediately upon being appointed surgeon of the Liberty Independent Troop.[51] Indeed wounds and injuries exacted a tremendous toll on both sides during the Civil War, but, owing to the inactivity of the unit, these troopers experienced no combat casualties. Moreover the command's orderly camp life occasioned few injuries. A total of eight, seven of which were bruises, were reported—five among the troopers and three among the camp servants.

In addition to these data the medical statistics for the Liberty Independent Troop include figures on a number of other ailments whose limited morbidity preclude any detailed examination. Yet these conditions were not without importance, since they were responsible for 21 casualties—all among the troopers. Ranked according to their incidence, these maladies were: skin conditions (4 cases), stomach and digestive complaints (3 cases), foot ailments (3 cases), hemorrhoids (3 cases), venereal disease (2 cases), diseases of the eye (2 cases), diseases of the ear (2 cases), cholera (1 case), and scrofula (1 case).

With its assignment to home guard duty, life in the Liberty Independent Troop settled into a routine, prompting Jones to complain: "We have but little to break the monotony of camp life."[52] He was complaining about the sameness of his duties and not a lack of them, however, for his medical practice continued to keep him on the go. But he did find time to pursue his study of southern diseases and to collect some new specimens for the museum of the Medical College of Georgia. A number of experiments with the effects of various poisons on animals were conducted at Maybank and Monte Video, the nearby Jones family homes. For the museum he assembled what was largely a collection of the skeletons of local vertebrata, although he did mount several birds and animals, including a six-foot whooping crane. Jones prided himself on his continued interest in the school, boasting in a letter to a former colleague there: "During my service in the Confederate Army I have not been unmindful of the Old Medical College of Georgia."[53]

For relaxation Jones took long walks in which he savored the pleasant memories of his happy home life before the war. Describing one of these interludes at Sunbury to Carrie, he wrote:

> After dinner I attended to the sick & then walked to the old fort & along the river bank that I might have some time for meditation & communion with you my own most precious wife. As I looked upon the green marsh rendered golden by the rays of the setting sun & upon the calm majestic river, reflecting his parting rays of gold & purple & mirroring back our white tents, beautiful Confederate flag & the green banks with their tall pines & spreading moss clad live oaks, & then out to the sound & still farther to the blue waters of the Atlantic Ocean, these calm & beautiful scenes rendered only more deep & intense my longings for you & my dear boy.[54]

Jones did miss them greatly. He often agonized over "the conflicting emotions which this cruel & long separation induces." On the one hand there was his desire "to serve my country & aquit myself honorably & worthily"; on the other there was his "intense longing to bridge over or annihilate these tedious days" which separated him from the ones he loved.[55]

By the beginning of November Jones was homesick. He requested, and was granted, a leave. It was to begin on November 4, providing he could be spared. He endorsed this condition with his usual patriotism, explaining to Carrie that as much as he longed to see her and his son that he could not "expose the life of a human being by leaving him in his hour of sickness & trial." "And I know," he added, "that my most noble & patriotic wife would not have me do otherwise."[56] As luck would have it, "27 vessels of the Lincoln fleet" appeared off Port Royal the day before his leave was to begin. All leaves were cancelled and an order was issued commanding every soldier "to hold himself in readiness to march at a moment's notice."[57]

The Union fleet bombarded forts Beauregard and Walker,

which guarded the entrance to Port Royal Sound, into submission and took control of this fine harbor. It provided an excellent base for the blockade of southern ports and subsequent Union operations along the coasts of South Carolina, Georgia, and Florida. Although within earshot of the battle the Liberty Independent Troop was not called into action. Instead, as we have seen, the troopers were ordered to evacuate their now vulnerable coastal position and to occupy a new one safely inland at Riceboro. This move was part of the general panic which seized coastal Georgia following the Confederate defeat at Port Royal. The citizens of Savannah expected an attack momentarily and many fled the city. Jones attributed this anxiety to a widespread realization of the poor condition of Georgia's defenses. "If we are preserved from this calamity," he asserted, "it will be through a merciful Providence & not through either the intelligence, honesty or energy of our officials. Our state defences have been shamefully neglected."[58]

The Union occupation of Port Royal placed a cloud over the future of the Liberty Independent Troop, making it uncertain when Jones would be able to obtain a leave. But the much-feared enemy invasion failed to materialize, and life in the troop soon settled back into its accustomed routine. At the end of November Jones resubmitted his request for a leave and was given five days beginning on December 2. He chose this particular time because it coincided with the opening of a General Assembly of Southern Presbyterians, scheduled to convene in Augusta on December 4, to establish a Presbyterian Church of the Confederate States of America. As an elder in his church Jones was anxious to attend at least the opening of this historic meeting. His father, who was to play an important role at this convention in the field of slave religion, accompanied him to Augusta.[59]

Before returning to camp Jones either asked Carrie or she persuaded him to allow her to accompany his brother-in-law, the Reverend Robert Quarterman Mallard, also a delegate at this convention, to Liberty County at the end of the meeting and to spend the remainder of his tour of duty with his parents. To Jones's dismay, upon his return he found the Liberty Independent Troop in the grip of an epidemic of measles which, of course, soon spread to the troopers' families in Liberty County. Not wishing to risk their exposure to this dangerous disease, he delayed his family's visit until the threat had subsided. He was most concerned with the journey to Liberty County since they would be traveling by train, throwing them together with soldiers. "The army," he pointed out, "is a great source of disease."[60]

Since it was now impossible for his family to visit him, Jones hoped for a second leave at Christmas to go see them. This plan fell through when Winn cancelled all leaves during the holiday in apparent fear of a surprise Union attack. The troopers countered with a Christmas Day "contribution dinner" honoring their families and relatives. Jones was even prevented from participating in this festive occasion owing to the recurrent sickness of his father and the needs of his patients. His Christmas was lonely.[61]

The New Year's holiday passed in a similar fashion with Jones busily engaged in treating the sick. The year had been a crucial one in his own personal history as well as that of the South and of the nation as a whole. On New Year's Eve he assessed its impact in a letter to his wife. "In the past year," he wrote, "we have had many, many changes—a nation has been divided, our peaceful land plunged in all the horrors of Civil War bringing distress & mourning to almost every heart in our land. During this year of horrors, even our sacred little circle has been broken, and I have been compelled to exchange my pen for the deadly rifle, my quiet study for the battle-field, and the sweet quiet intercourse of my dear wife & child for the rough converse of armed men." "And yet," he added happily, "through all these changes, through all these public & private afflictions, our hearts have remained united."[62]

Jones looked to the new year with renewed hope, for his wife and child were at last coming to Liberty County. They arrived at the middle of January and stayed until the end of his enlistment. He wanted them near him very much but did not demand it. Instead he repeatedly apprised his wife of the potential dangers facing her—the constant threat of a Union invasion, her unacclimated state, and the persistence of measles in the area. But he knew that Carrie would come. Writing her as she was making plans to join him, "I have a pre-sentiment," he observed, "that you will come, notwithstanding my faithful representation of the dangers which beset us." He made only one demand upon her— that she take great care in providing for the safety of his books before leaving Augusta, asserting: "My library is invaluable."[63]

Jones went on leave a second time in March 1862, shortly before the expiration of his enlistment. Its purpose was to help his brother move most of the family slaves to the safety of the interior. As early as the previous fall, with the commencement of the Union bombardment of Savannah's coastal defenses the Jones family had become fearful of raids on Liberty County from the sea and began to consider steps to safeguard their Negroes and to remove from them any temptation of fleeing to the Union navy. Three alternatives were examined: the slaves could be moved to a safer place in the interior, they could be hired out to planters in less dangerous areas, or they could be put to work on defense projects. After much deliberation the Joneses decided that they preferred to keep their bondsmen under their own control and elected to pursue the first alternative.

Charles Colcock Jones, Jr., assisted by his brother, conducted an intensive search for a suitable location. He eventually decided upon the relatively secure northeastern portion of the state and apparently rented (and later purchased) Buck-Head, a plantation in Burke County, slightly over a hundred miles north of Liberty County on the South Carolina border.[64] Beginning in March 1862 the steady evacuation of the Jones plantations began. It was an overnight railroad and wagon trip to the new plantation. Joseph Jones accompanied the Negroes, "who went cheerfully," as far as Augusta where they were met by his brother and escorted the rest of the way.[65]

The operations of the Union gunboats in the waters around Colonel's Island soon made Maybank totally untenable, and in the spring of 1862 it was abandoned. Moreover no crops were planted at Arcadia or Monte Video after 1861, and by the end of 1862 all the slaves, except the few necessary for caretaking duties, had been sent to Burke County. Because of the high cost of transportation most of the livestock, grain and cotton was sold. As soon as the slaves were safely moved to the new plantation the slow process of removing personal belongings began. This continued until 1863, when it was halted short of completion.[66]

By the time Jones returned from his second leave his enlistment was drawing to a close, and he was faced with a momentous decision. He had to decide whether to volunteer for further service with the Liberty Independent Troop, return to Augusta and resume his private practice, seek a commission in the Confederate medical service, or attempt to return to teaching. It was unlikely that he would elect the first of these alternatives. Jones had performed admirably as surgeon of the Liberty Independent Troop, and his comrades and many of their relatives he had treated urged him to stay on. At the end of his enlistment two of the county's most influential citizens presented him with a silver pitcher and two goblets on a silver waiter, each inscribed "Dr. Joseph Jones."[67] Jones deeply appreciated this "elegant expression of their kind feelings" but, believing that his talents were not being used to their fullest, he seriously questioned the wisdom of any further service with the Liberty Independent Troop. The last alternative had considerable merit but was in reality unfeasible. The war had wrought havoc with education in Georgia. Financial pressures combined with a shortage of faculty and students had already forced the closing of most medical colleges, and those attempting to hold classes were fighting a losing battle. By the end of the war all of the state's medical schools were closed and most had been converted into hospitals. Although not formally closed until 1863, the Medical College of Georgia suspended classes at the opening of the war. Jones insisted, however, that classes ought to be resumed, shrewdly noting that should the war continue the South would need a large number of trained physicians. "Now that Nashville is in the hands of the enemy, & the sea board cities threatened," he argued, "it is incumbent upon the professors of the Medical College of Georgia that they make every exertion to furnish the best means of instruction."[68]

For this reason Jones rejected an attractive offer for his laboratory equipment from an Augusta firm engaged in the manufacture of explosives for the South, rejecting funds that he could have used to good advantage. The offer, although made in good faith, angered him. The explosives firm was operated by two brothers, formerly of Philadelphia, who had chosen to support the Confederacy. Jones denounced their request as a "fine specimen of yankee impertinence." "It is amazing," he raved, "the brass & effrontery of these yankees. I consider his request equivalent . . . to a request for a house & home."[69]

This emotional outburst resulted partly from the mere thought that he would part with his beloved laboratory equipment. The beginnings of a war psychosis are also detectable, a product of Jones's basic personality and his blind, emotional defense of the South and southern institutions. He had long showed strong signs of paranoia, and the war aggravated this tendency. Jones's war psychosis was to become more apparent with the worsening plight of the South, but it was, for a man of science educated in northern schools, still claiming many close friends in the North, surprisingly strong from the onset of hostilities. Shortly after his induction into the Liberty Independent Troop, for example, he wrote his wife: "We can but believe that a just & merciful God will punish the cruel & blood-thirsty & utterly depraved & defiled northern tyrants. I have an unwavering confidence that God will protect those who contend for justice, liberty, & their homes. These cruel invaders would not only desolate & burn our houses, but they would excite our slaves to rebellion, & dishonor our wives & sisters & daughters." "Life," he continued, "would be utterly valuless under the cruel murderers & foul Pirates & it is the solemn duty of every man in the Southern Confederacy, to die, rather than to yield for one moment to the oppression of these vile freebooters whose cry is beauty & booty."[70] In a letter to his father a few days later he carried this argument a step futher, asserting: "If the enemy should invade it is my firm conviction that it is our duty to take no prisoners. . . . We should neither ask nor give quarter." He made this assertion while enraged by an article he had read in a local newspaper avowing the intention of the North to use Negro troops against the South.[71] Thus, in Jones's mind, it was the duty of every true southerner to give "the vile Pirates" of the North "a warm reception." "We must fight them," he exclaimed, "before they land, whilst they land, & after they land & give them no time to rest, night or day, until our soil is purged of the foul contamination of the rotten mercenaries."[72]

It was obvious that no matter what course of action Jones adopted he would be involved, and significantly so, in the struggle for southern independence. As his tour of duty neared a close he realized that he could make a far greater contribution in some capacity other than continued service with a militia unit relegated to local defense. Moreover a return to teaching was out of the question—at least for the time being. This left him two choices. He could accept a commission in the Confederate medical service and make a direct contribution through duty in a hospital or on the battlefield, or he could return to private practice and make a less direct, but still important, contribution through his research. But in reality the situation facing him was not this simple, for it was complicated by family and financial matters, making the path he should travel even more unclear. So on April 1, 1862, Joseph Jones was mustered out of the Liberty Independent Troop with his future very much in question.

Chapter 6
The Making of a Confederate Surgeon

The man who is raised up to discover the causes
and proper treatment of camp diseases will
be honored of God as a benefactor of his call.

Determining his personal contribution to the southern war effort was no easy task for Joseph Jones. It was not until eight months after the end of his tour of duty with the Liberty Independent Troop that his role became clear. This was unlike Jones. In the past his actions had been characterized by a decisiveness often bordering on impulsiveness.

Jones had not meant to be indecisive. On the contrary he had planned to return to Augusta as soon as he was mustered out of service to chart his future course. But he postponed these plans at the insistence of his parents, who urged him to spend some time with them to regain his strength before undertaking some new and strenuous project. What Jones viewed as a brief postponement turned into a lengthy one when measles, present in Liberty County since the preceding December, broke out among those slaves who had not been sent to Burke County. The disease appeared first at Monte Video, shortly before Jones was released from active duty. It quickly spread to Arcadia. Soon an epidemic was under way.

Jones immediately abandoned his vacation and moved to stem the epidemic's tide. He had his hands full running back and forth between Monte Video and Arcadia to treat the sick. As the number of cases mounted, he began to fear for the safety of his young son, and in mid-April he sent the youth and his mother to Augusta. Jones accompanied them as far as Millen, some two-thirds of the way, where it was necessary to change trains to complete the trip.

He then hurried back to Liberty County to resume his battle against measles. It was a great trial to Jones to leave his family and return to "these low-grounds of sorrow & sickness," but it was for the best that he did so, for he found the slaves at Monte Video and Arcadia "still in a most distressed condition" demanding his "undivided care & attention." Despite Charles Colcock Jones's fervent hopes and prayers that "it may please God to rebuke our diseases" so that his son could soon rejoin his family in Augusta, it was the beginning of May before Jones felt it safe to leave.[1]

While performing this service for his parents, Jones had his only confrontation of the war with the enemy. He had relished the thought of an active role in the defense of his beloved South when he enlisted as a private in the Liberty Independent Troop. In November 1861 it had appeared as if he would get the chance. The Union fleet began shelling Fort Pulaski, the gateway to Savannah, at the mouth of the Savannah River. Hearing the bursting shells, the Liberty Independent Troop was "for a time wild with excitement & the cry was onward to Savannah." Jones was among those most eager to march. "As soon as the firing commenced," he had reported to his wife, "I prepared my clothes & filled my cartridge box with amunition—my sword had been already sharpined—and filled my haversack with bread." But no Union attack ensued, and the services of the troopers were not needed.[2] Jones resented the lack of an opportunity to strike a blow for southern independence as a soldier. Ironically he got his wish shortly after becoming a civilian. In reality, however, the whole affair was more like a comic opera than combat.

Blockade-runners had long enjoyed the safety of the waters around Georgia's offshore islands. One, a steamer out of Halifax, Nova Scotia, had entered the North Newport River in search of a cargo about the time Jones had been mustered out of service. Several weeks later a Union gunboat appeared at the mouth of the river, apparently seeking the blockade-runner. The hostile vessel terrified Liberty County's coastal residents. Jones had started for Arcadia to treat the sick slaves there when he learned of its presence. He "posted back" to Monte Video. While his mother prepared him a hurried lunch and packed some rations for him, he got ready his blanket, camp clothes, and waterproofs. Armed with his grandfather John Jones's double-barreled gun, he bade his parents good-bye, put the spurs to Lewis, and "hurried away for the fight."[3] As he neared Colonel's Island he encountered an exodus of planters bearing conflicting stories. Some insisted that there was an invasion; others contended that the Union forces were only making a demonstration; all agreed that at the sight of the gunboat the Liberty Independent Troop, the area's only defense, "had thrown away their arms & were in full retreat." Jones found such a report hard to believe, for, although factionalism had caused the troop to split into two new units in early April, many of his former comrades were still serving, and he recalled a time six months earlier when several of them had boasted that they "would be willing to pay thousands, for the chance of being in . . . battle."[4] Any disbelief he may have had quickly disappeared when he reached Colonel's Island in late afternoon and discovered the Liberty Independent Troop retreating.

The gunboat, Jones observed, was anchored out of rifle range in the channel of the North Newport River. Anxious to halt its advance, he urged the troopers and a number of armed citizens accompanying them to make a stand, proposing the scuttling of the blockade-runner and the setting up of a defense on a commanding bluff between the mouth of the river and Riceboro. His plan was vigorously opposed by the troopers, who contended that the bluff was too low to be defended and could be easily raked with grapeshot. This reluctance to fight irritated Jones, prompting him to exclaim that "it was absurd to keep in the rear of an enemy & to have our homes exposed," that "our place was between danger and our homes," and that his proposed defensive site "was the only point of any strategic importance on the river" and was "an admirable place for [shelter] . . . whilst they picked off the Yankees." "If we [intend] to meet the invaders," he exhorted, "we must expect to run risks & if we [are] afraid of risking our precious Carcasses we [have] no busines to be playing the soldier." His appeal fell on deaf ears. It was a "very bad policy to fire on the Yankees," the troopers countered, "as they would then destroy all the private dwellings within reach of their shot & shell."

Jones's continued urgings resulted only in the sending of a detail to scuttle the blockade-runner and the volunteering of three troopers to accompany him to the high ground in question to maintain surveillance on the gunboat. By this time, however, night had fallen, and the four men lost their way in the woods and wandered about in the dark for nearly two hours before reaching their destination. Upon arrival Jones persuaded his companions to pledge that they "would fire on any-thing that passed, from a boat, up to a Gun-boat." He then divided his little command into two groups for the purpose of guard duty. His team drew first watch, but Jones soon became a solitary sentinel. "In ten minutes," as he put it, "my companion, as well as the remaining two, were blowing off steam at a terrible rate—running opposition lines to the steam Gun boats." Throughout the night he sat with his carbine and pistols close at hand "ready for a moments warning," but the only disturbance during his long vigil was the sound of muffled oars and low voices as some slaves escaped to the enemy.

Dawn found the gunboat still at the mouth of the river, being joined by a second one. The appearance of the second gunboat frightened away two of Jones's companions. He and the remaining trooper watched the movements of the enemy until mid-afternoon when they were summoned to Colonel's Island by Captain L. Walthour, the new commander of the Liberty Independent Troop, who intimated that the gunboats were to be taken under fire. Hurrying to Colonel's Island at a gallop, they arrived "in time to find that the Troop had . . . allowed the enemy to pass them unmolested." The gunboats were now ascending the North Newport River rapidly in search of the blockade-runner.

It was painfully clear to Jones that the Liberty Independent Troop would take no steps to repel the enemy. Out of patience he again resorted to personal action. In an effort to save the homes along the river he and his companion raced ahead of the gunboats, which were slowed down by the shallowness of the river and its frequent bends, and set the scuttled blockade-runner afire. Then, in a driving rain, he sped to Monte Video, giving Lewis "a ride that tested his bottom fairly," to warn his parents of the approaching danger. He quickly started them with his brother's young daughter for Arcadia and made plans to move the remaining slaves to safety. After a short rest he began evacuating his parents' personal belongings, determined that "if the Yankees came up, they should have a barren victory."

Jones sat up on watch a second full night. All he got for his vigilance was a thorough soaking up to his knees when he mired his horse in a spring bog while reconnoitering along the swamp between Monte Video and the river. He spent most of the next day riding up and down the river watching for the enemy gunboats, but they were gone. After steaming a short distance up the North Newport River the gunboats returned to the ocean, either seeing the burning blockade-runner or deciding that it was not there. On their return past Colonel's Island the Liberty Independent Troop mustered the courage to fire a parting volley.

Joseph Jones's brief encounter with the enemy was an exhilarating and satisfying experience for him. He wasted no time spreading the news, hurriedly penning his wife and brother lengthy blow-by-blow accounts. "Notwithstanding the great fatigue," he boasted, "the excitement sustained me & I was enabled to endure it without any discomfort." Recognition and praise of his heroics were immediately forthcoming. His parents were especially appreciative, asserting that in this crisis, as at the time of the measles epidemic, they did not know what they would have done without him. Relaying his congratulations through their parents, his brother praised him for his "energy and most valuable services." "I am sorry," Charles, Jr., added, "that he did not enjoy the opportunity of discharging at least both barrels well loaded with buckshot from Grandfather's genuine 'Mortimer' . . . full in the face, at easy range of the nefarious rascals."[5] Carrie rejoiced upon learning that her husband had had the chance to play the hero's role. "I don't think," she wrote his mother, "he would have ever gotten over it if such exciting events had taken place after his departure from the County."[6]

Jones was still basking in the pleasant afterglow of his heroic adventure when he returned to Augusta in early May, but the pressing issues of day-to-day life soon pushed this interlude into the background. Important decisions had to be made about how to recoup his personal finances and about what form his continued contribution to the southern war effort should take. The former demanded immediate attention. Financial insecurity was becoming Joseph Jones's constant companion, and it had to be dealt with again in the spring of 1862. Owing to his predilection for research and his aversion to the practice of medicine, he had been unable to secure a firm financial footing from the beginning of his professional career.

Jones's patriotism had exacerbated these difficulties, for his tour of duty with the Liberty Independent Troop wiped out any beginning he had made toward financial stability after he had turned to the practice of medicine in the spring of 1861. As fall gave way to winter his financial condition had steadily deteriorated. "I am economizing every dollar of my pay *small as it is*," he wrote his wife in December, "& expect to devote it religiously to the payment of my honest debts, & the support of my family. . . . Up to the present time even after I have taxed my health & strength to their utmost, I have not been able to make both ends meet." So precarious were his finances that he was forced to sell, against his banker's advice and at a considerable loss, the three thousand dollars in Confederate bonds which the Cotton Planters' Convention had given him in partial payment of his labors for this organization in 1860. "I will need every dollar of this & much more," he confessed, "to pay for the bare necessities of life, & for my pressing liabilities."[7]

Jones tried to remain optimistic in the face of continuing financial adversity. Admitting on the one hand that should the war and its "times of severe want & distress" continue he feared the suffering of "many privations," he maintained hope on the other for "a bright future." Thus upon his return to Augusta he renewed the quest for his "great & ardent wish"—"always to have a plenty for every want & comfort."[8] His options were essentially the same as they had been the previous year. He could practice medicine full-time or accept a commission in the Confederate medical department. Unsure what his true contribution to the southern war effort should be and still unwilling to undergo a lengthy separation from his wife and son or abandon his research, to Jones the former seemed the wiser choice—at least for the time being.[9]

In his free time Jones resumed his investigation of poisons as they related to his study of southern diseases. He also spent considerable time wrestling with the problem of how he could best aid the South in her struggle for independence. This was not an easy problem for him to solve, and the best solution that he could come up with at this time was the preparation of two articles. The first pointed out the location of important deposits of salt, sulphate of magnesia (Epsom salts), and sulphate of soda (Glauber's salts); the second outlined his method of making sulphuric acid and extracting sulfur. Jones approached these projects with his usual diligence, remarking: "These labors are necessarily tedious & require the expenditure of much time & labor."[10]

Jones pursued his medical practice with the same diligence, and he was heartened by his steadily growing number of patients. Then, at the middle of June, he had a stroke of good fortune which not only eased his financial distress but prepared the way for his major contribution to the southern war effort. Because of its heavy case load the Confederacy's general hospital in Augusta was shorthanded, and its director had been authorized to hire a civilian, or contract, physician. It is not clear how Jones learned of the opening but probably it was through the director, Dr. L. D. Ford, one of his former colleagues at the Medical College of Georgia. At any rate Jones applied for and received the position. It paid eighty dollars a month, the pay scale of an assistant surgeon in the Confederate army. Combined with his private practice, which he was able to continue on a limited basis, this position guaranteed Jones some measure of financial solvency. Most important it presented him with a new and inviting arena for research.[11]

This was the only Confederate general hospital in Augusta, and it was an important one. Located on the direct rail route from the upper South, it received numerous casualties from the Virginia front. Generally the sick and wounded received only temporary and often inadequate attention in the war zone. Therefore many of the nearly one hundred cases assigned to Jones were critical, and their treatment took much of his time. "The attention to this large number." he wrote his parents, "has left me but few moments of leisure during the day, & those portions of the nights devoted to rest have frequently been spent in resolving the best modes of treatment for the poor fellows."[12] Even a severe attack of fever and bronchitis at the end of June, which worried his wife and convinced his mother that he was again disregarding his health and left her "quite in despair," did not prevent him from making his appointed rounds.[13]

The immediate effect of Jones's duties in the Augusta General Hospital was to present the war in an entirely different light. Its romantic appeal waned as he constantly witnessed its horrors. "We know but little of war," he soberly exclaimed, "when we view it from the battle field covered with glory, & rendered attractive by deeds of valor. The work of the destroying angel goes on silently all the time, and the victories of disease exceed ten fold those of the sword." Although a member of the planter aristocracy, Jones was distressed at the disastrous effects of the hostilities on the South's yeoman farmers, observing that "the great curse of war is especially seen in its effects upon the small property holders who have entered our armies." "Many of the small farmers," he emphasized, "entered the service under excitement—expected to fight a battle or two & then to return home. Months have passed, they have remained encamped in swamps & marshes, their health has been destroyed, their crops unplanted—their children & wives suffering for the commonest necessities of life, & perhaps death has broken the circle—and still no bright future—not even the poor privilege of a short visit home." Despite this sobering reappraisal of the struggle Jones could still find no fault with the South. Southerners, he contended, could not be held responsible for "these great curses of war." Instead it should be "a great gratification to us of the South, that we are free from the blood of these men, at least as far as the origin & prosecution of this war is concerned." "However great may be the sacrifice of life by disease & by battle on our side," he added emphatically, "they are all martyrs in a great & glorious cause."[14]

The long-range, and by far the most important, outgrowth of Jones's practice in this large Confederate hospital was the effect it had on his research. Confronted constantly by the incursions of disease as he struggled to restore the sick and wounded to health, Jones became increasingly interested in the etiology, prevalence, and effect of camp diseases. The study of these disorders, which in many ways dovetailed with his investigation of southern diseases, soon became his primary research interest. Despite the complaint that it was difficult to do much with the large number of cases placed under his supervision, he launched extensive studies of the most prevalent disorders plaguing the southern soldiers. Augusta seemed ideal for this undertaking. There was an abundance of cases, and, of immeasurable importance, Jones had access to his laboratory and library. "I could not do more for the sick," he maintained, "if I were in Richmond for my time & strength are now fully occupied, & I may be able to do something in the way of investigations."[15] Charles Colcock Jones readily agreed with his son's stand, asserting: "You are indeed in a position to observe the infamous war in some of its most cruel and offending aspects."[16]

The Augusta General Hospital did without doubt provide Jones with the opportunity to study every major disease found in the Confederate armies. Traumatic tetanus was one of the first studied. No physician seemed able to cope with this acute infection of the central nervous system produced by *Clostridium tetani*, and it quickly became a frequent cause of death in Civil War hospitals. "To enumerate the means used for the relief of tetanus would require a volume," the authors of the southern *Manual of Military Surgery* wrote, "to record those entitled to confidence does not demand a line."[17]

Jones was confronted with his first case of traumatic tetanus in early July. The victim, a thirty-seven-year-old soldier "strong in health," had been wounded at the battle of Secessionville, South Carolina (June 16, 1862) when a minie ball passed through the three-inch plank wall of a house from which he was firing and wounded him in the fleshy portion of the right forearm. He was sent to Augusta for treatment where tetanus supervened on July 6. The clinical picture quickly became ominous as the disease's characteristic muscle spasms advanced from infrequent and mild to frequent and severe. With "a shrill, piercing cry," Jones observed, "the head and neck are drawn back and downwards towards the heels, whilst the lower extremities are drawn in like manner backwards towards the head with great violence." "The patient," he noted, "cannot lie down, even in the intermission of the spasms, and is compelled to sit upon the edge of the bed, his lower extremities being forcibly bent backwards over the bed. The jaws are very rigid; it is impossible, even during the most complete remissions, to protrude the tongue."

Typically unaware of the true nature of tetanus, Jones treated the case's most pronounced outward manifestations—pain, restlessness, and constipation. His primary treatment was a concoction of chloroform, sulphuric ether, and tincture of opium and a diet of chicken and beef soup, corn gruel, and milk punch. He supplemented this course of treatment when the situation seemed to demand it with large doses of calomel, quinine, and laudanum and enemas of molasses and common salt and water. The outcome of the case was understandably doubtful for the first week, but, almost miraculously, on July 15 the patient began to improve. By August 1 he appeared "to be entirely restored" and was sent home on convalescent leave. During the time that he treated him Jones made detailed notes on the disease's progress and constructed an elaborate chart showing temperature changes and the results of numerous urine analyses.[18]

Jones made his first extensive observations on pneumonia in Augusta. Unaware of its bacterial origin, surgeons on both sides generally fought this pneumococcal inflammation of the lungs with the accepted heroic therapeutic techniques of the day— bleeding, blistering, purging, and administering copious doses of dangerous drugs—with tragic results. But as time passed many surgeons, appalled by the high death rate from pneumonia, began to doubt the benefits of so rigorous a system of treatment and gradually turned away from it in favor of a supportive regimen based largely on diet. Jones, however, remained a traditionalist, insisting that statistics did not prove the wisdom of abandoning the lancet.[19]

He was more modern in his interpretation of a case in which a pneumonia patient inexplicably developed malaria. His views in this instance clashed strongly with those of many of his contemporaries in both armies who maintained that one disorder could develop into another. Jones argued strongly for the specificity of disease forms. A thorough examination of this case and later related ones convinced him of the validity of his stand. "That cases of fever should arise in a hospital, or in camp at any time, independently of the effects of exposure or fatigue, or the supervention of any recognizable inflammatory lesion," he explained, "may be accounted for in a measure by the fact, that tents and hospitals are often loaded with deleterious exhalations, which may be capable of inducing febrile excitement in the animal economy."[20]

Jones saw his first case of gangrene in the Augusta General Hospital. Seldom seen in the United States prior to the outbreak of the Civil War, this unsightly secondary infection became one of the conflict's most serious medical problems. It was classified as a surgical fever, along with erysipelas and pyemia, and was thought to be miasmatic in origin. Jones's gangrene victim was a young soldier from a Florida regiment who, during a saloon brawl, had been stabbed in the scrotum. He was brought to the Confederate hospital eight hours after the incident. The scrotum was greatly distended with blood, but a thorough physical examination revealed that the hemorrhage had stopped. Jones sutured the wound, suspended and elevated the enlarged scrotum with bandages, and applied cloths saturated with ice water. By the third day the wound had become gangrenous, and the infection had spread to the left thigh, groin, and lower portion of the abdomen. The clinical picture was ominous; the affected area "presented a swollen green, purplish, grayish, and in parts blackish look, as if the parts were undergoing rapid decomposition." The odor "became insupportable," and chlorine, nitric acid, and tar fumigations "only partially mitigated the stench."

The gangrenous area progressively increased, and soon "inflamed lymphatics and black distended veins" could be seen radiating from it in all directions. "When I plunged my lancet into this elevated purplish and greenish putrid-looking mass," Jones recorded, "it encountered no resistance; the integuments and tissues appeared to be completely dissolved, and a dark greenish and purplish, horribly offensive matter, mixed with numerous bubbles of air, poured out in large quantity." Shortly before the youth's death on the seventh day, the "entire mass of coagulated blood and infiltrated tissues . . . sloughed off, and left the white and apparently healthy testicles entirely exposed." Attempting to explain this malady, Jones posited: "The passage of the scrotum into the gangrenous state was due, not to the introduction of a special poison from without, but to the pre-existent state of the constitution, and the decomposition of effused blood in this hot climate, in a dependent organ, and in tissues of low vitality." This erroneous local and constitutional view of etiology of gangrene was strengthened by subsequent cases he treated in the Augusta General Hospital.[21]

Finally Jones observed what appeared to be a new disease. Most southern surgeons called it camp fever and attributed it to a combination of foul camp air, night exposure to the atmosphere of the swamps and marshes, bad water, and poor diet. Its symptoms were "low muttering delirium, loss of muscular & nervous power, & total derangement of the bowels & alteration & contamination of the blood." None of the standard specifics for fevers, such as quinine and calomel, had any noticeable therapeutic effect, and the more severe forms were uniformly fatal. Jones noted this disorder's similarity to typhus, or ship fever, which many of his contemporaries argued was its true identity. This explanation did not satisfy him, however, and he later correctly identified the disease as typhoid fever.[22]

By mid-summer 1862 Jones's position in the Augusta General Hospital was taking on an air of permanency, and his medical practice was increasing daily. Not only did he enjoy this new-found career as a contract surgeon and part-time general practitioner but, of even greater importance, he benefitted from it financially. Upon visiting him in the middle of July his brother observed that he appeared "to be getting along prosperously" and had "a very neat little carriage drawn by a fine horse: Titus as charioteer." After a second visit in early October Charles, Jr., reported that he was "getting a very clever practice, and tells me he thinks he will be able to make both ends meet without difficulty."[23] In fact so demanding did Jones's part-time practice become that he was forced to give up his idyllic honeymoon cottage on the outskirts of Augusta and rent a house on Broad Street nearer the more populous section of the town. Carrie recognized the reason for the move and acquiesced to it. "But," she lamented, "I give up this dear little *country* home with a pang."[24] Charles Colcock and Mary Jones rejoiced at the news of their son's success and, praising him for his perseverance, asserted: "Time & proper attention will secure all you want." But they worried about his tendency to ignore his health and warned him against taking on too large a practice.[25]

Joseph Jones continued in his dual capacity of contract surgeon and part-time practitioner until late November 1862, when the Army Medical Board for the military districts of South Carolina and Georgia invited him to Charleston, probably at Ford's request, to be examined for an appointment as a surgeon in the Confederate army. He passed the examination with ease and was immediately offered a commission as full surgeon with the rank of major. For reasons which are unclear he accepted it. The most logical explanation seems to be that while treating the sick and wounded southern defenders in the Augusta General Hospital Jones was overcome by a second wave of emotional patriotism, which prompted him to seek duty at the front. In making such a decision, he placed his promising study of the diseases of the southern Confederacy in jeopardy. But, as time would prove, this was one of the most fortunate steps Jones took during the entire war, for it ultimately opened to his examination all the principal southern armies, hospitals, and prisoner-of-war camps.[26]

Six weeks passed between Jones's commissioning and his receipt of orders. Although eager for an assignment he wisely used this delay to prepare for his new duties. He brushed up on anatomy and reviewed surgery, performing "upon the dead subject all the more important operations." Jones spent most of his time, however, writing up his observations of the past summer in the

Augusta General Hospital. He labeled this undertaking as "both pleasant & profitable," explaining that "it has served to fix the principles of practice in the most common diseases of camp life firmly in my mind, and to bring out at the same time the errors of diagnosis and treatment in bold relief." The only interruption in this routine came as the result of his brother's request that he take time out to go to Burke County and vaccinate the family slaves.[27]

Jones desired duty at the front and boasted: "Should I be ordered to Virginia I will go most cheerfully, and I may say with great pleasure, for it is a great honor to be permitted to contribute something towards the relief of the noble band of patriot soldiers who are guarding the homes & the defenceless ones of the entire Confederacy."[28] He actually expected to be stationed in Charleston, but his orders, dated December 22, 1862, retained him in Augusta "with a view of prosecuting certain professional investigations."[29] This assignment came as a complete surprise, for, according to Jones, "it is now against the rule to appoint any surgeon to duty in the town where he lives, and it is unusual to have two full surgeons in so small a Hospital as the General Hospital of Augusta." A likely explanation for Jones's unusual orders is easily discernible. He had undoubtedly discussed his research with the members of the Army Medical Board at the time of his examination and convinced them of its importance. They reported their findings to Surgeon General Samuel P. Moore, who also saw the merit of Jones's investigations and decided that they should be continued. Therefore this charge can be construed to be a testimonial to Joseph Jones's ability as a scientific investigator and a recognition of the potential importance of his research.

Jones interpreted his assignment in this manner, calling it "a great honor, and a most responsible trust."[30] His father viewed it likewise. "The man who is raised up to discover the causes and proper treatment of camp diseases," the Reverend Jones avowed, "will be honored of God as benefactor of his call."[31] Proud of this obvious confidence placed in him Jones was anxious to justify it, but he had to terminate his private practice first. This may have caused some hardship for his patients, but it posed no problems for Jones since his position as surgeon rendered him "perfectly easy in money matters" and enabled him "to carry on uninterruptedly his favorite investigations."[32]

Jones's first undertaking in his new capacity as a research

scientist for the medical department of the Confederate army was the writing up of his observations on the case of tetanus he had treated the previous summer in the Augusta General Hospital. He spent his every free moment during the remainder of December 1862 and throughout January 1863 preparing this report. It was ready at the beginning of February. Jones was proud of the completed manuscript and immediately sent it to the Surgeon General. It was his hope, he modestly entreated in the accompanying letter, that these observations, the result of much laborious investigation, would prove worthy of consideration.

Although exhibiting Jones's now familiar shortcomings as a scientific writer, the 150-page report was not without merit. Jones himself called attention to its greatest value when, upon reviewing the major previous research on tetanus, he pointed out: "I am unacquainted with the report of a single case of this disease, where a careful and full record was kept of the pulse, respiration, temperature, nervous and muscular phenomena, and physical and chemical changes of the urine throughout the course of the disease." Perhaps it was this lack of detailed clinical studies of tetanus which accounts for Jones's surprising eagerness, in an obvious departure from his usual cautious approach to the study of disease, to draw general conclusions from a single case. Whatever the reason, he pointed to the absence of the "essential phenomena of inflammation" and the presence of "exaggerated manifestations of nervous and muscular action." The latter, "attended by corresponding changes in the materials composing these structures," he argued, rendered it "probable that the two were intimately connected, and even dependent on each other, in the relation of cause and effect." In other words, the etiology of tetanus seemed to point to "a change in the electric conditions and relations of the nerves and muscles." This thesis, Jones acknowledged, was grounded heavily in the work of the eminent German physiologist Emil Du Bois-Reymond (1818–1896), who laid the foundations for modern electrophysiology with his studies of the electric currents in the nervous and muscular systems of the living body.

At the end of the report Jones informed Moore of his future research plans. His next project was to be a study of typhoid fever, a subject "of great importance, and worthy of the most careful study and investigation." He expected to produce a manuscript of several hundred pages and promised to forward his results.

Upon its completion he hoped to launch a thorough examination of the main forms of malaria.[33]

In his reply, dated February 17, the surgeon general made little mention of Jones's report. Instead he addressed himself to the subject of research on fevers. He was enthusiastic about the opportunities the war presented for "a free and thorough investigation" of the nature, history, and pathology of fevers caused by "animal effluvia," such as typhoid fever, as opposed to those, like malaria, attributable to "vegetable exhalations." "Your attention," he instructed Jones, "is especially called to this class of disease; and you are directed to make a thorough investigation." This study, Moore believed, promised valuable results, not merely from "a scientific point of view" but, more important, "of the greatest practical benefit to the army." To insure the success of such an undertaking he promised Jones any assistance he deemed necessary.[34]

The surgeon general's letter delighted Jones, for it gave his planned investigations official sanction. Labeling his assignment "a most difficult & important one," he launched it with a research trip to the detached cavalry commands serving between the Ogeechee and Altamaha rivers on the Georgia coast. In all he visited twelve units, including not only the Liberty Independent Troop but such colorfully designated commands as the Mercer Partisans, the Savannah Volunteer Guards, the Lamar Rangers, and Causton's Bluff Battery, compiled a brief history of each, and painstakingly copied their medical records.[35]

Jones's findings were largely an elaboration of what he had observed earlier as surgeon of the Liberty Independent Troop. In these twelve commands, with an aggregate strength of 1,081 during a nine-month test period, the average mortality was twenty-five. Deaths were lowest in units serving in sandy regions surrounded by salt water and highest in those stationed in the lowlands bordering on fresh water—a fact Jones accurately attributed to the presence of a malarial influence in the latter areas. Typhoid fever was virtually nonexistent among these troopers, strengthening his belief that this disease was a newcomer to the malarious regions of coastal Georgia. He suspected that a natural antagonism existed between the two fevers and that typhoid appeared only in the most healthy areas where malaria was dying out as the result of drainage and clearing operations. To account for the appearance of typhoid here, Jones, disputing the generally accepted view, suggested that the disease was contagious under certain circumstances and traced it to slaves returning from work on the fortifications around Savannah.[36]

This city was the last planned stop on Jones's itinerary. Here he hoped to interview the surgeons of the units manning the local defenses. Since the fall of Fort Pulaski in April 1862 the citizenry had lived in constant fear of an invasion from the sea. One seemed imminent on the morning of March 3, 1863, when a Union fleet of three ironclads, four gunboats, and several mortar boats began bombarding Fort McAllister, the South's last stronghold on the Georgia coast. Determined to be "on hand with the staff of surgeons if there should be a necessity," Jones interrupted his investigations among the detached cavalry commands and rushed to Savannah where he offered his services to H. V. M. Miller, the chief surgeon of the military district of Georgia. Jones seriously doubted, however, that there was any real danger, pointing out that since the capture of Fort Pulaski "the city has been completely isolated and turned into an island city." The events of the next few days proved the wisdom of his observation.[37]

After the invasion scare had passed, Miller, a former colleague of Jones's at the Medical College of Georgia, showed him some cases of cerebrospinal meningitis—the first either had seen. There were five cases, and all proved fatal. Jones examined three of them in their final stages, and he was struck by what he saw. Each patient presented an anemic, sallow hue, as if he "had been subjected to the prolonged action of malaria," and further investigation revealed that each had "suffered previously with chill & fever." Superficial evidence prompted Jones to speculate that the disorder might represent the sequelae of a severe, recurrent attack of malaria which had produced morbid changes in the blood and cerebrospinal structures. Intrigued by this mysterious killer he sought opportunities to study it further during the remainder of the war.[38]

Jones returned to Augusta around the middle of March. He had been home but a few days when he received an urgent telegram from his brother with the news that their father was critically ill. Since the early 1850s Charles Colcock Jones had been suffering from an incurable debilitating disease of the central nervous system, which had slowly sapped his strength. The outbreak of war, bringing new worries and aggravating old ones, greatly exacerbated its progress. His father's rapidly declining health had frightened Joseph Jones, and as early as the previous fall he had warned him that he must rest "from ever recurring and perplexing *plantation* cares" if he was to prolong his life.[39] This warning and subsequent ones went unheeded. On March 17 his condition became so grave that Charles Colcock Jones asked that his physician-son be summoned, refusing, and not without good reason, to send for any of the local physicians. Aware of their devotion to the accepted heroic therapeutic techniques, he was afraid they might misunderstand the seriousness of his case and kill him with their "rash practice."[40] It was too late: Charles Colcock Jones died later this same day. Joseph Jones was grief-stricken, deeply regretting that he was unable to reach his father before the end. He found solace, however, in the Reverend Jones's exemplary Christian life and the ending of his suffering. "Nothing but the peace & sunlight of heaven," he comforted his bereaved mother,

> rests upon his life and death, and we have reason to rejoice even in our deep mourning for however grevious the loss of his valuable counsels, Christian example & warm affection to us, the gain to him is infinite. That feeble weary body that struggled so long, with disease, has passed to its long rest, whilst that noble regenerated spirit, freed from the infirmities of life dwells in the full enjoyment of the glories of Heaven & exercises all its regenerated powers in new vigor, in worshiping & praising & loving God.[41]

A threatened naval attack against Charleston in early April curtailed Jones's mourning. Feeling it his "solemn duty" to offer his services "to our sister city," he hurried to South Carolina.[42] By the time he arrived the danger had passed. Jones was elated, and cheerfully shifting the purpose of his visit to research, he interviewed the surgeons of the units manning Charleston's defenses and inspected the city's large Confederate hospitals. He felt perfectly free to do this since the Augusta General Hospital was "just now not full" and he was sure that his absence "could be supplied."

His findings reinforced what he had observed previously among the detached cavalry commands serving on the Georgia coast: first, the greatest incidence of disease was found among the Confederate troops stationed within the unhealthy malarious rice-growing belt of the country; second, he noted the recent appearance of typhoid fever in this area too (the first death from it was not recorded until 1855); and, third, there was accordingly a similar natural antagonism here between typhoid fever and malaria, which in this instance he attributed to either the dilution of the malarial poison or the creation of an artificial atmosphere by the amassing of large numbers of men and horses in the area.

Drawing on his own personal experiences and those of other Confederate surgeons, Jones urged the adoption of less traditional methods in the treatment of typhoid fever, pneumonia, and gunshot wounds, holding that these conditions were most successfully treated "in the open tents of the field & regimental hospital than in the crowded wards of the General Hospital." Using typhoid fever as a case in point, he argued: "We cannot conceive of a more favorable position for the treatment of Typhoid fever than the exposed sandy points along the sea-coast." "The constant circulation of the cool refreshing seabreezes secures if any attention is paid to ventilation," he explained, "that constant circulation of fresh air which is so beneficial in the treatment of Typhoid fever." This notable example of empiricism is commendable, especially when one takes into consideration the faulty theories and practices which characterized contemporary medicine. Jones's powers of observation were even more apparent when he pointed out that the increasing tendency to crowd the injured into the large, unsanitary general hospitals often led to wounds attracting hospital gangrene. "This disease," he suggested, "appears to follow, crowding & inattention to hospital hygiene, as surely as the night follows the day."[43]

Jones left for home at the middle of the month. Before leaving he exacted a promise from the surgeons of the various commands around Charleston to furnish him with subsequent accounts of the diseases they treated and furnished them with forms for this purpose. He also visited his brother, whose unit had been ordered to James Island (a large island on the southern side of Charleston harbor) to help bolster the city's defenses when invasion from the sea seemed immenent.[44]

Back in Augusta Jones began writing up his observations of the past two months for the surgeon general, devoting his "undivided time & strength" to the task. Neither a severe cold accompanied by his mother's renewed warnings about impending broken health nor the birth of his second child, Susan Hyrne, on April 28 distracted him. Acting under the provisions of Moore's instructions

of February 17, Jones viewed this report as but the first of several
on the fevers "which have proved far more fatal to our poor soldiers than the balls of the enemy." It was finished on June 27 and
sent to the surgeon general by express the next day.[45] This manuscript was a truly extraordinary piece of work—not as much for
its contents as for its vivid testimony to Jones's remarkable concept of and dedication to scientific research. Filling 900 large
pages of his script, it had been researched and written in four
months. At the same time Jones had, with but few exceptions, fully discharged his duties as surgeon. In his case this meant responsibility for half the cases in the Augusta General Hospital. The report, inductive in approach, was concerned primarily with
typhoid fever and tetanus, those fevers thought to be caused by
"animal effluvia," and was based on Jones's investigations in the
various hospitals and camps of the military districts of South Carolina and Georgia. It was profusely illustrated by numerous cases
Jones had selected from the more than one thousand he had either
treated or observed and twenty colored plates he had painstakingly drawn of the liver, intestines, Peyer's patches, and mesenteric glands in fatal cases of typhoid fever.

There is little really new in this report. Its only noteworthy
conclusion was Jones's determined denial of the existence of
typhus fever in the areas of the Confederacy he had visited. There
had been much controversy among southern surgeons about the
identity of a highly fatal fever which appeared early in the war.
Some argued that camp fever, as this disorder was called because
of its obvious connection with the large southern armies, was
a new disease; others insisted that it was typhus. Jones believed
that both sides were in error, his research having convinced him
that camp fever was in reality a virulent form of typhoid fever.
"I feel myself warranted in making this assertion," he explained,
"only after a personal examination of the sick in the majority of
the Camps & Hospitals, and after personal conferences with the
Surgeons." Despite its absence, typhus was still a matter "of
great moment to our army," he maintained. The prerequisite
conditions for its appearance and spread, crowding and filth, were
present in the Confederate camps and hospitals. Therefore it
seemed highly probable that typhus would eventually become a
health hazard. The continued importation of typhus-ridden
Irishmen for soldiers by the "Lincoln despotism," he added,
greatly increased the likelihood of its outbreak. In this situation

effective treatment depended upon early recognition and continued investigation.

Perhaps the most important feature of this report was Jones's recognition that it was, at best, "preliminary to a more extended investigation of this class of diseases" in the various geographic divisions of the Confederate army. Follow-up studies embracing "the diseases of armies under all variations of climate and soil and under all the varied circumstances of toil, exposure, and changes of diet" to which the Confederate soldiers were subjected would, he hoped, lead to the establishment of "facts & principles of universal application & permanent value" by settling for all time the "true character & modes of treatment" of diseases attributable to "animal effluvia."

Jones realized that this would not be an easy undertaking. Indeed "many embarrassments . . . and great expenditures of health & strength" had already arisen and would continue to arise. "The complicated nature of the phenomena demanding investigation" and "the peculiarities of the struggle in which we are now engaged with a powerful, cruel and relentless enemy who has blockaded our ports, surrounded us with a wall of fire, and thus cut us off from implements & materials of research" were further impediments to be overcome. But he was willing to push ahead with his investigations in the face of these considerable difficulties, provided he had the support of the surgeon general.

Jones sought two things from Moore—new orders and a promise of financial support. He desired an order admitting him "into any military district or division of the Confederate Army," permitting him "to examine & investigate the sick in Camps & Hospitals," conferring upon him "the right of seeking information from the various medical officers of the Confederate Army, and when practicable performing Post Mortem examinations." Such instructions were necessary, he argued, for two important reasons. First, diseases "arising from Animal exhalations" were very rare in the military district of Georgia. Second, "the true character" of these diseases, "the great facts of their uniformity or diversity, of their contagion or non-contagion, of their relations to climate and soil," and "the circumstances most favorable to their production & spread" could be determined only "by an examination of their phenomena in different localities, and by the careful examination of the experience & testimony of numerous intelligent observers widely separated." "It was in vain," he insisted, "to attempt to obtain the needed information from the surgeons by circulars & letters; reliable facts upon these questions which will be of importance to the army in all time to come can be accumulated only by visiting the various divisions of the army, investigating the nature of the diseases in person, and by carefully examining, sifting, analyzing and recording the testimony of the various medical officers of the Army in charge of Regimental & General Hospitals." He explicitly wanted to visit the large hospitals in Richmond at the earliest moment where "the most valuable materials for investigation" were to be found. He believed that he would find the necessary information here to confirm or disprove the results set forth in his present study.

These investigations, Jones pointed out, would be necessarily expensive, "far beyond the limited pay of a surgeon in the Confederate Army." Therefore the financial support of the surgeon general's office was essential to their success. He sought only necessary expenses. Paper and field notebooks headed the list. In peacetime, he asserted, such items would be unworthy of notice, but the South's spiraling inflation had increased the price of paper by more than 1000 percent. In addition he would need the services of one or more assistants and a servant. The assistants would aid him in his research while the slave would cut fuel, keep up fires, obtain water, assist in heavy laboratory work, and carry his instruments and chemicals. Next he sought an allowance of fifty dollars a month to purchase chemicals and laboratory apparatus. The commonest chemicals, like paper, seemed almost too basic to mention, but here again inflation had increased prices 1000 percent. Finally Jones asked for a travel allowance for himself and a servant during those periods when it was necessary for him to be away from Augusta, where he planned to keep his base of operations owing to its central location and the presence of his library and laboratory here.[46]

Several weeks passed before Moore acknowledged receipt of the report. The "pressing importance of a vast variety of official engagements," he confessed, had permitted "only a brief and desultory investigation" of the manuscript. But even this cursory examination revealed sufficient evidence "to justify the belief that much very valuable acquisition to the science and art of medicine is contained therein," and he extended Jones the thanks of the medical department for his "zeal, untiring energy, [and] laborious industry." It is not clear from the available sources, but Moore seems to have taken a compromise stand on Jones's request for permission to extend his research to any part of the Confederacy and for research support. He seems to have limited his response to Jones's first request for permission to visit the hospitals in Virginia. Moore was inclined to believe that they offered little for the advancement of his investigations. "Still," he wrote, "you might come and see for yourself." As for research support, he apparently authorized Jones to requisition paper, notebooks, and chemicals from the nearest medical supplier and permitted him to hire a servant and two draft-exempt assistants but denied his request for travel expenses.[47]

The surgeon general's invitation excited Jones, and he immediately made plans to extend his epidemiological studies to the hospitals of the Army of Northern Virginia. All his previous typhoid fever research had been done in the malarious coastal plain of South Carolina and Georgia; now he had the opportunity to test his conclusions in a nonmalarious climate. He also hoped to determine the numerical relationship of typhoid fever to other diseases, to ascertain the existence or nonexistence of typhus, and to persuade the surgeons in Virginia to assist in his research by recording the results of their experiences and forwarding them to him. Accompanied by Titus, who continued to prove "invaluable & as ever faithful to the fullest degree of human capability," Jones left by train for Richmond on August 5, carrying with him the necessary chemicals and apparatus for sixty pathological, microscopic, and chemical analyses.[48]

He scheduled short layovers in Charleston and Columbia. Upon arrival in the South Carolina port city, he changed into his Confederate uniform and hurried off to see the Confederate casualties from the batteries on Morris Island, a small desolate island lying at the south side of the mouth of Charleston harbor. The Union had launched a seaborne invasion of the island at the end of July. The attack was supported by a savage naval bombardment which frequently forced the southern defenders to seek the safety of underground shelters. Often more than one thousand men were crowded into them for long periods. The weather was intensely hot, and the air in these poorly ventilated subterranean passages quickly became fouled. To worsen matters, the only available water was brackish, and the ferocity of the Union shelling made it impossible to supply the island except for occasional night forays. Moreover meat and other perishable supplies quickly spoiled in the hot foul air of the underground shelters. An appalling situation ensued as hundreds of the defenders were felled "by shere exhaustion & bowel affections" induced by "the heat, foul air & continuous labors & excitements." "How much honor," Jones exclaimed, "should be rendered to our brave men who have so long contended upon Morris Island against such terrible odds."[49]

Charleston was in the grip of a sweltering summer heat wave during Jones's short stay. But neither the oppressive heat nor the hurried pace of his research had any apparent ill effect on him. Instead Jones boasted of his high state of health, asserting: "I feel as well, through a merciful Providence, as I ever did in my life." For relaxation and relief from the heat he took long evening walks along the Battery. He sat for hours enjoying the refreshing sea breeze and watching the Confederate batteries' methodical harassment of the Union invaders on Morris Island. This artillery display excited him. "The flash of the Guns," he wrote home,

> resembled a distant flash of lightening & the track of the shell could be traced by the burning fuse as it mounts up towards the stars, as it reaches the highest elevation its progress is very slow, it appears to stand still for a moment, & then slowly descends for a few seconds, & now more rapidly until it attains very nearly the same momentum with which it left the mouth of the gun. Now just as you think it has reached the ground a brilliant flash—you listen for the sound but none reaches your ear until the dull heavy explosion.

"Stanhope," he added, "would have begged his papa to catch the big firefly for him."[50]

In the large and busy hospital at South Carolina College in Columbia he observed many of the wounded, both Union and Confederate, from the siege of Charleston. Here, as in Charleston, he was struck by the noticeably superior recuperative powers of the northern soldiers, a fact he accurately attributed to their better state of health at the time they were wounded. The Union soldiers had benefited immensely from their access to the salubrious outer range of sea islands while the Confederate defenders had been cooped up in underground shelters laden with "offensive & noxious exhalations."[51]

Jones arrived in Richmond "safely without accident in the enjoyment of good health" on August 11. His first impression of the Confederate capital was distinctly unfavorable. Two years of war had exacted a heavy toll of this historic southern city. In fact, according to one historian of her wartime years, Richmond had become "downright shabby-looking." "Paint had begun to peel on steps and porticoes. Shingles were loose here and there, clapboards bulging. Missing palings made fences gape; and vines and shrubberies showed the need of shears." Her population, nearly 40,000 at the outset of the war, had more than tripled, and she now teemed with more government workers, soldiers, and refugees than could be properly housed.[52] It was with great difficulty that Jones found suitable quarters. His search was complicated by the almost unbearable summer heat which impelled him to become necessarily slow in his movements. After much searching he succeeded in renting a room in a boarding house apparently run by the relative of a personal friend. Room and board, owing to Richmond's galloping inflation, were almost prohibitive. Jones was forced to pay $125 a month for himself and another $50 for Titus. "This is an enormous tax," he complained, "& will have the effect of shortening my stay."[53]

A meeting with Surgeon General Samuel P. Moore did a great deal to restore Jones's morale. Moore has been described as "a brusque man who offended fellow officers and private citizens with equal facility."[54] Many of his subordinates did indeed view him in this light. Joseph Jones did not. He was able to see Moore for what he really was—a strict disciplinarian and a highly efficient and extraordinarily capable administrator who demonstrated and demanded professionalism. Alike in many ways, the two men became immediate friends and enjoyed a warm working relationship.

Although harried by the medical aftermath of Lee's disastrous defeat at Gettysburg a month earlier, Moore took time to discuss Jones's research with him. He was genuinely impressed with his youthful lieutenant's accomplishments and plans and moved to grant him research conditions for his investigations in Virginia as nearly ideal as the fortunes of the Confederacy would allow. Unfortunately there were no funds to meet his heavy expenses, but Jones was given access to every medical facility in Virginia, excused from any hospital duty, told to pursue these investigations according to his own plan and at his own pace, and reminded to safeguard his health, even at the expense of his research. Jones was thankful for the surgeon general's "kind interest" in his investigations and the renewed confidence placed in him, boasting to his wife that he had been made "master of the situation."[55]

There were twenty Confederate hospitals in the Richmond area. Jones began his research at Camp Winder, one of the largest, which covered over 125 acres and had facilities to accommodate 5,000 patients. In addition to his planned investigations, the "inviting field of labor" which the high incidence of gangrene in these hospitals offered captured Jones's attention, and he spent much of his time studying this much-feared and generally misunderstood killer. "With my microscope in hand," he later wrote, "I visited all the cases, & subjected the matter from the best marked to a careful microscopic examination & executed drawings of the gangrenous matter." He also tried to involve the local surgeons, urging them to try to determine whether this appalling condition, by now a major problem in Confederate hospitals, was caused by local or constitutional factors and whether it was contagious or not. Gangrene, probably owing to its unsightly appearance and ghastly horrors, seemed to upset Jones more than any other disease he encountered during the war. "It would make your heart bleed," he exclaimed, "to see our poor soldiers suffering with this severe disease, with in many cases the flesh dissolving into putrid fluid without any apparent cause, & leaving frightful gaping wounds, exposing the trembling muscles & beating vessels."[56] Yet, he maintained, these brave men bore their misery without "one word of discontent or despondancy." "As long as such noble men compose our armies," he boasted, "we can never be conquered."[57]

Jones's stay in Richmond was both enriched and enlivened by the offer of his friend Colonel Isaac M. St. John, head of the Mining and Niter Bureau, to show him the places of interest in and near the city. St. John's eagerness to make his visit an enjoyable one was unexpected but much appreciated. His tour of Richmond greatly improved Jones's impression of the Confederate capital. He found of particular interest visits to Castle Thunder, the foreboding prison for unruly soldiers, deserters, and political prisoners, and to Libby Prison and Belle Isle, where the Union prisoners of war were confined. But he most enjoyed having breakfast with General George W. Randolph, a grandson of

Thomas Jefferson and a former Confederate secretary of war. Jones was flattered, considering this "rather a singular honor for a stranger."

Another pleasurable experience was an afternoon boat ride down the James River to Drewry's Bluff, a commanding promontory overlooking a narrow place in the river's channel some seven miles below Richmond. The fortifications here, a combination of artillery and channel obstructions, were the keystone in the defense of the James River. Jones believed them virtually unbreachable, asserting: "Our fortifications at the Bluff are most formidable, and from the river impregnable. They can only be turned by a land attack simultaneously with an attack by the river."

The high point of Jones's sight-seeing was an excursion to Seven Pines, the site of the opening battle of the celebrated Peninsula Campaign. Here on May 31 and June 1, 1862, the South under General Joseph E. Johnston had decisively defeated General George B. McClellan's larger Union army. Jones found the "calm & beautiful" setting to be deceiving, observing that it "seemed to be a fit resting place for only the husbandman with his peaceful flocks." A walk over the battlefield rekindled his fiery southern patriotism, and he exulted at the sight of "numerous bones, skulls &c. of dead Yankees scattered in every direction."[58]

Jones completed his investigations in the Confederate capital at the beginning of September. He was pleased with his accomplishments: he had advanced his study of typhoid fever and typhus, he had increased his knowledge of gangrene, and he had been able to copy many of the medical statistics from the field reports on file in the surgeon general's office. On September 3, as he was preparing to leave, Moore presented him with new orders. His mission remained unchanged—an extended investigation of the nature, history, and pathology of fevers caused by "animal effluvia" as opposed to those produced by "vegetable exhalations"—but now he was permitted to "visit those parts of the Confederate States and prosecute his Investigations in those Cities and Regimental and General Hospitals, which he may deem necessary, as affording suitable fields for the establishment of the results indicated in this Order." Confederate surgeons and medical officers were not only informed that they were to cooperate with him in his research, but were ordered to "respond as far as possible to his inquiries by letter and circular." Jones was elated. "Whilst the general tenor of these orders is similar to those previously received," he remarked, "they are more liberal & explicit, in fact I could not desire more liberal orders."[59]

From Richmond Jones traveled by train to Charlottesville in central Virginia where there was a large general hospital. He broke his journey in Gordonsville, the site of a small receiving hospital. Armed with a letter of introduction from a Colonel Reves to Dr. James L. Cabell, the surgeon-in-charge of the Charlottesville General Hospital, Jones arrived in Charlottesville on September 5. Cabell, however, was out of town, and Jones was greeted by Dr. John S. Davis, professor of anatomy, materia medica, and botany in the Virginia medical school and Cabell's chief assistant. In Charlottesville Jones received one of his warmest receptions of the war. Davis, brushing aside Jones's "great delicacy" over accepting his generous hospitality "in such times of war & scarcity as these," quartered him in his own house on the University grounds and extended to him "every hospitality & kindness." From this beginning blossomed a friendship which was to last for the remainder of the two men's lives.[60]

Jones was surprised and highly pleased with the "organized system of investigation" he found at the Charlottesville General Hospital and the "most valuable assistance" he received from the "intelligent & energetic Surgeons." This hospital, owing to its proximity to "the grand armies" and "the great battles" and its "ample accommodations" and "skillful management," Jones learned, "received more than its just proportion of seriously sick & severely wounded." "For these reasons," he asserted, "this was one of the best, if not the very best field for medical observations in the Southern Confederacy." Jones spent most of his time copying the hospital's records which had been "carefully collected & preserved . . . under the intelligent action & supervision of Professors Cabell & Davis," convinced that these figures would furnish "the most reliable data for the determination of many important points in the history of various diseases."[61] He also availed himself of the opportunity to select "typical cases of uncomplicated typhoid fever" abounding in this "elevated region of Piedmont Virginia," which he felt were suitable "in all respects for the critical study of the characteristic phenomena of the disease."[62]

All was not work. In Charlottesville, as he had done previously in Richmond, Jones relaxed by touring local points of interest. He paid an early morning visit to "Mr. Jeffersons residence at Monticello on the Mountain" and was enthralled by the beauty of the Virginia countryside. "When I ascended the Mountain in the morning," he wrote, "a dense fog surrounded the bases of the Blue ridge & the peaks appeared like islands in a great white ocean. The fog of dense whiteness driven by the winds would break over the mountain ridges like the waves of the sea. The heat of the sun aided by a wind dissipated the fog & before I descended the whole valley with the city & University surrounded with the splendid ampitheater of mountains were spread out in clear view."[63] Jones spent many of his leisure moments walking the tranquil grounds of the University of Virginia. "Everything," he observed, "has been erected with a view to elegance & effect." On a tour of Charlottesville Davis took him to a citizens' meeting at the courthouse. He watched with intense interest as this assemblage, chaired by another of Jefferson's grandsons (probably Thomas Jefferson Randolph) and attended by James B. Holcombe, a Confederate representative and former law professor at the University of Virginia, and Louis T. Wigfall, a Confederate senator from Texas, passed four resolutions aimed at aiding the Confederate government in its fight to control speculators and extortioners. The citizens of Charlottesville and Albemarle County cheerfully pledged to pay the government tax of one-tenth of their produce, to sell another one-tenth to the government at prewar prices, to live economically in order to sell as much of the remaining eight-tenths to the families of soldiers and the government at prices set by the government, and to cease buying Negroes and land, investing this money instead in Confederate bonds. Jones was pleasantly surprised, remarking: "If every community in the South would pass similar resolutions, the effects would be most salutary." Undoubtedly he had his native Georgia in mind, where Governor Joseph E. Brown seemed to delight in defying Jefferson Davis. "I find," Jones asserted, "that the people nearest the seat of the war, & those who have felt its horrors in ernest are the most warm in the support of self Government."[64]

Jones ended his Virginia research in mid-September at Lynchburg, a small town southwest of Charlottesville at the southern end of the war-torn Valley of Virginia, where there was a large convalescent hospital. From Lynchburg he had planned to continue his southwesterly course into Tennessee and visit the

Army of Tennessee before returning home through Chattanooga. But the enemy's advance into eastern Tennessee forced Jones to cancel these plans. In fact to return to Augusta he had to retrace his steps to Richmond.

Just as he was preparing to leave the Confederate capital for Augusta, Jones was handed a telegram from his wife containing the alarming news that their son was seriously ill. Although he was greatly worried, there was no way Jones could hurry home. The only available rail transportation was a troop train—in reality a collection of boxcars in which there was "scarcely room to stand or sit"—transporting soldiers to northern Georgia to reinforce the Army of Tennessee which was engaged in the crucial battle of Chickamauga. The train's progress was excruciatingly slow. It was involved in two accidents and was further delayed by several broken-down trains. At Kingsville, a major railroad junction near Columbia, everyone was forced to spend the night in an open depot. Many of the passengers were exchanged prisoners returning home from Fort Delaware, a well-known Union prisoner-of-war camp located on Pea Patch Island in the Delaware River. The night was rainy and the area was swampy. The prisoners coughed incessantly. Their pitiful condition enraged Jones. "We have," he fumed, "scarcely received one sound man in our recent exchanges from the North. It would be but just retaliation if we confined the Yankee prisoners in the rice-fields around Savannah."[65] Soon, he would visit Andersonville.

Despite the "great anxiety & discomfort" of his trip home Jones could not avoid reflecting on his stay in Virginia. He was pleased with the results. "My trip to Virginia," he wrote, "has been very valuable to me not merely in the fruits of investigation but also in securing to me the . . . liberal order from the Surgeon General."[66] Armed with this mandate, he looked forward to carrying his research to other parts of the Confederacy—as soon as his young son was restored to health.

Chapter 7
Surgeon Jones

*I hope and believe that yr. labors will
enhance yr. reputation, already exalted, and
contribute largely to the progress of our science
and the welfare of mankind.*

By the time Joseph Jones arrived home in late September 1863 his son was much improved. The youth was soon out of danger, and Jones resumed his research. On October 9 he left for Charleston, considering it important to visit "this low malarious region during the last and most unhealthy months of the fall" if he were to determine the relationship between malaria and typhoid fever. Specifically he planned to test the hypothesis advanced by many of his contemporaries that "remittent fever of malarious origin can be converted by an actual change into typhoid fever." Jones was adamantly opposed to this view and hoped to disprove it. "The establishment of the transmutation of a disease due to malarious poison, into another excited by a different poison," he asserted, "would produce the same derangement in the classification of disease that would follow the establishment of the proposition that *measles* may be converted into small-pox."[1]

Shortly after his arrival in Charleston Jones suffered an attack of malaria, which he attributed to the combined effect of his "continuous exertions" and the sudden change from "the elevated regions of Piedmont Virginia" to the "low malarious plain of coastal South Carolina." His strength was temporarily impaired, but the prompt and energetic use of quinine minimized the disruption of his research. Jones conducted his investigations in the hospitals of Charleston and Summerville. The latter, a small town west of Charleston on the South Carolina Railroad, had accommodations for 280 patients. The selection of cases to prove the specificity of typhoid fever and malaria occupied the major part of his time. He found ample evidence to undergird his contention that these fevers were separate diseases. Two pathogenic poisons, he postulated, existed in the area—one caused typhoid fever, the other caused malaria. The former had been introduced into the South's coastal plain by the soldiers from the southern mountains; the latter had long been endemic there. The typhoid poison, he continued, was the stronger of the two, but the malarial poison, owing to its indigenous nature, often manifested its symptoms first. At a later date, however, it was not surprising to see the more virulent typhoid poison seem "to preoccupy the ground to the exclusion of the malarial poison." Completing his argument, Jones asserted that after the typhoid symptoms had abated the weaker but longer lasting malarial symptoms frequently became apparent again. It was the relative virulence of two distinct pathogenic poisons, then, which produced the illusion of the transmutation of disease forms.[2]

Jones spent almost three weeks in South Carolina, returning home near the end of October. He arrived in Augusta at the height of a gangrene epidemic among the Confederate wounded from the battle of Chickamauga. These soldiers had experienced a disastrous odyssey. Chickamauga, the last important southern victory in the West, had been fought September 19–20, but the 1,050 casualties sent to Augusta did not arrive there until eight to ten days after receiving their wounds. They were transported from the scene of the engagement in northwestern Georgia, some 300 miles away, in filthy crowded railroad cars. Upon arrival they had been left unattended in the railroad station for another forty to eighty hours because the Augusta General Hospital and the various regimental hospitals could accommodate only a few of this large number of casualties without serious overcrowding. Eventually many were consigned to temporary hospitals hastily set up in churches and private residences. Even these stopgap measures were inadequate, and soon both the regimental and the temporary hospitals were frightfully overcrowded. The Second Georgia Hospital, with an official capacity of 165, received 273 of the wounded; the two divisions of the larger Third Georgia Hospital, with combined accommodations for 292, were sent 590; the Presbyterian church, with room for 112 in improvised bunks on the seats and floors of the pews, crowded in 240; and Augusta's small Catholic church, with space for only 50, housed 130.

A majority of the injuries were slight wounds of the extremities and should have posed no serious health hazard; but, as the result of poor treatment on the battlefield, the torturous journey to Augusta, the neglect upon arrival, and the crowding and poor sanitary conditions in the hospitals (especially the temporary ones), gangrene soon became rampant. Painfully aware of these factors, Jones noted: "The number of cases of hospital gangrene appeared to increase in proportion to the distance which the wounded were transported from the battle-field."

This sad spectacle dismayed him, but there was little he could do. Hoping to determine the disease's "laws & to trace as far as possible its cause," he visited the various hospitals, real and makeshift, where he selected the most interesting gangrene cases and carefully recorded "the changes of the secretions, excretions, temperature, pulse, and respiration, and . . . pathological alterations after death."[3] Jones's findings strengthened his growing suspicion that this infection could be traced to "over-crowding & inattention to ventilation." "If I am enabled to establish these causes beyond controversy," he warned, "it will throw a fearful responsibility upon those surgeons who over-crowd their hospitals & neglect the ventilation of their hospitals."[4]

Jones worked hard to complete this study by mid-November when the annual synod of the Presbyterian Church in Georgia was to convene in Athens. He had been chosen to represent his church and was eager to attend. At the close of the meeting Jones planned to delay his return home long enough to visit the Chickamauga casualties who had been sent to the hospitals in Atlanta and to travel to the battlefield itself to study its medical topography. But his investigations progressed at a much slower pace than anticipated and were only partially completed when the time for his departure for Athens arrived. Convinced of the importance of this research and afraid that he could not interrupt it without "losing all his work," Jones canceled his trip.[5]

Upon the eventual easing of the gangrene epidemic in Augusta Jones turned to his investigations for the surgeon general and spent the remainder of 1863 and the first six months of 1864 assiduously carrying out his recent instructions. Two important projects and the writing of a third report for Moore occupied Jones's time. First, he completed his study, begun earlier in Charleston, of the interrelations between typhoid fever and malaria in the lower South's coastal plain. This necessitated visiting all the military encampments in Georgia and northern

Florida east of a line formed by the Charleston & Savannah, Savannah, Albany & Gulf, and Atlantic & Gulf railroads. In all he covered over 1,000 miles. Second, Jones drafted, duplicated, and distributed a twenty-four page questionnaire to the Confederacy's principal surgeons designed "to excite investigations, secure uniformity of action amongst the medical officers, and rescue from destruction valuable records, and experience, which if not now preserved in a systematic manner would be entirely lost."[6]

By the beginning of 1864 Jones was ready to begin the writing of his third report for the surgeon general, the most ambitious one to date. His progress was not as fast as he would have liked for it to have been. Some delay, caused by periodic interruptions to do additional research and to check sources, was unavoidable. At least two retarding factors, however, were products of the war. Despite Moore's permission to requisition these items, he experienced great difficulty in obtaining essential supplies and equipment, such as test chemicals, paper, pens, and ink, for the completion of his research and the writing of his report. He was totally frustrated, for example, in his quest for a set of dissecting instruments. His own had long since given out, forcing him to rely on borrowed instruments. "I would state," Jones complained to the medical supplier for the military district of South Carolina and Georgia, "that I have tried in vain in every city of the Confederacy to obtain a suitable case." Frustrated in the hope of securing a dissecting kit, he asked for a set of amputating instruments, pointing out that they could be made to answer the same purpose. Another kind of delay occurred when Jones laid aside his work to help his mother look after family interests in Liberty County. With the death of his father and the stationing of his brother in South Carolina he was the only one available to assist her.[7]

Jones finished the report near the end of June. He could not have completed it nearly this quickly had it not been for the valuable assistance of Louis Manigault, his secretary. He met Manigault, the descendant of a prominent South Carolina Huguenot family, during one of his trips to Charleston. Desperately needing help with the voluminous paperwork associated with his research and reports, Jones made him his secretary. Manigault was an ideal choice: he was exempt from conscription and his thorough education and extensive mercantile experience in Charleston and Canton, China had prepared him well for the organizing and copying of material which the position demanded. In the hiring of Manigault, Jones exercised the authority granted him by Moore in July 1863 to employ, at government expense, up to two assistants to facilitate his investigations. At various times he was assisted by others, always temporarily or permanently disabled soldiers who were detailed to his service, but of all his assistants Jones worked best with Manigault.[8]

During the final stages of preparation of the report, Jones anxiously followed events in northern Georgia where General William Tecumseh Sherman was threatening to strike a mortal blow to the heartland of the Confederacy. Sherman had launched his attack, one strongly resembling modern total war, from Chattanooga in May. Outnumbered almost two to one, his Confederate opponent, General Joseph E. Johnston, was forced to adopt the Fabian policy of strategic withdrawal. He gave ground slowly and played Sherman for time in the hope of maneuvering him into a position where his outmanned Army of Tennessee could deliver a decisive counterstroke. By late June the battle lines were within twenty miles of Atlanta.

Joseph Jones was apprehensive about the seriousness of Sherman's invasion. His fears were heightened at the end of May by the urgent appeal from Atlanta of his sister and brother-in-law for permission to store their books, winter clothing, and all the furniture that could be spared in his home "so that if the army does not make a stand at this place, we will not lose everything."[9] Curious and concerned and having several weeks of free time while waiting for Manigault to prepare the final draft of his manuscript, Jones decided to go to the front to determine the true state of things for himself and to offer his services to Dr. Andrew J. Foard, medical director of the Army of Tennessee.[10]

Upon his arrival in Atlanta on June 23 he learned that the opposing forces were deployed near Marietta girding themselves for the next encounter, which was to come in a few days (June 27) on Kenesaw Mountain. A tour of the southern defenses convinced Jones that the enemy would be decisively repulsed. This confidence was grounded in an unshakable faith in the generalship of Joseph E. Johnston, a faith not shared by many of his contemporaries. Jones defended Johnston's tactics as sound, contending that they were governed "by his knowledge of the relative strength of the two armies, by his knowledge of the topography of the country & by his wise determination to husband the strength of his army, to prolong the struggles to the utmost, to weaken his adversary by a carefully conducted defense, to draw him from his base of supply, & finally defeat and annihilate him."[11] "The army," he exclaimed, "has the most unbounded & enthusiastic confidence in General Johnston, & would I believe march, fall back or retreat through the streets of Atlanta without any demoralization or straggling."[12]

Because of his deep admiration for Johnston, Jones was deeply distressed when on July 17 Jefferson Davis, motivated by personal distrust, pressure from the Confederate government, and the frenzied appeals for help from the panic-stricken Georgians, ordered Johnston to hand over his command to General John B. Hood. Despite his towering reputation as a fighter Hood's offensive strategy proved even less successful than Johnston's defensive maneuvers. Jones had feared this. "General Hood," he later wrote, "combined with unbounded energy and dauntless courage and glowing patriotism a fiery ambition for military glory which led him to overestimate his own military genius and resources and at the same time to underestimate the vast resources and military strategy of his antagonist." Jones held Hood personally responsible not only for the loss of Atlanta but for the opening of the heartland of the South to Sherman and the subsequent collapse of the Confederacy. "When Hood," he inveighed, "ceased to confront General Sherman, and opened way for his desolating march through the rich plantations of Georgia, the Empire State of the South, the fate of the Confederacy was forever sealed. The beleaguered Confederacy, torn and bleeding along all her borders, was in no position to hurl her warworn, imperfectly clad and poorly armed and provisional battalions upon fortified cities."[13]

Jones's reputation as an investigator was well known in the medical department of the Army of Tennessee, and he was invited to inspect the army's hospitals rather than to serve as a surgeon. The ensuing contest for Kenesaw Mountain and the Confederate withdrawal inside the final defenses of Atlanta afforded him an excellent opportunity to observe health conditions in this large Confederate army and to inquire into the experiences of the medical director and many of the chief surgeons of the various corps, divisions, brigades, and regiments. Throughout this trying period of bloody combat and disheartening retreat Jones was both deeply touched by the courage and devotion of the hard-pressed southern soldiers and bitterly appalled at the devastating effect of disease and battle on the rapidly thinning Confederate ranks. "By day," he wrote, "these men were exposed in the trenches with their attention constantly strained to avoid shells, or the minnie balls of the sharp shooters. By night their rest was broken by the bursting shells, and the repeated real and feigned attacks of the enemy." To add to these problems there was a shortage of food and a lack of sanitation in the camps and trenches. The result was a general weakening of the individual soldier, making him easy prey for the prevailing diseases.[14]

An inveterate preserver of the Confederacy's medical records, Jones used much of his month's stay in the Army of Tennessee to begin compiling its medical statistics for the crucial last two months of the Atlanta campaign. He finished the task during a second visit to this army in October 1864. Despite their two-month limitation these figures provide many insights into the effect of disease and battle on the Confederate soldiers futilely struggling to repel Sherman. Indeed the wealth of information they contain is astonishing. They are clearly superior to the figures for Sherman's army in depicting medical conditions. Rather than merely listing the total number of cases and deaths reported by the more than sixty hospitals serving the Army of Tennessee Jones meticulously recorded the medical returns for each of them. He also distinguished between new and readmitted cases and between deaths from an original injury or disease and those which were the result of some secondary or supervening infection. Jones concluded his statistics with a detailed summary, which not only reviewed the monthly activity in these Confederate hospitals but also revealed the disposition of cases treated.

A number of significant conclusions can be drawn from the Confederate medical statistics for the Atlanta campaign. Most important, they clearly indicate the effect of disease and injury on the Army of Tennessee. The 46,332 southern soldiers (24,384 in July and 21,948 in August) hospitalized starkly portray the enormity of suffering. These figures become even more meaningful when casualties are compared to effective strength. This comparison reveals that one of every two Confederate soldiers fit for battle was incapacitated each month. These were losses the Army of Tennessee could ill afford.

In addition, the leading forms of disease and injury are identified. Chief among the diseases were the war's most dangerous disorders—malaria, typhoid fever, and diarrhea and dysentery. They were closely followed in importance by bone-and-joint and other exposure-aggravated disorders, digestive complaints, and various childhood ailments such as measles, chicken pox, and mumps. The primary cause of injury, of course, was gunshot wounds.

The medical statistics of the Atlanta campaign are an eloquent testimonial to the admirable work performed by the surgeons of the Army of Tennessee. Without doubt these surgeons labored in the face of insurmountable handicaps. Not only was Sherman's pressure oppressive but by mid-1864 the war was rushing to a close and the Confederacy was beginning to disintegrate. Medical stores, already in short supply, became almost impossible to obtain. Even when they were available the collapsing Southern transportation system, the obstruction of Georgia's states' rights-supporting governor, Joseph E. Brown, and the involved Confederate red tape made them virtually inaccessible. Southern surgeons, therefore, were often forced to find substitutes or to do without. Finally there was the constant shifting of hospitals in order to escape the advances of Sherman and to treat the large number of sick and wounded in each new sector. These repeated moves not only necessitated the abandonment of excellent hospital sites but also caused the crowding of hospitals, one upon the other. In addition the frequent breaking up and moving of hospitals led to the loss of much valuable and irreplaceable equipment and stores. Worse yet the confusion accompanying these forced moves was responsible for the unavoidable crowding of the sick and wounded into boxcars and temporary hospitals, where they suffered from shock and exposure to other diseases.

Despite the handicaps under which they operated the surgeons of the Army of Tennessee kept at their tasks and compiled an enviable record. Counting the cases in the various hospitals at the beginning of each month, they handled a grand total of 40,038 cases in July and 39,671 in August. Of these nearly 80,000 cases an average of 20 percent were returned to duty and only 2 percent died. But these long-suffering surgeons were fighting a losing battle. In the face of their remarkable achievements Jones's statistics indicate a general breaking down of medical services as the contest for Atlanta rushed to a climax. The mounting intensity of the operations, their disrupting effect on the medical department of the Army of Tennessee, and their debilitating influence on the individual Confederate soldier began to show. More soldiers were sent to the large, rear-area general hospitals in August; there was a significant decrease in the number of soldiers returned to active duty; desertions mounted; and convalescence furloughs increased as chronic cases were sent home in order to make room for the new cases.

The medical statistics for the Atlanta campaign help round out the story of this epic struggle. The military side is well known, but the medical aspect has been largely neglected. Yet disease and injury were significant reasons for the fall of Atlanta, especially when one considers that Jones's statistics clearly show that the Army of Tennessee lost over 45 percent of its effective strength to disease and injury in July and almost 50 percent in August. This proud southern army had presented only a thin gray line at the outset of the campaign in May, and every casualty from battle or disease further thinned it. It broke at the opening of September; and, as Sherman had predicted, the capture of Atlanta was "the death-knell of the Southern Confederacy."[15]

Manigault finished copying Jones's manuscript at the end of July. Desiring to get it in Moore's hands as soon as possible, Jones postponed any further research in the Army of Tennessee until fall.[16] The uncertain state of communications between Augusta and Richmond, coupled with the fear that the report contained "much matter which would prove of value to our enemies" should it fall into their hands, convinced him that it was his duty to deliver the volume in person. His concern was well founded for like Atlanta, Richmond was a beleaguered city in the summer of 1864. At the beginning of May Grant, in conjunction with Sherman's invasion of Georgia, had launched a determined assault against the Confederate capital. Lee quickly moved his smaller Army of Northern Virginia across Grant's line of march. A series of bloody encounters ensued, starting with the battle of the Wilderness on May 5 and 6, and terminating in the siege of Petersburg a little over a month later. In addition to the large-scale attacks of Sherman and Grant the increasing vulnerability of the South late in the war prompted a number of daring Union cavalry raids. Richmond, for example, was threatened by the Kilpatrick-Dahlgren raid in late February and early March 1864 and by General Philip Sheridan in May. Determined to safeguard his manuscript at all costs, Jones left for Richmond on August 2, arriving there four days later.[17]

This report was his most ambitious undertaking for the surgeon general to date. It consisted of almost 600 crowded pages and was liberally illustrated with tables, maps, and hand-drawn colored plates. Although it dealt ostensibly with typhoid fever, the manuscript's greatest value lay in Jones's analysis of the medical statistics for the Confederacy during the nineteen-month period, January 1862–July 1863. These calculations were based on the field and hospital reports, which he had meticulously copied in Georgia, Virginia, South Carolina, and Florida.

This test period saw an average of 160,231 officers and men carried on the field reports, 17,300 (10.8 percent) of whom had died. During this same time the general hospitals reported 17,059 deaths (4.2 percent of the cases treated). Jones pointed out, however, that these figures encompassed neither all the Confederate forces nor the total activity of the South's general hospitals. The field reports, he believed, reflected but two-fifths of the southern strength while the hospital statistics accounted for only two-thirds of the total cases treated. His adjusted statistics showed that there were 43,250 deaths in the field and 25,588 in the general hospitals, a total of 68,838 fatalities. Jones felt that these corrected figures were still conservative and suggested that the true total might be as much as 25 percent higher, raising deaths to almost 86,000.

As for the causes of death Jones's research revealed that one-fourth resulted from typhoid fever and another fourth from pneumonia. "The great mortality of Typhoid Fever and Pneumonia, amongst the Confederate Forces invests these diseases with peculiar interest and importance," he remarked, "and should lead to a *thorough examination of the different modes* of treatment now before the Profession." He insisted that every southern medical officer should be urged to test the value of all available forms of treatment and pointed to his own interest in the study of pneumonia. His comparison of the cure rate in European and Confederate hospitals showed that deaths were two to four times greater in the latter, a fact he erroneously attributed to the growing trend to abandon traditional heroic principles for less rigorous dietetic and nature-supporting regimens.[18]

Jones spent only a few days in Richmond, staying just long enough to present his report to Moore, to have his orders of the previous September reaffirmed, and to discuss future research plans. He informed the surgeon general that he had collected a great deal of material on hospital gangrene, malaria, pyemia, spurious vaccination, and the relations between and classification of fevers and promised to report on his findings at the earliest possible moment.[19] First he wanted to extend his investigations to the Federal prisoners confined at Andersonville.

This prison, located in southwestern Georgia near Macon, had been opened in early 1864 to ease the overcrowding in the prisons around Richmond. It quickly became the South's principal prisoner-of-war camp as Union pressure on the Confederate capital mounted. Constructed to hold 10,000 prisoners, the stockade originally encompassed seventeen acres but was soon enlarged by ten acres to accommodate the ever-increasing number of prisoners. The first 860 Union soldiers arrived in the middle of February; by August the total population had reached 33,000, far beyond even the expanded facility's capacity. Soon overcrowding, exposure, inadequate diet, and filth produced an appalling situation, and Andersonville became a living hell.[20]

Persistent reports of the exceptionally high mortality among these Union prisoners aroused Jones's curiosity, and he sought the surgeon general's permission to visit Andersonville "with the design of instituting a series of inquiries upon the nature and causes of the prevailing diseases." The opportunities for the study of fevers were especially appealing. "It was believed," Jones explained, "that a large body of men from the northern portion of the United States, suddenly transported to a warm southern climate, and confined upon a small portion of land, would furnish an excellent field for the investigation of the relations of typhus, typhoid, and malarial fevers."[21]

Moore viewed this request favorably, for he too believed that "the field of pathological investigation afforded by the large collection of Federal Prisoners in Georgia is of great extent and importance." Believing Jones's standing orders which authorized his wide-ranging research to be insufficient for such an unusual undertaking, he provided him with special instructions. Jones was sent to Andersonville in the hope "that results of value to the Profession may be obtained by a careful investigation of the effects of disease upon this large body of Men subjected to a decided change of Climate, and to the circumstances peculiar to prison life." Further the surgeon general instructed Isaiah H. White, the surgeon-in-charge of the prison hospital, to accord Jones every facility and complete cooperation in the prosecution

Joseph Jones
(*from the Joseph Jones Collection,
Tulane University*)

Charles Colcock Jones
*(from the Joseph Jones Collection,
Tulane University)*

Mary Jones
*(from the Joseph Jones Collection,
Tulane University)*

Joseph Jones at Princeton

*(from a lithograph by
F. Michelin & Shattuck)*

POPULAR
Lectures on Chemistry,
BY JOSEPH JONES, M. D.,
AT THE
SAVANNAH MEDICAL COLLEGE,
COURSE TICKET.—ADMIT ONE.
Lectures on Mondays and Thursdays, at 8 o'clock.

Ticket of Admission to Joseph Jones's
Popular Lectures, 1860

*(from the Joseph Jones Collection,
Tulane University)*

JOSEPH JONES'

LABORATORY

For Practical Instruction in Medical Physics, Chemistry
and Pharmacy, Toxicology, Microscopy, Experimental
Physiology and Comparative Anatomy.

MEDICAL COLLEGE OF GEORGIA,

AUGUSTA.

PHYSICS. EXPERIMENTAL AND ANALYTICAL CHEMISTRY.

THE Student will be furnished with the Apparatus and Chemical Re-agents, and will be instructed
in the modes of Experiment and Analysis, and will be exercised in those Experiments and Analyses,
which are necessary for the thorough and practical knowledge of Medical Physics and Chemistry. The
Therapeutic applications of Heat, Light and Electricity will receive special attention.

PHARMACY.

THE necessary Apparatus and Chemical Re-agents will be furnished, and the Student will be exercised in the abstraction and preparation of the Alkaloids; and in the preparation of Inorganic Medicines,
and in the demonstration of the Chemical relations of Remedial Agents.

TOXICOLOGY.

THE Actions of Poisons and Medicines will be illustrated by Experiments upon Animals; and
the Student will be furnished with the necessary apparatus and tests, for the analysis of poisons and the
demonstration of the Chemical relations and modes of action of remedial agents.

PHYSIOLOGICAL AND PATHOLOGICAL CHEMISTRY.

SPECIAL INSTRUCTION will be given in Physiological and Pathological Chemistry. The Student
will be furnished with the necessary apparatus, and with the solids and fluids of man and animals; and
special instruction will be given upon the Chemical Constitution, physiological and pathological relations,
and methods of analysis of the Blood and Urine.

MICROSCOPY.

THE Student will be furnished with a Microscope, and instructed in the appearance, and mode of
examination of healthy and diseased structures, secretions and excretions. The microscopic examination
of the Blood and Urine, will receive special attention.

COMPARATIVE ANATOMY.

The Student will have free access to the Private Collection of Dr. Joseph Jones, which numbers
more than Fifteen Hundred Anatomical Preparations, and Minute Injections, illustrating the structure
and development of the Animal Kingdom; and will be carefully instructed in the art of Minute Injection.

LECTURES.

ONE HUNDRED LECTURES will be delivered, during the Course of the year, on Physics, Inorganic,
Vegetable, Animal, Physiological and Pathological Chemistry, Pharmacy, Toxicology, and Comparative
Anatomy.

TERMS.

Laboratory Fee, for one year,..$100.00
Laboratory Fee, for one month,................................... 20.00
Fee for One Hundred Lectures,................................... 30.00

For further information apply at the Medical College of Georgia, corner of Washington and Telfair Streets, or at the residence of Dr. Jones, No. 90 Green-street.

JOSEPH JONES, M. D.

Professor of Medical Chemistry and Pharmacy in the Medical College of Georgia

AUGUSTA, GA., February, 1860.

Advertisement for Joseph Jones's
Private Laboratory, 1860

*(from the Joseph Jones Collection,
Tulane University)*

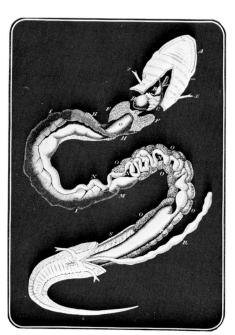

Jones's woodcut
of the Congo snake

(*from* Contributions to Knowledge,
Smithsonian Institution, 1856)

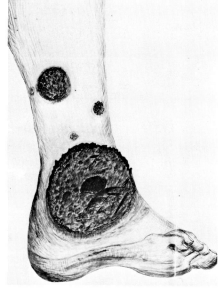

Jones's drawing
of a gangrenous
foot & leg

(*from the Joseph Jones
Collection, Tulane
University*)

Louis Manigault's sketch of Joseph Jones
at Andersonville

(*from the Joseph Jones Collection,
Tulane University*)

Andersonville Prison
(*from the Library of Congress*)

of his investigations "in order that this great . . . field may be explored for the benefit of the Medical Department of the Confederate Army."[22]

Jones excitedly hurried to Augusta to prepare for his visit to Andersonville, but several obstacles forced him to delay his trip for almost a month. The biggest was the scarceness of research supplies. Jones had exhausted most of his test chemicals, medicines, and office supplies in the compilation of his recent report. Replacements were secured, but with great difficulty. Even then he had to prepare most of his own chemical solutions, including the mineral acids which he used in his investigations. At Moore's suggestion he also took time to prepare a brief outline of his study of gangrene, promising a future full report "supported and illustrated by cases, experiments, and . . . chemical and microscopical investigations."[23]

Jones's weakened state of health further postponed his start for Andersonville. Exhaustion growing out of his constant research of the past two years and a prolonged diet of salt meat and too few vegetables were beginning to exact an ominous toll on both his physical and mental well-being. Physically Jones complained of spongy, bleeding gums—unmistakable signs of scurvy. He attributed his malady to the war. "The Confederate currency had depreciated to such an extent," he explained, "that officers were not much better off than the privates of the Confederate army, and were in most cases confined to the ordinary ration of cornmeal and salt pork or bacon, with occasional small issues of fresh beef, rice, pease, and molasses; and the tendency of this diet without change was to induce a scorbutic state of the system."[24] From an early age Jones had demonstrated only a limited ability to cope effectively with adversity and stress. By the summer of 1864, as the pressure of his research and the strain of the war mounted, he began to show the symptoms associated with combat fatigue—most notably, irritability and anxiety. In fact as early as the previous fall he had confessed to his wife that he had not treated her as "good & pleasant" as he should have upon his return from Virginia and apologized for his "unkind & petulant speeches." "You must forgive them all," he pleaded, "for I am nothing but a poor imperfect man."[25]

Carrie was also a casualty of the war. From the very first she dreaded being left alone with only her children and the servants for company while Jones pursued his investigations. Dutifully she made the best of her plight. "I have," she wrote Mary Jones in November 1863, "to get accustomed to lonely evenings & indeed nights—this roving commission takes the Doctor away so much, so I accustom myself to spending my time in this great house without a soul nearer than the kitchen except the two babies."[26] But try as she might she never adjusted to these long periods of loneliness and anxiety. Added to this unhealthy situation were the problems and frustrations of maintaining a household as shortages mounted and inflation soared late in the war. Carrie taxed her energies even further in the summer of 1864 when she joined a group of local ladies in the demanding project of supplying refreshments to the sick and wounded in the Augusta hospitals. In late August, after two months of daily hospital visits, her health gave out. She was struck down by what seems to have been acute nervous exhaustion. Jones was worried about her condition but did not consider it sufficiently serious to postpone his visit to Andersonville, now in its final stages of preparation. At the middle of September he left her in the care of his mother and, accompanied by Manigault and Titus, set out for this southwest Georgia prison.[27]

With the labor of several paroled Negro soldiers Jones set up his camp, consisting of two tents and cooking and mess facilities, on a heavily wooded site near the post headquarters and a safe three-quarters of a mile away from the alleged miasmatic environs of the prison. It was necessary to maintain a permanent guard, "not against Yankees," according to Manigault, "but thieves, cows, hogs and dogs."[28] As soon as his camp was in order Jones eagerly launched his investigations. He had no trouble gaining access to the hospital and morgue (or dead house as it was called), both of which were located outside the prison walls. Despite his orders, however, Captain Henry Wirz, the prison commandant, flatly refused him admission to the stockade. Jones appealed to Brigadier-General John H. Winder, the commander of Andersonville post, calling his attention to his special instructions from the surgeon general. Winder intervened on his behalf, and Wirz backed down.[29]

A detailed examination of Jones's Andersonville investigations is the subject of a later chapter. In brief he found himself confronted with a "field of great extent and of extraordinary interest." There were more than 5,000 seriously sick Union soldiers in the stockade and prison hospital, and deaths ranged from 90 to 130 daily. Almost 10,000 deaths had occurred in the seven months between the establishment of the prison and his visit, nearly one-third of the prison population. Desirous of learning the true reasons for the prisoners' plight, Jones judiciously utilized his two-week stay to study the medical topography of the area, to screen many of the prisoners (both healthy and sick), to perform numerous postmortem examinations, and to execute frequent drawings of the diseased structures which his autopsies uncovered.

He conducted his pathological studies in a "small structure surrounded at the sides with old tent cloth, and covered with boards" which the surgeon-in-charge had ordered "erected extemporaneously for the occasion" in an open space just outside the hospital grounds. To Jones this makeshift dissection room "afforded but indifferent facilities" for these investigations. "In this confined, unventilated room, exposed to the burning autumnal sun," he asserted, *"post-mortem* examinations of the thoroughly poisoned and rapidly decomposing bodies of those who had died from hospital gangrene, diarrhoea, dysentery, and scurvy, were not unattended with discomfort, and with even some danger." Fearful for their health, Jones did not demand the assistance of the Andersonville surgeons as authorized in his instructions from Moore. Instead he merely invited their cooperation. Consequently many of these medical officers showed an "apparent indisposition" to engage in "such unpleasant, and to a certain extent, hazardous labors." To safeguard his own health Jones adopted the policy of immersing his hands in a strong solution of alum, which he allowed to dry thoroughly, before undertaking any postmortem examination or handling any diseased structure. At the completion of each autopsy he washed his hands in successive strong solutions of alum, chlorinated soda, and tincture of camphor, allowing these to dry completely. Every cut or abrasion was painted with tincture of iodine.[30] Jones's prophylactic measures, representing a combination of unfounded feelings and commendable empiricism in this prebacteriological era, was of understandably mixed value. Alum and camphor are of little or no use as antiseptics, while chlorinated soda and iodine are effective germicides.

His investigations showed that diarrhea, dysentery, scurvy, and hospital gangrene were chiefly responsible for Andersonville's extraordinary mortality. Hospital gangrene received Jones's special attention. This killer was so rampant that almost every amputation to remove a gangrenous limb was followed by a return of the disease and eventual death. He spent much of his time observing the origin and progress of individual cases and conducting postmortem examinations to determine the pathological changes of the organs and tissues.[31]

The unmitigated suffering of the Andersonville prisoners was a heartrending sight to both Jones and Manigault. Manigault aptly described the prison as "a Hades on Earth." "In my travels in China, and various sections of the Globe," he wrote, "I have witnessed many an awful sight, and beheld the dead and dying in various stages. I even now recall to mind most vividly some fearful scenes of death within the Prison at Shanghai, and also cases of Cholera in the North of China, but all is nothing to what I am now beholding."[32] Jones was equally moved. In marked contrast with his earlier views on Union prisoners, he exclaimed: "Whilst the Yankees have no claim upon our sympathies & upon our charities, still if prisoners are to be sacrificed let the fact be distinctly stated beforehand or else let the black flag be raised."[33]

Jones firmly believed that "the fear of great suffering in imprisonment only renders our enemies more vindictive & more stubborn in battle." His Andersonville research, he hoped, would provide "the means of mitigating some of this suffering."[34] In this same vein he planned "to make a similar inspection of all the Confederate military prisons, and to draw up an extended report upon the causes of diseases and death, together with observations upon the best methods of remedying existing evils."[35] But as commendable as his goals were, Jones's research was not universally appreciated in the Confederacy. One notable critic was Dr. Samuel H. Stout, the most famous medical director of the Army of Tennessee under whose jurisdiction the medical services at Andersonville were administered. Jones, he later wrote, "was noted for a disposition to find fault, and never proposed a rational remedy for anything. He was . . . to be seen everywhere *flickering* about and furnishing aid no where to the over worked surgeons."[36]

Jones left Andersonville at the end of September, moving to Macon, a short distance away in central Georgia, to resume his investigations in the Army of Tennessee which he had commenced the previous summer. He pitched his tents on an open lot behind the town's Female Academy and between the two principal roads connecting Macon and nearby Vineville. Owing to this central location the little camp was continually enlivened by "numerous passers-by" and "various equipages." There were at least ten large hospitals in Macon and Vineville, prompting Manigault to remark that "a man may witness here at present almost any and every disease."[37]

Jones was primarily interested in the effect of gangrene on the Army of Tennessee. He found the research opportunities very promising, for this large Confederate army had experienced a marked increase in the incidence of this disorder since the evacuation of Atlanta four weeks earlier. "The Gangrene Hospital here," he reported, "furnished a most extensive & interesting field for the determination of the phenomena of the disease in all its various stages."[38] He examined hospital records, studied cases of interest, tried to determine the effects of location and change of climate, questioned medical officers, made numerous analyses of the blood and excretions, and executed lifesize drawings of gangrenous limbs. Most of his research was conducted in a special hospital for gangrene patients, a practice originated in the Army of Tennessee. Jones denounced this policy as "doubtful if not dangerous and disastrous," believing that the congregating of several hundred cases of gangrene in one crowded hospital threatened recovery because of the concentration of the pathogenic poison responsible for the disorder.[39]

During the course of these investigations Jones became increasingly intrigued with what he described as the "engrafting of smallpox" upon gangrene patients and spent considerable time studying this phenomenon. The smallpox ward, he discovered, was located in a pine grove some three hundred yards to the rear of the gangrene hospital. Nurses circulated freely between them. Since smallpox had first appeared among the nurses in the gangrene hospital, Jones held them responsible for spreading it to their patients. He studied the two diseases "side by side in the same manner" and compared the results of analyses of the excretions and postmortem examinations, hoping to distinguish "between the actions of two poisons." This study, he concluded, had "clearly established that small-pox would attack patients suffering with gangrene, and even pyemia, when they were greatly reduced in flesh and strength."[40]

Jones spent six weeks, first in Macon and then in Columbus, carrying out research in the hospitals of the Army of Tennessee.

Often he received no assistance whatever from the harassed, over-worked medical officers and was compelled to perform his examinations alone, frequently working ten to twelve hours a day. After a two-month absence, broken only by a brief visit home in mid-October, Jones returned to Augusta in the middle of November. He began writing up his Andersonville research and started his fourth report, on gangrene, for Moore, planning to finish it by mid-1865.[41]

Although his gangrene investigations had been limited to Virginia, South Carolina, and Georgia, he hoped to describe its effect on all the southern armies. To do this he prepared and distributed a detailed eight-page questionnaire entitled "Inquiries upon Hospital Gangrene." Jones introduced this survey by calling attention to Moore's orders instructing him to study the diseases of the Confederacy and with a personal appeal for assistance from his comrades in arms. "Generalizations upon the history, origin and causes of diseases, and their relations to the climate and soil," he entreated, "cannot be perfected without *testimony* from various competent medical officers viewing the same diseases under varied circumstances." There followed a series of eight questions, with numerous subdivisions, calling for the responding surgeon's total experience in combating gangrene. Jones asked for a general description of the origin, progress, and characteristics of this infection; reports of cases followed throughout their course; opinions as to whether the disease was local or constitutional in origin; views on its contagiousness and the method by which the infection was spread, should it be thought contagious; views on the underlying conditions and causes of the disease, should it not be considered contagious; a listing of characteristic lesions, if any, discovered during autopsies; and accounts of the best means of treating gangrene. A table set forth the desired pattern for reporting cases of particular interest. Jones concluded the questionnaire with a reminder that all these questions were "open for discussion and investigation" and could be settled "only by the most careful record of the cases."

Although admirably thorough and the product of much hard work, Jones's questionnaire was unrealistic. Few of the beleaguered southern surgeons had the time to answer its involved questions. Most of them ignored it. Many of those who did respond chose to do so in a very general manner. In addition Sherman's movement eastward from Atlanta isolated Jones from a large number of the surgeons to whom the questionnaire had been sent. The responses that he did receive, however, generally confirmed his own findings, prompting him to proceed with his report.[42]

Sherman stirred from Atlanta as Jones was making his way back to Augusta from the Army of Tennessee. He had been inactive since capturing this southern citadel at the beginning of September, allowing his victorious army to regain its strength. Although everyone, North and South, had an opinion, no one, not even Lincoln and Grant, knew his next move. Lincoln reluctantly gave his approval when Sherman revealed his intention to march eastward through Georgia to the sea. Grant, however, insisted that Hood be destroyed first. To placate him General George H. Thomas, who was headquartered in Nashville, was detached and ordered to contain Hood. Then, vowing to live off the land, Sherman severed his lines of communications and on November 10 began his famous march to the sea. He moved southeasterly, paralleling the Ogeechee River. Jones had ample time to cross his line of march and reach the safety of Augusta, thus avoiding capture or isolation in central Georgia.[43]

Much has been written about the wanton destruction which Sherman's army perpetrated as it moved through central and eastern Georgia. These charges are, in large measure, true. In general, however, the senior officers and most of the division and brigade commanders, conducted themselves well and tried to control the actions of their men. The glaring exception was Brigadier-General Judson Kilpatrick, Sherman's cavalry commander. His troopers, ranging far in front of the main body, seemed to revel in pillage and destruction. Kilpatrick's "notorious immoralities and rapacity set so demoralizing an example to his troops," one of his colleagues has confessed, "that the best disciplinarians among his subordinates could only mitigate its influence."[44] Even Sherman is said to have considered him "a hell of a damned fool" but requested his services during the Georgia campaign because of his masterful operations under fire.[45]

It was this band of marauders that overran the plantations of coastal Georgia. Ostensibly these bummers, as they were called, were foraging for Sherman, but plunder and ruin were their trademarks. First appearing in mid-December they terrorized large parts of eastern Georgia for over a month. It was not until February 1865, when Sherman moved north into the Carolinas, that the depredations eased. The Jones family plantations lay in their path and paid a terrible price.

Buck-Head in Burke County was the first to feel the brunt of Kilpatrick's savagery. His troopers poured into northeastern Georgia in early December after executing a successful feint against Augusta. The overseer, upon learning of the enemy's presence, hid the slaves, mules, and horses in a nearby swamp, only to have their location betrayed by a young Negro. In two visits, on December 2 and 5, the raiders almost denuded the plantation. Kilpatrick's departure did not end the plundering, for on the very next day, December 6, Major-General Jeff Davis's Fourteenth Corps passed. "The grand army," Jones later learned, "stole & destroyed what the raiding thieves had left." One group used magnets and magnetic needles to search every inch of the grounds for silver and buried treasure; another "even tore the little silver pieces from the necks of the negro children." The clothing was "jerked . . . from the backs of the women & men & either used for bags, or tore . . . up for strings, or also put . . . on for garments." Housewares were wantonly destroyed. Strong efforts, including the threat of death, were made to induce the slaves to leave. With the exception of the youthful betrayer all refused. The coup de grace was the torch. "As the last of the grand army passed at dark," the overseer told Jones, "the bugle sounded at the end of the lane & the wick was applied to the Gin house & Cotton house & screw."

As soon as it was safe, Jones hurried to Burke County to assess the damage. He was outraged. The "degraded wretches" had dealt a costly blow. In addition to the losses by fire 16 mules, 2 horses, 10 oxen, 72 hogs, 3 wagons, 4,000 bushels of corn, 200 bushels of rice, 25 bales of cotton, and the entire potato and molasses crop had been confiscated or destroyed. Fortunately, however, sufficient provisions were salvaged to support the plantation until new crops could be planted and harvested. Jones successfully sought to restore some semblance of order, remarking: "Before I left the plantation was restored to its usual quiet & regularity."[46]

Kilpatrick's host overran Monte Video on December 13. Their only opposition consisted of Mary Jones, her granddaughter Ruth Jones (whom she had raised from infancy), her pregnant daughter Mary S. Mallard (who was to give birth during the occupation) and her three children, and a family friend and her two children who had taken refuge at Monte Video after their own home had been put to the torch.

Mary Jones, unlike most of the inhabitants of Liberty County, had refused to flee before the advancing Union forces because of her emotional attachment to the area. Instead she chose to put her faith in Sherman's published orders guaranteeing the protection of life and private property. "I did not," she later wrote, "anticipate immunity from distress or from the common losses and spoliations of war. I expected to suffer with my suffering country, but I did believe through those orders that I would be protected in my own home from private invasion and pillage." No belief could have been further from reality. During a four-week period, with the exception of only two days, Monte Video was invaded "three and four times a day by numbers of soldiers varying from forty to two and three at a time." When the doors were unlocked they literally swarmed through the house; when the doors were locked to protect the captive colony of females and children within they were burst open or entered with skeleton keys. Every inch of the house was searched repeatedly. "Not the minutest box or trunk," Mary Jones exclaimed, "escaped scrutiny; and all that was deemed valuable in furniture, library, household effects, clothing, knives, forks, silver, crockery, or jewelry, etc., was subtracted or injured." Even a small cache of food which she had hidden was sought out and stolen. Her pleas that it was to feed her helpless guests were allegedly dismissed with rejoinders such as: " 'You deserve to starve to death, and we mean you shall do it. You have no right even to have wood or water. We will *crush* and humble you in the dust.' "

The denudation of the plantation was equally complete. All the cotton was destroyed; with the exception of some unshelled corn and unthreshed rice every particle of food, right down to seed potatoes, was taken; every conveyance—whether carriage, wagon, or cart—was confiscated, as well as all harness; and the plantation was stripped of all livestock and poultry. "In a few days," Mary Jones lamented, "over my once cheerful home was cast the pall of death." But as wanton as the destruction at Monte Video had been, that at Maybank, the Jones family's summer home on Colonel's Island, surpassed it. The dwelling, outbuildings, and even the fences on this abandoned plantation were senselessly reduced to ashes. The blow she and her family had been dealt by the Yankees added to Mary Jones's deep-seated hatred of them. "Such desolation and ruin," she lashed out bitterly, "pervaded my native county as might satisfy the deepest revenge."[47]

The invasion of Liberty County and the uncertain fate of his mother made Joseph Jones ill with anxiety, but there was nothing he could do but pray for her safety. Not until Sherman's forces had withdrawn could he even reestablish contact with her. In the meantime he and his brother, now in Augusta, devised plans to move her to safety as soon as circumstances should permit.[48]

Sherman occupied Savannah on December 21, 1864, and presented the city to Lincoln as a Christmas present. Panic-stricken that a similar fate awaited their city, the residents of Augusta deluged Governor Joseph E. Brown with frantic appeals for help. Jones, expecting to be forced to flee at any moment, worked feverishly on his gangrene report. To the relief of all the anticipated attack did not materialize. In his eagerness to carry the war to what most northerners considered to be the heart of the rebellion, South Carolina, Sherman bypassed Augusta when he moved north on February 1, 1865.[49]

Chapter 8
Defeat

*I cannot express to you the pain which I feel in
being compelled to use my labors which were
pressed solely for the advancement of the course
of Humanity & my profession, in the
prosecution of criminal cases.*

By the opening of 1865 Joseph Jones's confidence in the inevita-
bility of southern victory had given way to despair. He was ready
to accept, and indeed hoped for, a negotiated peace. Many on
both sides shared this hope. Several attempts in the summer of
1864 to end the war had failed, but the prospects for peace
seemed almost promising in February 1865, when a three-man
southern delegation headed by Vice President Alexander H.
Stephens met with Lincoln and his secretary of state, William H.
Seward, on board a Union transport anchored at Hampton
Roads, Virginia. During the course of these negotiations Lincoln
laid down his conditions for a cessation of hostilities—reunion,
emancipation, and the disbanding of all Confederate forces. Although unyielding on these three points he adopted a liberal
attitude toward other pressing issues, most notably the possibility of compensating slave owners, and assured the southerners of
a lenient executive policy. Unfortunately the meeting ended without reconciling opposing views, and hopes of peace were dashed.[1]

Shortly after the Hampton Roads conference Jones requested
and received a leave of absence to move his mother and sister to
safety. The combined atrocities of the liberated slaves and the
occupation troops which Sherman had left in Savannah made life
in the Georgia rice country a nightmare. Broken in spirit, Mary
Jones gave in to family pressure and agreed to take shelter at her
brother's home, Refuge, in Baker County, over 200 miles away
in far southwestern Georgia.[2]

Jones returned home in the middle of April after a 500-mile journey on horseback. Refreshed by this respite from his exhausting labors and sedentary life, he was ready to pursue his research with renewed vigor. The most pressing matter was a fourth report for the surgeon general. Encompassing his gangrene investigations, it had not been scheduled for completion until June or July, but Sherman's threatening operations in Georgia and the Carolinas had prompted Jones to shorten the study in hopes of getting it to Moore before Georgia was completely cut off from Virginia. In his absence Manigault had finished the abbreviated manuscript, and Jones, unaware of the fall of the Confederate capital, busied himself with plans to carry it to Richmond.[3] These plans were obviously futile, for the war was at an end. The failure of the Hampton Roads conference had convinced Lincoln that there was to be no end to the fighting short of a clear-cut Union victory. Consequently he met with Grant and Sherman in late March at City Point on the James River below Richmond to plan a massive assault to end the war.

Lee had held Grant at bay before Petersburg for almost a year, but the Confederate line was so stretched that it could no longer withstand a large-scale thrust. The attack, the last important battle of the war, came at Five Forks on April 1. Lee was defeated and the shaky southern defenses crumbled. Petersburg was evacuated on the night of April 2. With the loss of this bastion Richmond, now untenable, was abandoned. Lee rapidly moved his weary troops westward in a frantic attempt to outdistance Grant and to join General Joseph E. Johnston and the remnants of the Army of Tennessee in North Carolina. Grant pursued the retreating Confederates with dogged determination and cornered them in central Virginia. With all hope of escape gone Lee surrendered his battered Army of Northern Virginia at Appomattox Court House on April 9. Two weeks later the war, except for isolated incidents, ended when Johnston surrendered to Sherman.

Joseph Jones had enthusiastically and wholeheartedly embraced the Southern Confederacy, and he despaired at its collapse, but he squarely faced defeat and vowed to make the best of the ensuing chaos in the South, filing away his wartime research to contend with "the pressing necessities of the times." "Broken in health, fortune, and spirits," he desired only "peace and rest."[4] This, however, he was not to enjoy. There were many in the victorious North who in their outrage at the carnage of battle and the rumored atrocities in Confederate prisons adamantly insisted that the rebellious South be punished. A nineteenth-century witch hunt seemed imminent as demands to bring the Confederate leaders to trial echoed throughout the North. Yet in the end neither Jefferson Davis, nor Robert E. Lee, nor any other well-known southerner was formally charged with war crimes. Instead those demanding a scapegoat unleashed their wrath against Captain Henry Wirz, the commandant of Andersonville prison. That Wirz's arrest, condemnation, and execution were unwarranted has virtually become a historical truism. The most recent historian of Andersonville, for example, has labeled the affair "an indefensible travesty of justice."[5] Ella Lonn probably best characterized the Wirz tragedy when she wrote: "The verdict of history is that he doubtless did the best he could with what the Confederacy could provide him, but the inflamed war feeling demanded a sacrifice."[6]

The decision to prosecute Wirz for the horrors of Andersonville placed Joseph Jones in an uncomfortable position, for he feared that his research among the Union soldiers imprisoned there would be revealed and construed as documented evidence of Confederate atrocities. "I desired especially," he later asserted, "that the report on the Federal prisoners at Andersonville should never see the light of day, because it was prepared solely for the eye of the Surgeon-General of the Confederate States Army; and the frank manner in which all the subject had been discussed, would only engender angry feelings, and place weapons in the hands of the victors." His worst fears materialized. On September 22, without any warning, he was ordered to report in Washington to Colonel Norton P. Chipman, judge advocate and prosecuting attorney in the Wirz case, as a witness in the trial and to take with him "all papers, reports, records, etc., of every kind in his possession, pertaining to the Andersonville Prison."[7]

It is unclear how United States authorities learned of the existence of Jones's report. He later insisted that they had been made aware of his Andersonville investigations "through information clandestinely furnished by a distinguished member of the medical profession of the North, who, after the close of the war, had shared the hospitality of my own home."[8] Chipman, on the other hand, held that he had heard of Jones and his research among the Federal prisoners confined at Andersonville through southern sources.[9] At any rate, whatever the channel of information, the North knew of the manuscript and demanded that it be surrendered.

Jones immediately appealed the summons of the Wirz tribunal to General James B. Steedman, provost marshal of the Department of Georgia, whose office had issued it, insisting that he had *"none* of the *original* records of Andersonville" in his possession. He did admit to having copies of some of the prison's hospital records which had been incorporated in an unfinished report but questioned whether the order applied to "matter which had never been formally and officially presented to the Medical Department of the Confederate States." Steedman rejected Jones's appeal, informing him that the summons was irrevocable and pertained to everything in his possession connected in any way with Andersonville. This material, including his unfinished report, was to be immediately surrendered to the judge advocate. Jones was dismayed, since he had no recourse but to comply with Steedman's instructions. "To a paroled prisoner of war," he remarked, "there was neither option nor appeal in the matter."[10]

With a heavy heart Jones left for Washington at the end of September. "I cannot express to you," he wrote his wife, "the pain which I feel in being compelled to use my labors which were pressed solely for the advancement of the course of Humanity & my profession in the prosecution of criminal cases."[11] The destruction of rail transportation throughout the Carolinas and Virginia forced Jones to detour to the west through Ohio, Indiana, and Pennsylvania. At every stop along the way he was impressed with "the wonderful energy & boundless resources of this great Northern people." "The poor distressed South," he bemoaned, "had but an imperfect idea of the gigantic power against which they were contending. The only wonder is that they should have held out so long & so well." As the train passed through Pennsylvania he saw the young but rapidly developing oil industry, signifying the new America which the South had fought so long, in and out of the Union, to hold back.

Jones arrived in Washington on October 2. Unfamiliar with the city he took a room at Willard's, one of the best-known but most expensive hotels in the capital. He was furnished transportation but had to pay his own living expenses. It is not surprising, then, that he considered the $4.50 daily rate exorbitant and planned to move to a less expensive hotel as soon as he could find an acceptable one. In the meantime he made the most of his luxurious surroundings, remarking: "It does a hungry Confederate good to set down to . . . sumptous bounds. . . . I will eat my head off every two or three days."[12]

One of Jones's first acts in Washington was the drafting of a lengthy appeal to Chipman in a last-ditch attempt to prevent the use of his Andersonville report against Wirz. He began by pointing out that he had gone to Andersonville "to determine the causes of the great mortality amongst the Federal prisoners" and included a copy of his orders from Moore to prove the trip's official nature. This being the case, he professed a deep distress at the likelihood that his labors were to be diverted from their intended purpose and used as evidence in a criminal case. As for the Federal prisoners, Jones argued that they had been moved to southwestern Georgia not only for reasons of security *"but also to secure a more abundant and easy supply of food."* That this humane action was accompanied by such high morbidity and mortality rates was indeed tragic, but these developments, he was convinced, were the result of "the exhausted condition of the Confederate Government" and not the product of a heinous plot on the part of the southern leaders to destroy a hapless captive enemy. "The same principle," Jones asserted, "which led me to endeavor to deal humanely and justly by those prisoners, and to make a truthful representation of their condition to the Medical Department of the Confederate States army, now actuates me in recording my belief that as far as my knowledge extends there was no deliberate or wilful design on the part of the Chief Executive, Jefferson Davis, and the highest authorities of the Confederate Government to injure the health and destroy the lives of these Federal prisoners."[13]

Again Jones's appeal fell on deaf ears; once more he was ordered to hand over his report. Sensing the futility of protesting further, he visited the Old Capitol Building, the scene of the court, on October 3 and surrendered his manuscript to Chipman, who "expressed himself as greatly pleased & pronounced it exceedingly valuable."[14]

There was to be a delay of several days while the report was read and abstracted. Jones used this time to visit the Smithsonian Institution, the Patent Office, and the Medical Museum. He especially enjoyed his trip to the Medical Museum. "The Yankees," he observed, "have preserved an immense number of fractured bones & even entire limbs. Generals have sent their amputated legs with their compliments." He was struck by the many examples of "magnificent operations" performed by the Union surgeons, pointing out that they were "in striking contrast to our cramped & imperfect labors." Jones made friends with the museum's director, who allowed him to examine exhibits in which he was interested and promised to lend assistance in attempting to locate his reports for the Confederate surgeon general which had been lost when the South evacuated Richmond.[15]

On October 7, near the end of the three-month trial, Jones was sworn as a witness. While the former Andersonville inmates were encouraged to paint a devastating picture of the prison and Wirz, Jones was neither asked nor allowed to report mitigating or extenuating circumstances of any kind. His brief testimony was largely limited to the identification of his report. Chipman questioned Jones for the prosecution. His initial questions were mere formalities—education, occupation, current position, role in the rebellion, reason for visiting Andersonville, and disposition of his findings. At this point Jones was confronted with the prosecution's abstract of his manuscript, which was subsequently offered in evidence. To his surprise and dismay the 600-page report had been reduced to a mere 20 pages. Much of the material deleted had indeed been extraneous, but Jones was justifiably upset when he discovered that any passage favorable to the Confederacy and even those in which he had attempted to explain the reasons for the abominable conditions at Andersonville had been expunged.[16] He considered the abstract to be "a most unfair & garbled statement" of his labors, complaining to his wife: "Everything relating to the climate, health, purity of the waters, & to the privations & sufferings of the Confederate Armies, as well as to the reports of the various surgeons, showing the difficulties with which they contended, were carefully excluded."[17] The remaining portion presented Andersonville at its worst. Chipman later readily admitted this, pointing out that "for our present purpose it furnished indubitable proof that the horrors of Andersonville have not been overdrawn . . . . in fact, for graphic and harrowing description of human suffering, it excels anything spoken by witnesses who were themselves victims."[18]

The remainder of Chipman's examination was aimed at clarifying several terms and points in the report generally favorable to the prosecution. The following exchange concluded the judge advocate's inquiries:

Q. Have your sympathies been with the rebellion during the war?

A. Entirely so.

Q. Then your report was made out in the interest of the confederate government?

A. In the interest of the confederate government; for the use of the medical department; in the view that no eye would ever see it but that of the surgeon general. I beg leave to make a statement to the court. That portion of my report which has been read is only a small part of the report. The original report contains the excuses which were given by the officers present at Andersonville, which I thought it right to embody in my labors; it also contains documents forwarded to Richmond by Dr. White and Dr. Stevenson and others in charge of the hospitals. Those documents contained important facts as to the labors of the medical department and their efforts to better the condition of things.

Q. Are your conclusions correctly stated in this extract?

A. Part of my conclusions are stated; not the whole. A portion of my conclusions and also my recommendations are not stated.

Q. Touching the subject of exchange?

A. Yes, sir; the general difficulties environing the prisoners and their officers.

Q. But the condition of things at Andersonville you have correctly described in the report of which this is an extract?

A. I endeavored to do so in that report so far as my means of investigation would allow. I would also state that the results of my examination of gangrene, scurvy, and other diseases have been omitted from the report. They were very extended. I was there for three weeks and made some score of post-mortem examinations. I endeavored, in this report to the surgeon general, to condense the results of all those labors; in fact that was the end and aim of the investigation.

Otis Baker, the defense counsel, did nothing to exploit this opening, and his line of questioning appeared to do little to aid Wirz. He asked: What had become of Jones's original report? Had he prepared the abstract himself? When had he gone to Andersonville? How long had he remained there? Did he examine prisoners in both the hospital and stockade? What type of cornbread were the prisoners fed? Had he seen any cases of starvation? Why had the Union prisoners been forced to act as their own nurses? Had he seen Wirz while at Andersonville? Why had Wirz refused him permission to enter the stockade? The only discernible opportunity Jones was given to aid Wirz was the following exchange:

Q. Would these prisoners have died in the same numbers if they had been at home instead of at Andersonville?

A. I should say not.

Q. Was it a general thing there for the prisoners to curse the general government, or was it only done by a few?

A. If I recollect aright, it was the time when there was a good deal of excitement about General McClellan's election, and that excitement seemed to pervade even the prisoners. Many of them were desirous of voting for McClellan, in the belief that they would be exchanged, and they spoke about the government in that connection.

Baker's final question was one of the most telling in the entire examination, for it clearly revealed the direction of the trial. "You have stated that in your original report you made some remarks upon the conduct of the officers at Andersonville?" The judge advocate objected to the question, arguing that cross-examination "must be confined to the report that had been produced in the court." The question was withdrawn. The implication was clear: not only had Jones's report been robbed of its true significance but any attempt to restore any portions favorable to the South were to be quashed.[19]

Participation in the Wirz trial was one of the most painful experiences of Jones's life. He viewed Chipman with unmitigated animosity, believing that he had "deliberately endeavored to arouse the hatred of the entire North" against him and the medical officers of the Confederacy.[20] The judge advocate's closing argument readily lent itself to such a charge; his assessment of Jones's investigations is a good case in point. Chipman saw no humanitarian interest in this research. Instead he professed outrage that Jones was ordered to Andersonville. "When we remember," Chipman charged, "that the surgeon general had been apprised of the wants of that prison, and that he had overlooked the real necessities of the prison . . . it is hard to conceive with what devilish malice, or criminal devotion to his profession, or reckless disregard of the high duties imposed upon him—I scarcely know which—he could sit down and deliberately pen such a letter of instruction as that given Dr. Jones." Warming to the issue, he emotionally inveighed:

Was it not enough to have cruelly starved and murdered our soldiers? Was it not enough to have sought to wipe out their very memories by burying them in nameless graves? Was it not enough to have instituted a system of medical treatment the very embodiment of charlatanism? Was not this enough, without adding to the many other diabolical motives which must have governed the perpetrators of these acts, this scientific object, as deliberate and cold-blooded as one can conceive?

"The surgeon general," he continued,

could quiet his conscience, when the matter was laid before him . . . by indorsing that it was impossible to send medical officers to take the place of the contract physicians on duty at Andersonville. Yet he could select, at the same time, a distinguished gentleman of the medical profession and send him to Andersonville, directing the whole force of surgeons there to render him every assistance, leaving their multiplied duties for that purpose! Why? Not to alleviate the sufferings of the prisoners; not to convey to them one ounce more of nutritious food; to make suggestions for the improvement of their sanitary condition; for no purpose of the kind; but, as the letter of instructions itself shows, for no other purpose than "that this great field for pathological investigation may be explored for the benefit of the *medical department* of the confederate armies."

"The Andersonville prison, so far as the surgeon general is concerned," Chipman concluded, "was a mere dissecting room, a clinic institute to be made tributary to the medical department of the Confederate armies."[21]

It was impossible for Joseph Jones to stomach this harsh assessment of his work and vilification of his esteemed friend, Samuel P. Moore. He had no recourse, however, but to bear up under both. There was little to comfort him, except for the belief that his every action during the ordeal of the Wirz trial had been "in entire sympathy" with his "distressed fellow Countrymen."[22]

Dejected and bitter, Jones returned to Augusta where he resumed teaching at the Medical College of Georgia.[23] He remained a defender of the South's recourse to war the rest of his life, but as time passed his bitterness toward the North slowly faded. Moreover he was caught up in a paradoxical development that greatly assuaged the sting of defeat. Instead of attempting to obliterate all recollection of this appalling fratricidal struggle which had brought irreparable loss of life and property and had nearly destroyed the Union, Americans enshrined it as a cause celebre. This was especially the case in the South with the rise of the cult of the lost cause.

The lingering interest in the war made Jones a minor celebrity, since no one, with the exception of Surgeon General Samuel P. Moore, was as well informed on the medical history of the Confederacy. He had been on intimate terms with and had worked directly for Moore; he had traveled extensively throughout the eastern theater of the war; he had done research in the main southern hospitals; he had the only remaining copies of many of the records of the Confederate medical department (making him a leading authority on southern numbers, losses, and diseases); he had carefully studied the effects of the most important diseases—pneumonia, gangrene, diarrhea and dysentery, the various fevers, and tetanus—upon the Confederate armies; and he was the undisputed authority on Andersonville.

Jones took full advantage of his unique position and wrote extensively on his wartime experiences and Confederate medical history. His studies on the medical aspects of the war in the South appeared not only in the leading medical journals, both North and South, but were also included in such northern memorabilia as the United States Sanitary Commission's *Sanitary Memoirs of the War of the Rebellion* and *Surgical Memoirs of the War of the Rebellion*. In addition his expertise on Confederate casualties was recognized by the compilers of the official *Medical and Surgical History of the War of the Rebellion*. Jones's most ambitious undertaking was a full-scale medical history of the Confederacy, which he was writing at the time of his death in 1896.[24]

Much of Joseph Jones's literary output on the war is of little value. But some of it is of considerable importance, for it adds a sobering dimension to this much-romanticized rebellion. "Every great war," Allan Nevins has reminded us, "has two sides, the

glorious and the terrible." Too long has the glorious side of the
Civil War been eulogized and the terrible suppressed. This conflict was not a glory road as Bruce Catton would have us believe
but "a terrible reproach to American civilization."[25] The tremendous toll of battle and disease prove this point beyond contention. An examination, even a cursory one, of Jones's studies
of Andersonville, gangrene in the Confederate armies, southern
numbers and losses, and Confederate medical history makes one
starkly aware of the terrible. Although a defender of the war
Joseph Jones never forgot its horrors, not just the horrors of
battle but "the depressing effects of prolonged muscular exertion upon soldiers scantily clothed & improperly fed, & subjected to all the depression & efforts of a hopeless contest
against overwhelming odds."[26]

Chapter 9
Andersonville

The haggard, distressed countenances of these
miserable, complaining, dejected living
skeletons crying for medicine and food . . .
formed a picture of helpless, hopeless misery,
which it would be impossible to portray by words
or by the brush.

The arrest, condemnation, and execution of Henry Wirz spurred
a heated debate about Andersonville prison. On the one hand
outraged northerners have vehemently contended that Andersonville's unspeakable horrors were the result of a cold-blooded
conspiracy by leading Confederates to murder helpless prisoners;
on the other, the southern apologists, although fewer in number,
have vociferously countered, attributing the suffering and death
to the prostrate state of the Confederacy. The arguments on
both sides are painfully lacking in objectivity. The inevitable
result has been a confusion of voices.[1]

Yet one voice stands out from all the rest—that of Joseph
Jones. He too was partisan, absolving the South of all blame for
Andersonville. But unlike most, whether in the North or the
South, Jones painstakingly portrayed conditions there in a full
and frank fashion from firsthand knowledge. His motive for
going to Andersonville was equally commendable. Far from using
these prisoners for guinea pigs, as his detractors have loudly
claimed, Jones genuinely hoped that an exhaustive investigation
of "the causes of the great mortality amongst the Federal prisoners" would reveal "the best methods of remedying existing evils."[2]

Gradually the true significance of Jones's Andersonville investigations was recognized—even by his former foes. This recognition began as early as 1867, when the United States Sanitary
Commission included his report in the first volume of its *Sanitary*

Memoirs of the War of the Rebellion. He was the only southern author so honored. The published manuscript was essentially a copy of the one confiscated and emasculated by the Wirz tribunal. Jones's only additions were the completion of several unfinished sections and a short preface in which he introduced his investigations. With the exception of some abridgment necessitated by its great length, the report was published without alteration. The deleted portions—a number of unnecessary tables, a large amount of extraneous background material, a chapter on postmortem findings in cases of diarrhea, dysentery, scurvy, and gangrene, and a chapter on hospital gangrene—neither detracted from nor changed the nature of the study. Indeed, almost as if he wished to rectify the injustice handed it at the Wirz trial, the editor emphasized: "In making the necessary abridgement nothing has been excluded of importance as affecting either the investigations or the conclusions deduced therefrom by Professor Jones."[3]

The report began with an exhaustive examination of the medical topography of Andersonville and the surrounding countryside, encompassing geology, soils, waters, flora, fauna, and climate. The only natural health hazard Jones uncovered was an abundance of vermin and insects. The sandy soil provided "a most suitable and healthy habitation" for fleas, and mosquitos swarmed "in untold myriads," making life at night "all but intolerable by their everlasting buzzing and troublesome bites." Like many of the prisoners, Jones was "so stung by these pestiferous insects" that it looked as if he was "suffering from a slight attack of measles." Reportedly this region had not been troubled by fleas and mosquitoes before the establishment of the prison, and Jones postulated that their proliferation might be attributable to the immense amount of filth generated by the prisoners.[4]

The emphasis, however, was upon salubrity. "No blame," Jones was convinced, "can be attached to the Confederate authorities for the collection of the Federal prisoners at this elevated and healthy locality, which was more salubrious than one half of the territory of South Carolina, Georgia, Alabama, Mississippi, and Louisiana."[5] He was especially impressed with the remarkable quality of the waters around Andersonville. For contrast he compared the stream which served as the prisoners' principal water supply and sole sewage system as it entered and exited the stockade. At the former point it was "of great purity";

at the later it was "loaded with filth and human excrement" and emitted "an intolerable and most sickening stench." "Standing as I did over these waters in the middle of a hot day in September, as they rolled sluggishly forth from the Stockade, after having received the filth and excrements of twenty thousand men," Jones recalled, "the stench was disgusting and overpowering; and if it was surpassed in unpleasantness by any thing, it was only in the disgusting appearance of the filthy, almost stagnant, waters moving slowly between the stumps and roots and fallen trunks of trees and thick branches of reeds, with innumerable long-tailed, large white maggots, swollen pease, and fermenting excrements, and fragments of bread and meat."[6]

This sickening state of affairs was man's doing, not nature's, a fact which served to bolster Jones's belief that the real reasons for Andersonville's frightful mortality were not to be found in natural factors but in human ones. "As far as my physical and pathological investigations extended," he asserted, "I was compelled to believe that the diseases which proved so fatal to the Federal prisoners confined at Andersonville, Georgia, were due to causes other than those connected with the soil, waters and climate." That the heat "may have promoted the rapid decomposition of the filth which, in violation of all hygienic laws, was allowed to accumulate in the Stockade and hospital grounds . . . and may have proved a cause of debility" was indisputable. "But still," he reiterated, "the fearful mortality could not properly be referred to this condition of climate, or to all the other elements of climate combined."[7] The true culprits, Jones suspected, were to be found within the prison walls.

The unsightly horrors of war he had witnessed in the armies and hospitals of the South had, Jones thought, inured him against human suffering, but he was totally unprepared for the sad spectacle which confronted him upon entering the stockade. From wall to wall there was a churning sea of sullen, suffering humanity. It took only a cursory perusal to spot the physical sources of this incredible misery: they were everywhere apparent —overcrowding, inadequate shelter, and filth. These things, when coupled with the effects of the prisoners' faulty diet and protracted confinement, made Andersonville's mounting morbidity and mortality readily understandable.

Overcrowding and its results were especially noticeable. Constructed to accommodate 10,000 prisoners, the Andersonville stockade, as we have seen, encompassed seventeen acres when it was opened in February 1864. Four months later it was enlarged by ten acres in order to make room for the ever-increasing numbers of prisoners sent there. Still, as table 3 shows, the burgeoning prison population soon outgrew the expanded facilities and over-crowding became steadily worse. The actual situation, Jones found, was even more distressing than these figures indicated, for much of the land lying along the stream which bisected the stockade "was low and boggy and was covered with excrements of the men and thus rendered wholly uninhabitable." Consequently a great deal of much-needed space was lost. Overcrowding forced the prisoners "to perform all the offices of life,— cooking, washing, urinating, defecation, exercise, and sleeping" within the confines of a few square feet.[8] The health hazard was obvious.

The lack of adequate shelter was equally noticeable. The prison had been built in a sparsely wooded area and was soon denuded by the prisoners in search of firewood. The few "old, torn, and rotten" tents which the prison officials distributed did little to help matters. Left to their own ingenuity to protect themselves from the sun, rain, and extremes of the Georgia climate, the prisoners constructed all manner of makeshift shelters. They were monuments to man's imagination, for as Jones noted, the surface of the stockade, with the exception of the uninhabitable portion along the stream, was covered with "huts and small, ragged tents, and parts of blankets and fragments of oil-cloth, coats, and blankets stretched upon sticks."

Because of the already large number of prisoners and the con-

TABLE 3

Overcrowding at Andersonville

Month 1864	Mean strength, Federal prisoners	Area of stockade in sq. feet	Average number of sq. ft. to each prisoner
March	7,500	740,520	98.7
April	10,000	740,520	74.0
May	15,000	740,520	49.3
June	22,291	740,520	33.2
July	29,030	1,176,120	40.5
August	32,899	1,176,120	35.7

stant influx of new ones Wirz and his lieutenants were unable to exercise supervision over the construction of these hovels. The ensuing hodgepodge arrangement, where there was "scarcely room for two men to walk abreast between the tents and huts," would have threatened a highly organized program of camp and personal hygiene. At Andersonville internal affairs—security and sanitation in particular—were left up to the prisoners. Thus, even basic sanitary procedures were nonexistent. The result was both disgusting and disastrous. Jones observed men "urinating and evacuating their bowels at the very tent doors and around the little vessels in which they were cooking their food"; small pits "not more than a foot or two deep nearly filled with soft offensive faeces" were found throughout the stockade and "emitted, under a hot sun, a strong and disgusting odor"; and "masses of corn-bread, bones, old rags, and filth of every description" were piled or scattered everywhere.[9]

Personal hygiene was also shamefully neglected as one of Jones's personal experiences vividly depicted. One night during his stay a heavy rain fell. The next morning while walking down one of the stockade's narrow streets he was startled "at seeing a bold full-length figure of a man upon the smooth, well-beaten street." "There was," he exclaimed, "the well-defined nose, open mouth, and flowing beard in strong profile. It looked as if an exact daguerrotype of the man had been taken upon the filthy soil, saturated with urine and the washings of the food. The impression was life-like in all its proportions, and was of a much darker color than the surrounding soil." "Upon inquiry," he continued, "I found that the dead, as was the usual custom, had been removed out of the tent, and had remained there during the night. The descending rain washed off the filth from the clothes and body, and the carbon deposited from the smoke of the pine wood used in cooking. From each point of the body, and the scant covering of clothing, poured a stream of black filth, which painted the body full-length upon the ground."[10]

The prisoners, Jones asserted, appeared to be "utterly callous" to the filth around them, making it "utterly impossible" to impose proper hygienic rules "without the constant presence of a Confederate guard within the stockade."[11] Despite the absence of such a force Jones did not hold the South responsible for Andersonville's filth, nor its overcrowding, nor its lack of shelter. On the contrary he laid the blame on circumstances over which the

Confederacy had little or no control. "Sorely pressed on every side," he contended, the southern leaders were simply unable to provide for "this large number of prisoners, which they have ever been anxious to exchange, and which [they] . . . believe to be forced upon their hands by the persistent action of the United States Government."[12]

No matter where the responsibility lay, conditions at Andersonville were horrifying. Sadly the treatment of the sick was little better than that accorded the well. At first all of the sick were treated in the stockade, but in May, three months after the opening of the prison, a hospital was established outside the walls. Two major problems prompted this move: the overcrowding in the stockade, where the prisoners' makeshift shelters were "clustered thickly" around the medical facilities, made it impossible "to secure proper ventilation or to maintain the necessary police"; and second, the frequent forays the other prisoners made upon the hospital stores, food, and clothing of the sick. Subsequently patients were divided between the hospital and the stockade: acute cases were treated in the former and less serious ones in the latter.[13]

The sick in the prison were housed in several long sheds located in the northern end of the stockade. Originally built as barracks, they were two-story but were open on all sides. Those patients treated here, Jones discovered, "lay upon bare boards, or upon such ragged blankets as they possessed" without, as far as he could tell, any bedding, not even straw. Pits designed to serve as latrines had been dug within a few feet of the lower floor but were seldom used because of neglect and the debilitating effect of scurvy, diarrhea, and dysentery.[14]

Conditions in the hospital were perhaps even more distressing. Situated on a five-acre site near the southeastern corner of the prison, it was plagued by all of the stockade's major problems. The water supply, a stream also, had been quickly turned into an "immense cesspool." The ensuing stench was exacerbated by the proximity of the stockade, for the marsh into which its filth-laden stream emptied lay nearby, producing "deleterious influences" upon the sick.

More than 2,000 patients and attendants had been crowded into this confined area with predictable results. There was such a shortage of space that many of the sick were forced to pitch their tents within a few yards of the stream, even that portion used for a privy. Shelter was grossly inadequate. In general the patients were "poorly supplied with old and ragged tents," but Jones reported that some of them had neither protection against the elements nor bunks and "lay upon the ground, ofttimes without even a blanket."

Sanitary measures were worse, if possible, than they had been in the stockade. Wooden boxes placed along the streets between the tents for the use of those patients who were unable to walk to the privies over the stream were not emptied until completely filled. Time and again Jones saw men he felt to be strong enough to utilize the outdoor facilities urinating at the doors of their tents. Not surprising, he found the air of the tents "foul and disagreeable in the extreme." "In fact," he added, "the entire grounds emitted a most nauseous and disgusting smell." The cooking arrangements, which Jones denounced as miserable and defective, were a further source of filth. "Two large pots, similar to those used for boiling sugarcane," he revealed, "were the only cooking utensils furnished by the hospital for the cooking of near two thousand men." Forced to rely in great measure "upon their own miserable utensils," the sick cooked in their tent doors and in the streets.

The total lack of concern for camp police and sanitation was well illustrated by a large pile of molding cornbread, bones, and all manner of filth, some thirty feet across and several feet high and swarming with "myriads of flies," which dominated a vacant area near the cooking pots. And if mosquitoes made the patients' lives miserable at night, then flies did the same during the day, for owing to the extreme filth these bothersome insects were everywhere. "Millions of flies," as Jones graphically put it, "swarmed over every thing and covered the faces of the sleeping patients, and crawled down their open mouths and deposited their maggots in the gangrenous wounds of the living and in the mouths of the dead."[15]

That there was an important connection between filth and disease was obvious to Jones, and he found conditions at Andersonville frightening. But he was outraged by the almost absolute neglect for the personal cleanliness of the sick throughout the prison. To the man, they were "literally incrusted with dirt and covered with vermin." Moreover it was a frequent sight, Jones asserted, to see dying men brought to the hospital from the stockade "begrimed from head to foot with excrements, and so black from smoke and filth that they resembled negroes rather than white men." Most of this problem was a product of the general low state of hygiene in the prison; some of it grew out of a general lack of concern for the diseased by their fellow prisoners; but far too much of it was attributable to the hospital attendants, usually paroled prisoners, who "neglected the comfort and cleanliness" of the sick "in a most shameful manner."[16]

An extreme shortage of medical officers worsened the plight of the sick. The surgeon-in-charge found it virtually impossible to induce physicians to come to Andersonville. Jones attributed this situation to a variety of factors: the absence of necessary facilities, the consequent unsatisfactory results of practice and distressing nature of the duty, the remoteness of the area, the pressing medical problems in other parts of Georgia created by Sherman's invasion, the scarcity of physicians in the Confederacy, and, finally, the nature of the conflict, which tended "to excite such prejudices as would disincline medical officers from voluntarily seeking service amongst the captive enemies, who are the representatives of those who are seeking to conquer and desolate their native land." Those that did come frequently became so thoroughly discouraged that they "endeavored to get transfers to other fields of labor, preferring the hardships and exposures of service at the front." Those who braved the obstacles and stayed were often unable to perform their duties because overwork and "exhalations from the sick and filth" disabled them. This was especially true of the surgeons serving in the stockade.[17] To help compensate for the shortage of medical personnel the surgeon-in-charge had a number of prisoners paroled or pressed into duty as nurses and attendants. The results of this policy were mixed. The basic idea was sound; but as we have mentioned, far too often the parolees ignored or mistreated the sick. Jones preferred to view their shortcomings as "the result of carelessness and inattention rather than of malignant design."[18]

The magnitude of suffering at Andersonville was staggering; and as table 4 shows, Joseph Jones objectively reported it. He warned, however, that these carefully prepared statistics gave only part of the picture, for owing "to the insufficiency of medical officers and the extreme illness, and even death, of many prisoners in tents in the stockade without any medical attention or record beyond the bare number of the dead" they were "far below the truth."[19] Jones also called attention to the fact that Anderson-

TABLE 4
Consolidated Report of Sick Prisoners at Andersonville, March–August 1864

	March	April	May	June	July	August
Remaining last report	—	636	1,022	2,621	4,078	6,412
Cases during month	1,530	2,425	8,583	7,969	10,624	10,915
Supervening diseases	—	—	—	—	210	431
Aggregate	1,530	3,061	9,605	10,590	14,912	17,758
Returned to duty	353	1,463	6,276	5,311	6,548	9,443
Died	283	576	708	1,201	1,952	2,992
Remaining	894	1,022	2,621	4,078	6,412	5,323
Mean strength	7,500	10,000	15,000	22,291	29,030	32,899
Percentage of mean strength incurring illness during month	20.4	24.3	57.2	35.5	36.6	33.2
Ratio of sick to mean strength—one sick in every:	4.9	4.1	1.7	2.8	2.7	3.0
Percentage of sick dying during month	18.5	23.8	8.2	15.1	18.4	27.4
Percentage of mean strength dying during month	3.8	5.8	4.7	5.4	6.7	9.1
Ratio of deaths to mean strength—one dead in every:	26.3	17.2	21.3	18.5	14.9	11.0

TABLE 5

Consolidated Report of Sickness among the Confederate Guards at Andersonville, July–August 1864

	Cases	Deaths	Mean strength
July	1,258	29	3,881
August	1,236	33	3,629
TOTALS	2,494	62	

ville's rampant sickness was not limited to the prisoners; it had seriously undermined the health of the Confederate garrison too. Although statistics, shown in table 5, were available for the southerners during July and August only, he accepted them as indicative of their general health profile.[20]

The most glaring disparity between these two sets of figures is in the mortality of the two groups. Almost 41,000 Union soldiers, Jones learned, had been sent to Andersonville from the opening of the prison in February 1864 to the time of his visit in September. Of this number 9,479 (23.3 percent or 1 in nearly every 4) had died. The death rate had climbed precipitously, rising from 3.8 percent in March to a perilous 9.1 percent in August. The Confederate garrison, on the other hand, sustained less than 2 percent fatalities during the two-month period for which statistics were available. The reasons for the marked difference in mortality, Jones felt, were easily discernible. There were two main ones: first, there was the portentous accumulation of "the sources of disease" in the stockade and hospital—"the increase of excrements and filth of all kinds," "the concentration of noxious effluvia," and "the progressive effects of the bad diet, crowding, and hot climate"; the second reason, "home-sickness and the disappointment, mental depression, and distress attending the daily longings for an apparently hopeless release," was, he contended, "as potent . . . in the destruction of these prisoners as the physical causes of actual disease."[21]

For the sake of discussion Jones divided the diseases found at Andersonville into three categories according to alleged origin: those produced by climatic changes and exposure, those caused by a specific poison, and those attributed to protracted confinement and poor diet. The chief climatic disorder was thought to be malaria. The incursions of this great southern endemic at Andersonville presented a curious anomaly. "The march of malarial

TABLE 6

Effect of Malaria on the Prisoners at Andersonville,
March–August 1864

	Cases	Deaths
March	72	7
April	49	5
May	1,162	19
June	662	22
July	506	24
August	515	42
TOTALS	2,966	119

fever amongst these Federal prisoners," Jones discovered, "did not conform to the almost universal law of the progressive increase of these diseases during the months of May, June, July, August, and September in the Southern States." Indeed, as table 6 shows, after a high of 1,162 cases in May the incidence of malaria decreased sharply during subsequent months.[22]

A similar contradiction did not occur among the Confederate guards who sustained almost 600 cases during July and August. In fact, findings from his extensive wartime research showed that malaria prevailed to a far greater extent among southern soldiers serving in all sections of the South than it did among the Union prisoners at Andersonville. Jones was puzzled, for the reverse should have been the case since these prisoners were held captive in "a hot, and to a certain extent, malarious climate" and were "to a great extent unaccustomed to either the extreme heat, or the malaria of the swamps" while the Confederate troops "were natives of the soil" and had, in many cases, been "subjected to these influences from birth." Unable to unravel this mystery he erroneously conjectured: "We can only account for the comparative immunity of the Federal prisoners on the supposition that the artificial atmosphere created by the immense accumulations of filth and human excrements within and around the Stockade and Hospital counteracted or destroyed in some unknown manner the malarial poison."[23]

Exposure-related diseases, attributed to continuous imprisonment without proper clothing or shelter, included pneumonia, pleurisy, bronchitis, catarrh, laryngitis, tonsillitis, and rheumatism. As was to be expected the ratio of these disorders to the

TABLE 7

Effect of Diseases Caused by Specific Poisons on the
Prisoners at Andersonville, March–August 1864

	Typhus		Typhoid fever		Smallpox		Measles	
	Cases	Deaths	Cases	Deaths	Cases	Deaths	Cases	Deaths
March	0	0	67	28	28	5	10	0
April	0	0	56	18	73	34	6	1
May	0	0	92	17	13	10	40	3
June	0	0	18	32	1	10	8	2
July	0	0	39	58	4	8	3	0
August	0	0	200	32	0	1	1	1
TOTALS	0	0	472	185	119	68	68	7

total number of cases steadily diminished as the weather became warmer, declining from 24.3 percent in March to 11.1 percent in August. Deaths from them followed a similar pattern, falling from 32.8 percent to 2.3 percent during the same period. Of these diseases pneumonia was the most important. This pneumococcal inflammation of the lungs attacked only 2.5 percent (528 cases) of the prison's mean strength but almost 50 percent of those affected died. These figures, Jones reported, corresponded closely with the effect of pneumonia on the Confederate armies.[24]

Specific poisons produced by the crowding and the "foul exhalations" of the prison were thought to cause typhus, typhoid fever, smallpox, and measles. As table 7 reveals, the incidence of these disorders varied greatly.[25] Jones quickly dispensed with typhus. He had heretofore searched diligently for this scourge of European armies without success, uncovering only a few misdiagnosed cases of typhoid fever. But he had not visited Andersonville where the conditions for its presence seemed ideal—so ideal, in fact, that Jones "supposed that if typhus fever existed anywhere in the Confederate States it would be found at Andersonville, and especially amongst the foreign element of the Federal armies, which had been but recently imported from the bogs of Ireland, and from the hovels of the densely populated European countries." His careful search yielded no trace of typhus, convincing him that it was not to be found in the southern armies, hospitals, or military prisons.[26]

The incidence of typhoid fever at Andersonville was surprisingly low. It accounted for slightly more than 1 percent of the total number of cases treated. Moreover the ratio of typhoid cases to mean strength was well over twice as great among the Confederate guards as it was among the prisoners—1 in 37 as opposed to 1 in 86. Jones had a ready and probably accurate explanation for this disparity, pointing out that these southern soldiers were mainly reserves who had been recently inducted and had not yet "passed through the diseases of the camp" while most of the prisoners had been held captive for as long as two years and those who had not had this fever previously either contracted it during their confinement or else long exposure had made them immune.[27]

The occurrence of smallpox was also slight, a fact Jones attributed to the foresight of the Confederate medical officers who acted quickly to halt its spread through mass vaccination. "Untoward results" followed in a number of cases. Large unsightly ulcers resembling those of gangrene appeared at the points of vaccination, "causing extensive destruction of the tissues, and necessitating amputation in more than one instance." These aberrations led to the widespread belief among the prisoners that the physicians "had intentionally introduced poisonous matter into their arms"—a charge frequently made at the Wirz trial.[28] Jones denounced this allegation, labelling it "as malicious as it was false." He freely confessed that in every collection of men it was possible to find some unprincipled individual and that the Confederate medical officers at Andersonville probably represented no exception to the general frailties of mankind. "But this I do know by personal observation," he avowed, "that they deplored the distressing fate of these unfortunate victims . . . and earnestly desired to do their duty in the cause of suffering humanity."[29]

Spurious vaccination, as the secondary infections arising from vaccination were called, was no stranger to Jones; he had seen numerous cases in the Confederate armies and hospitals. In fact, this phenomenon had become so widespread by 1864 that Moore ordered the southern surgeons to make it the subject of a special investigation. Jones's research unveiled a variety of causative factors: a scorbutic condition of the blood, the use of vaccine matter from subjects who had been only partially protected or who were suffering from erysipelas or secondary syphilis, and the use of vaccine matter which, owing to the effects of the warm, humid southern climate, had started to decompose.

Applying these findings to spurious vaccination among the Andersonville prisoners, Jones concluded: "These accidents were . . . referable in a great measure, if not wholly, to the scorbutic condition of their blood and to the crowded condition of the Stockade and Hospital." In support of this assertion he called attention to the increased incidence of gangrene at Andersonville. Its prevalence, he maintained, was concrete proof that the blood of the prisoners was in such a scorbutic state that similar infections "would most probably have attacked any puncture made by a lancet without any vaccine matter or any other extraneous material." In fact the "foul ulcers" and gangrene which followed the slightest injuries prevented Jones from drawing blood from the prisoners for use in his scientific experiments. "I did not feel justified," he explained, "in subjecting these prisoners of war to the inconvenience and dangers of bloodletting for purely scientific purposes."[30]

Scurvy, diarrhea, dysentery, and hospital gangrene, Jones learned, were the diseases responsible for the extraordinary mortality of Andersonville. He attributed them to poor diet and protracted confinement. Dietetic disorders—scurvy, anasarca, ascites, marasma, and debility—were commonplace. Of these scurvy was not only the most prevalent but was also the most dangerous, since, according to Jones, a scorbutic condition "modified the course of every disease, poisoned every wound, however slight, and lay at the foundation of those obstinate and exhausting diarrhoeas and dysenteries which swept off thousands of these unfortunate men."[31] "The effects of scurvy," he remarked, "were manifest on every hand, and in all its various stages, from the muddy pale complexion, pale gums, feeble, languid, muscular motions, lowness of spirits, and fetid breath; to the dusky, dirty, leaden complexion, swollen features, spongy, purple, livid, fungoid, bleeding gums, loose teeth, oedematous limbs, covered with livid vibices and petechiae, spasmodically flexed, painful and hardened extremities, spontaneous hemorrhages from mucous canals, and large, ill-conditioned spreading ulcers covered with a dark purplish fungous growth."[32]

Pointing to the "remarkable healthy and strong appearance of the paroled prisoners, who were allowed an extra ration, and who were able to supply themselves with whatever vegetables the country afforded by the sums of money which they made in trade with their fellow-prisoners and the Confederate soldiers,"

TABLE 8

Effect of Scurvy on the Prisoners at Andersonville,
March–August 1864

	Cases	Deaths
March	15	0
April	50	0
May	1,221	14
June	2,097	68
July	3,092	195
August	3,026	722
TOTALS	9,501	999

Jones correctly attributed the great prevalence of scurvy, shown in table 8, to the character rather than the quantity of the food, or, as he put it, "the effects of salt meat and of farinaceous food without fresh vegetables."[33] The Andersonville prisoners in both the stockade and the hospital, Jones claimed, "received the same ration in kind, quality, and amount issued to the Confederate soldiers in the field." Such fare—"corn-bread, rice, bacon, and beef, with occasional supplies of green pease, molasses, and vinegar"—was insufficient to ward off scurvy. "As far as my experience extended," he contended, "no body of troops could be confined exclusively to the Confederate ration without suffering materially in their health, and without manifesting symptoms of the scurvy."[34] A marked increase in the incidence of this disorder in the southern armies late in the war supported this contention. Had it not been for an "immense amount of extra supplies" furnished by friends, relatives, state agencies, and benevolent societies and obtained through foraging, the Confederate soldiers would have been stricken by the severe and fatal forms of scurvy which preyed upon the prisoners.[35]

Diarrhea and dysentery, as table 9 shows, were the most persistent causes of disability and death at Andersonville. It is difficult indeed to overestimate their impact, for as Jones observed, "almost every prisoner was afflicted with either diarrhoea or dysentery." He offered a variety of reasons for the "great prevalence of bowel affections." These included the adverse effects of exposure, inadequate shelter, and accumulations of dust, smoke, and filth on the functioning of the body and skin; the noxious odors of the stockade; scurvy and its sequelae; im-

TABLE 9

Effect of Diarrhea and Dysentery on the Prisoners at Andersonville, March–August 1864

	Diarrhea		Dysentery	
	Cases	Deaths	Cases	Deaths
March	481	77	185	41
April	1,149	335	184	76
May	2,337	422	1,277	101
June	2,476	777	811	103
July	3,145	847	1,179	242
August	2,502	1,072	1,046	436
TOTALS	12,090	3,530	4,682	999

properly cooked food; and a prolonged diet of salt meat and coarse unbolted cornbread.[36]

Jones placed especial emphasis on the role of the prisoners' inadequate diet. In general they had been reared on wheat bread and Irish potatoes. Indian corn, a mainstay of the southern diet, was unknown to them prior to their capture. The prisoners found it disagreeable and distasteful, and Jones was sympathetic. He insisted that southern cornbread was "one of the most wholesome and nutritious forms of food, as has been clearly shown by the health and rapid increase of the southern population, and especially of the negroes, previous to the present war, and by the strength endurance, and activity of the Confederate soldiers" but at the same time admitted that "it is nevertheless true that those who have not been reared upon corn-meal, or who have not accustomed themselves to its use gradually, become excessively tired of this kind of diet when suddenly confined to it without a due proportion of wheat bread."[37]

A scarcity of sieves in the Confederacy further complicated matters as the prisoners were forced not only to eat cornbread but cornbread prepared from meal from which the husk had not been removed. The husk of the Indian corn seemed to produce "a decided irritant effect" on their intestinal canals. Soon, as might be expected, "immense piles" of decaying cornbread were found throughout the stockade and hospital. Those prisoners who became "so disgusted with this form of food that they had no appetite to partake of it" were quickly reduced to the condition of men slowly starving. "In this state," Jones observed, "the muscular strength was rapidly diminished, the tissues wasted, and the thin, skeleton-like forms moved about with the appearance of utter exhaustion and dejection." "In many cases," he continued, "even of the greatest apparent suffering and distress, instead of showing any anxiety to communicate the causes of their distress, or to relate their privations and their longings for their homes and their friends and relatives, they lay in a listless, lethargic, uncomplaining state, taking no notice either of their own distressed condition or of the gigantic mass of human misery by which they were surrounded." "Nothing," he exclaimed, "appalled and depressed me so much as this silent, uncomplaining misery."[38] That diarrhea and dysentery ensued is not surprising.

The therapeutic measures taken to combat these disorders were inadequate at best. Jones dismissed them as of "little or no beneficial effect." Admittedly opium "allayed pain and checked the bowels temporarily," but this "frail dam was soon swept away" and the hapless victim "appeared to be but little better, if not the worse, for this merely palliative treatment." "The root of the difficulty," Jones asserted, "could not be reached by drugs; nothing short of the wanting elements of nutrition would have tended in any manner to restore the tone of the digestive system." "My opinion to this effect," he added, "was expressed most decidedly to the medical officers in charge of these unfortunate men." He pointed to the "robust condition" of the paroled prisoners as proof of the validity of his contention.[39]

Gangrene was Jones's pet research project at the time of his visit to Andersonville, and thus it was guaranteed special attention. The bacterial origin of this unsightly much-feared killer was unknown to Civil War physicians. Jones attributed its appearance at Andersonville to those same factors which were responsible for dietetic disorders, diarrhea, and dysentery. "In the depraved and depressed condition of the systems of these prisoners, in the foul atmosphere of the stockade and hospital, reeking with noxious exhalations," he observed, "small injuries— as the injury inflicted by a splinter running into a hand or foot, the blistering of the arms or hands in the sun, or even the abrasions of the skin in scratching bites of insects—were sometimes followed by extensive and alarming gangrene ulceration."[40] The poisonous air of the prison was so virulent, he maintained, that its harmful effects extended to a considerable distance outside and was responsible for several cases of gangrene among the guards who had not entered the stockade but had only occupied the sentry boxes along its top.[41]

"The almost total absence of records" and "the imperfect organization of the hospital" prevented Jones from compiling accurate statistics on the incidence and mortality of gangrene at Andersonville. Available figures, which he viewed as "far below the truth," showed 267 cases and 25 deaths. Of these cases 102 were listed as supervening upon gunshot wounds, 12 followed vaccination, and the remainder attributed to a "scorbutic and deranged condition of the system." Only 67 amputations for gangrene were recorded. Jones also dismissed this figure as too low, remarking: "After careful inquiry, and personal examinations of the wards and patients, I was convinced that the number of amputations for hospital gangrene reached, and perhaps exceeded, one hundred." "The depressed condition of the prisoners" and "the foul atmosphere of the military prison hospital" unfortunately reduced amputation to a worthless procedure as the infection almost invariably returned. "Almost every amputation," Jones bemoaned, "was followed finally by death, either from the effects of gangrene or from the prevailing diarrhoea and dysentery."[42]

Conditions in the prison hospital insured that the fight the harried surgeons were waging against gangrene was to be a losing one: the uncontrolled filth and crowding made it impossible to protect the injured against infection; when a gangrenous wound needed cleaning "the limb was thrust out a little from the blanket or board or rags upon which the patient was lying, and water poured over it, and all the putrescent matter allowed to soak into the ground floor of the tent"; flies swarmed over wounds; the supply of rags for dressings was pitifully inadequate, and "the most filthy rags, which had been applied several times and imperfectly washed," were used in dressing recent wounds; and sponges and washbowls were also scarce—"the same wash-bowl and sponge serving for a score or more of the patients." There was, therefore, "such constant circulation of the gangrenous matter," Jones contended correctly, that the infection "might rapidly be propagated from a single gangrenous wound." In addition he displayed an early and commendable awareness, albeit empirical, of the vector role of flies in the transmission of gangrene, when he pointed out that "the numerous flies which swarmed around and over every ulcer without doubt formed efficient agents for the spread of hospital gangrene." His empiricism is all the more remarkable when it is recalled that it was not until the closing years of the nineteenth century, well after the onset of the bacteriological revolution in medicine, that the importance of carriers in the propagation of disease was generally understood.[43]

Joseph Jones sympathized wholeheartedly with the prisoners in their desperate struggle against disease and death. "In truth," he lamented,

> these men at Andersonville were in the condition of a crew at sea, confined upon a foul ship upon salt meat and unvarying food, and without fresh vegetables. Not only so, but these unfortunate prisoners were like men forcibly confined and crowded upon a ship tossed about on a stormy ocean, without a rudder, without a compass, without a guiding star, and without any apparent boundary or end to their voyage; and they reflected, in their steadily increased miseries, the distressed condition and waning fortunes of a devastated and bleeding country which was compelled, in justice to her own unfortunate sons, to hold these men in this most distressing captivity.[44]

Despite the South's waning fortunes Jones warned against overt malice toward these helpless victims of the war and hoped that his findings would provide the means of mitigating some of the misery. "With a sincere appreciation of the great difficulties of the situation," he presented for the consideration of the surgeon general those changes which he believed "essential to the relief of these suffering prisoners." There were five of them—an increase of the available area for each prisoner by at least fivefold and the establishment of an effective system of hygiene enforced by "a regularly appointed and accountable guard," the construction of suitable barracks and hospital buildings, an enlargement of the medical staff and the appointment of one or more chaplains, the detailing of disabled Confederate soldiers as nurses, wardmasters, and pharmacists, and the liberal issuing of fresh fruit and vegetables and milk to combat scurvy.[45]

Jones was, however, painfully aware of the limitations of the Confederacy late in the war. Much that needed to be done for the relief of the Andersonville prisoners simply could not be carried out. He was without doubt overly apologetic for the South, but he expressed the southern dilemma in a very convincing manner, writing:

As long as the Confederate government is compelled to hold these prisoners as hostages for the safe return and exchange of the captive men of its own armies, it is difficult to devise efficient measures for the mitigation of much of the suffering of such an immense army of prisoners (equal at least to one fourth of the Confederate forces actively engaged in the field, east of the Mississippi), in a purely agricultural and sparsely settled country, with imperfect lines of communication, with but few manufactories, without commerce, cut off from all communication with the surrounding world, deprived of even the necessary medicines which have been declared by its enemies "contraband of war," with torn and bleeding borders, with progressively diminishing powers of subsistence and resistence, with its entire fighting population in arms, and yet being steadily driven back and overpowered by the hosts of the enemy, with a constant driving in of the population from the constantly contracting borders upon the overcrowded and distressed centre, and with a corresponding increase of travel upon the delapidated railroads, already taxed far beyond their capacity with the transportation of troops, the munitions of war, and the sick and wounded.

"In Georgia, especially," he continued,

the very State in which these prisoners are confined, is the pressure of the Confederate disasters felt with daily increased force. The disastrous campaign in Northern Georgia has been attended with the desolation of the fairest portions of the State. Thousands of families from the devastated regions, and from all the towns and villages from Chattanooga to Atlanta and beyond, have fled to the regions considered more safe from invasion, and are occupying old cars, depots, sheds, and tents along the entire railroad system of Georgia. Thousands of old men, delicate women, and defenseless children, have not only lost all their earthly possessions, but are without a roof to cover their heads, and are dependent for their daily bread upon the charities of the State government. The hospitals attached to the army of Tennessee are in a constant state of motion, and the poorly fed and imperfectly treated wounded are suffering with the worst forms of hospital gangrene and pyaemia. Every available building, including churches and colleges and schoolhouses, suitable for hospital purposes, in all towns and villages, are crowded with the sick and wounded, and Georgia may with truth be said to be one vast hospital.[46]

Jones was in earnest when he insisted that the horrors of Andersonville were attributable to the Union's summary suspension of prisoner exchange and the Confederacy's subsequent inability to provide for an ever-increasing number of captives as it tottered on the brink of collapse. Therefore it would be unfair to dismiss his work as a mere whitewashing of the South. To do so would be to lose sight of its considerable value, because Joseph Jones has provided historians with the most complete account of the hell that was Andersonville. Nor should it be forgotten that he was sincerely grief-stricken at the plight of these prisoners and did everything in his power as a research scientist to improve their wretched lot. In fact he became so emotionally involved that he was never able to forget Andersonville; it was indelibly etched upon his mind. As long as Jones lived he would remember how "the haggard, distressed countenance of these miserable, complaining, dejected living skeletons crying for medicine and food, and cursing their government for its brutality in refusing to exchange prisoners, and the ghastly corpses with their glazed eyeballs, staring up into vacant space, with the flies swarming down their open and grinning mouths, and amongst the sick and dying, formed a picture of helpless, hopeless misery which it would be impossible to portray by words or by the brush."[47]

Chapter 10
Hospital Gangrene

*Abundant supplies of nutritious animal and
vegetable food, free ventilation, with the
largest possible supply of fresh air to each
patient, with scrupulous cleanliness of the
wounds, as well as of the person's clothing and
bedding, and apartments of the wounded, are
the great prophylactic measures against hospital
gangrene.*

Little known in the United States prior to the outbreak of the
Civil War, gangrene became one of the conflict's most serious
medical problems. In reality the generic term *gangrene*, or *hospital
gangrene* as this disorder was most commonly called, included a
wide range of streptococcic, staphylococcic, and other dangerous
infections. The prevalence of these secondary infections is readily
understood when one considers the general lack of knowledge
of the principles of antisepsis and asepsis, the unsanitary condition of hospitals, and the improper attention accorded wounds.
Unfortunately for the injured Civil War soldier Lord Lister's
revolutionary discoveries revealing the life-saving antiseptic
treatment of trauma came too late to be of help.

As we have seen, Joseph Jones first encountered hospital gangrene in July 1862, when he unsuccessfully treated a case while
serving as a civilian surgeon in the Augusta General Hospital.
This unsightly killer both shocked him and excited his interest,
and he sought opportunities to increase his knowledge of it.
Subsequently he studied gangrene's ravages in the Confederate
armies and hospitals in Georgia, South Carolina, and Virginia and
among the Union prisoners confined at Andersonville.[1]

The horrors of gangrene and the general impotence of the
southern surgeons in preventing or controlling it are painfully

clear in the following cases which Jones observed. A private from the 25th Regiment of Georgia Volunteers lost an arm during the battle of Chickamauga. He was sent to Augusta for treatment, where gangrene supervened. As was often the case in southern hospitals, his wife came to help nurse him. She wore a pair of new shoes which blistered her left foot just above the instep. For relief she walked about the hospital barefooted. Gangrene of a severe form soon appeared in the blister and spread rapidly, involving the bones of the tarsus. "As the floor, especially just under the gangrenous stump of her husband, contained more or less gangrenous matter, it is highly probable," Jones postulated, "that the matter was introduced directly into the foot through the blistered surface."[2]

A twenty-eight-year-old private from the 9th Mississippi Regiment, wounded on September 2, 1864, during the battle of Jonesboro, Georgia, was sent to Macon for treatment. His wound was caused by a minie ball which had passed through the muscles of the neck and shoulder above and almost parallel to the scapula. Gangrene supervened on September 20, and Jones examined the patient ten days later. The muscles of the neck, he discovered, were "extensively denuded," and the clavicle was exposed throughout a considerable portion of its anterior surface. "In the act of swallowing," he remarked, "the play of the muscles could be most distinctly seen and studied." Death mercifully ended this doomed soul's suffering on October 2 through a massive hemorrhage. An autopsy revealed that the infection had almost completely destroyed the external jugular vein.[3]

Toward the end of October 1864 a twenty-two-year-old soldier was admitted to the Ocmulgee General Hospital in Macon for advanced pneumonia. He was given ipecac and opium and blistered. A second blister was administered on November 7. That same evening a nurse mistakenly dressed the blister with a cloth which had been used in dressing a gangrenous wound. Within twenty-four hours there were unmistakable symptoms of gangrene in the whole blistered surface. The youth died of pneumonia, however, before gangrene had time to kill him.[4]

"Two stout negro women" were assigned to wash the rags used in dressing gangrenous wounds in Macon's gangrene hospital. They laundered these soiled dressings in a small stream over a half-mile from the hospital and never once entered the hospital enclosure; yet both were attacked by gangrene. The first to be stricken had abraded the backs of her wrists in washing the gangrenous rags, and gangrene appeared in the scratches within two or three days. Unaware of the identity of her malady, she complained to the wardmaster of sore wrists. He too was ignorant of the cause and ordered her to tramp the rags in a tub of water. Several days later gangrenous sores appeared on her feet.[5]

It was impossible, Jones learned, "to determine from the sick reports of the Confederate armies, either the date of the origin, or the number of cases of gangrene." Two things were responsible for this situation: gangrene did not appear as a separate pathological entity in the southern table of diseases until the middle of 1864, and the frequent transferring of gangrene cases from one general hospital to another precluded accurate statistics.[6] A careful study of available medical records convinced him, however, that gangrene had probably appeared during the summer of 1862. He found what he considered to be the first cases among Stonewall Jackson's wounded in the Charlottesville (Virginia) General Hospital following the battle of Port Republic, Virginia (June 8–9, 1862). Thereafter this "disease" progressively increased, although no case was officially recorded until July 1863—more than a year after its initial appearance.[7]

The full impact of gangrene on Confederate military operations cannot be determined, but Jones's investigations afford some interesting insights into its incursions. As the struggle for Atlanta rushed to a climax during July and August 1864, for example, the hospitals serving the Army of Tennessee reported 824 cases of gangrene. "If we assume," Jones advanced, "that one half of these cases were permanently disabled by this disease, then four hundred men were lost to the Army of Tennessee." The true situation, he believed, was far worse, for his personal inspection of many of the general hospitals had convinced him that this estimate was too low. Many gangrene cases were entered upon the sick reports as gunshot wounds. Moreover, in those cases in which this infection supervened the fact of its supervention was frequently not recorded. "I think that it would be fair to assume that during the months of July, August, September, and October 1864," Jones concluded, "about three thousand cases of hospital gangrene occurred amongst the wounded of the Army of Tennessee, and of this number about half, or fifteen hundred, were disabled, for the war at least, by the disease."[8] This estimation was without doubt inflated but should it be only half true it presents a distressing picture and adds a new dimension to the history of the Atlanta campaign.

Jones embodied the findings from his exhaustive study of gangrene—based on the examination of more than 1,000 cases—in a 900-page report for Surgeon General Samuel P. Moore, but the war ended as he was making plans to carry it to Richmond. All was not lost, however, because in 1871 the United States Sanitary Commission included the manuscript in its *Surgical Memoirs of the War of the Rebellion.* The report was published in its entirety without editing. This was unfortunate, since it presented Jones at his worst as a scientific writer. The study reflects much hard work and contains a great deal of valuable information, but these things are lost sight of in a meaningless mass of extraneous material. What emerged was not a much-needed informative account of a diligent researcher's findings on gangrene as it appeared in the Confederacy but a wordy, disjointed anthology of the writings on this infection from antiquity to the Civil War. As one exasperated reviewer aptly put it: "No one can, with justice, accuse Prof. Jones of haste, or of too great brevity, in his consideration of the matters which occupy his pen; but, on the other hand, a charge of prolixity might, we fear be maintained with some show of reason."[9]

The published report, covering over four hundred pages, consisted of an introduction and six substantive chapters. In his introduction Jones gave a brief history of his interest in gangrene and stressed the study's value. He had admittedly prepared this report for the benefit of the Confederacy, but now that the war was over he held that it might be of practical use to the reunited nation. "Apart from the large amount of original material presented in this report, and the interest which it may possess from the time and circumstances of its production," he suggested, "it is worthy of consideration, that hospital gangrene was almost unknown upon the American Continent up to the time of the recent gigantic contest; and as we have no reason to believe that the military operations of the American people will cease with this age, we are led to hope that the experience now recorded will prove of value in the conduct of future wars."[10]

Gangrene, Jones believed, was an old disease. "A disease similar in all respects to hospital gangrene," he reported, "appears to have been known to the most ancient writers."[11] Despite its antiquity this infection was shrouded in mystery and gave up its secrets grudgingly. Indeed the complete comprehension of "the complicated phenomena" of a single case of gangrene, he insisted, demanded a thorough grounding in physiology and pathology, the determination of the cause of the infection, an accurate account of the victim's state of health at the time of infection, the discovery of the pathological and structural changes produced by the disease, a knowledge of the relations of the various stages of gangrene to the corresponding stages of other diseases, and an understanding of the process by which nature sought to limit or to arrest the destructive progress of gangrene.[12]

Students of gangrene through the ages had advanced four theories for its appearance. One group thought it was constitutional in origin; another argued that it was a local disease; a a third held that it was both local and constitutional; and a fourth claimed that it was produced by the action of a specific poison. Jones, like most of his contemporaries, subscribed to the third view. He supported his stand with an impressive array of illustrative cases and with the opinions of the profession's luminaries, past and present.[13]

The chief constitutional cause of gangrene was thought to be "a debilitated and cachectic state of the constitution." Jones judged this condition to be the result of "exposure, fatigue, bad diet, and impure water, and also of the rapid and slow action of a special poison in a low, humid, and miasmatic atmosphere." "In the earliest periods of the present war," he elaborated,

> the Confederate armies were composed in large measure of men who had been accustomed to an abundant and varied diet, a large portion of which consisted of animal food. Notwithstanding the unavoidable crowding of the hospitals, and the existence of all the circumstances most favorable to the development and spread of hospital gangrene in the first months of war, this disease appears to have been almost unknown, until a change had been wrought in the constitution of the soldiers by fatigue, exposure, and reduced rations, from which both coffee and vegetables were universally absent.

It was an irrefutable fact, he concluded, that hospital gangrene would "arise most readily" in soldiers "on scanty and poor food" and "exposed to fatigue, loss of rest, the constant excitements of battle, and the unhealthy atmosphere of crowded, filthy camps, and besieged cities."[14]

Jones enumerated two local causes of gangrene. The first was "the exhalations which contaminate the atmosphere of the crowded, badly ventilated, and filthy tent, hospital, or ship." "In the present condition of the Confederate troops, exposed as they have been to unparalleled labors and fatigue, with short and unvaried rations," he asserted, "the crowding of the wounded into badly ventilated and filthy hospitals will uniformly be attended by the appearance of hospital gangrene." He was further convinced that crowding deteriorated and poisoned the air of hospitals to such an extent that any wound was likely to become infected and that the rapidity with which gangrene spread depended in large measure upon the hygienic condition of the hospital. So pestilential were the effects of crowding that hospital gangrene could "at any time arise *de novo*" when wounded soldiers were crowded together.[15]

A second local cause of gangrene was "the contact of the gangrenous matter with diseased and wounded surfaces, as in using unclean sponges, bandages, wash-bowls, and surgical instruments." Foreshadowing one of Koch's famous postulates, Jones voiced his agreement with a sizable number of his contemporaries who held that "hospital gangrene may be readily communicated by actual contact of the matter from one wound to another, and that the matter may be inoculated into the healthy subject, just as the case of the matter of small-pox, and produce a poisoned wound exactly similar to the one from which the matter was taken."

He based his support of this view on experiments carried out on dogs and on personal observations made in the Army of Tennessee's gangrene hospital in Macon. Many of the deaths in this hospital were the result of a second or third attack. A careful examination convinced Jones that the recurrence of gangrene in these instances was not entirely due to "the condition of the constitution of the patient" nor to "the infected atmosphere of the hospital and the exhalations from the neighboring cases of gangrene." Instead much of the blame was attributable to the absence of a division of labor among the nurses who were required to treat all classes of patients, the shortage of hospital equipment which prevented each patient from having his own washbowl, and the indiscriminate use of improperly washed dressings on convalescent cases. "When nurses infected with the foul odor of the worst gangrene cases," he remarked, "went directly to a healthy granulating wound, and with the same fingers which but a moment before were employed in cleaning and pulling away gangrenous sloughs, the recurrence of the disease was almost inevitable."[16]

It is interesting that Jones, during the course of numerous detailed microscopic examinations of pus from gangrenous wounds, saw the bacillus responsible for gangrene but dismissed any connection between it and the infection. "Animalcules of simple origin, and endowed with active rotary action," he noted, "abound in hospital gangrene." Further examination of "various vegetable and animal matters exposed to the atmosphere under similar circumstances of temperature and moisture" convinced him, however, that "in the present state of our knowledge we are unable to demonstrate that these animalcules are in any way connected with the origin and spread of hospital gangrene." "The gangrenous matter," he postulated, "appears to afford a nidus in which these simple forms of animal and even of vegetable life are rapidly generated and multiplied."

Jones's failure to connect the bacteria he observed with gangrene is easily understandable when one recalls that the miasmatic theory of disease was still firmly entrenched in America during the Civil War. In addition his microscope magnified to only 250 diameters, making it virtually impossible for him to distinguish among the various bacteria he saw. To his credit, however, Jones became one of the leading American exponents of the new science of bacteriology after being won over to the "germ theory" when exposed to the work of Pasteur and Koch in 1870, while on a trip to Europe. He promptly recanted his wartime stand, now boasting of having been among the first to see the gangrene bacillus and claiming credit for discovering the microorganism responsible for typhoid fever as well.[17]

The onset of gangrene was marked by both constitutional and local symptoms. The constitutional signs were systemic, including "loss of appetite, depression of spirits, constipation of the bowels, and such an enfeebled, irritative action of the circulatory apparatus as denoted a depression of the vital, nervous, and muscular forces."[18] Local symptoms varied. At times there might be severe and darting pains in the wounds; at other times a stinging or itching sensation was felt; but in many cases there was little or no change in the sensation of the part affected. Frequently the approach of gangrene could be seen in the wound. "In some cases, in the earliest states," Jones pointed out,

> the wounds presented a dark-red glazed surface; the granulations became altered in appearance, and rapidly disappeared; the discharge of healthy pus disappeared, and was followed by a reddish and greenish sanious fetid discharge. The parts around the wound became painful and swollen, and frequently a well-defined red and purplish indurated border in the sound skin surrounded the wound. The wound itself rapidly assumed a swollen, ragged appearance (the gangrenous matter often rising several lines above the surrounding tissues), with swollen, ragged, everted edges.[19]

As the infection spread, or entered its active stage (as Jones called it), the glazed, dark-red appearance of the wound disappeared, and the gangrenous mass presented a greenish and grayish color. The surrounding areas also became swollen and infiltrated with serum and their temperature rose. During its active stage hospital gangrene rapidly destroyed the cellular and adipose tissues. The muscles, nerves, large blood vessels, and the bones resisted its incursions for a longer period of time. "It is not uncommon," Jones remarked, "to see large surfaces of muscles and even of bones exposed, the skin and cellular tissue having been completely dissected away by the disease." There was also frequent sloughing of dead tissue. "I have seen the skin in the affected spot melt away in twenty-four hours into a grayish and greenish slough," he asserted, "whilst a deep blue and purple, almost black areola, surround the dead mass, spread rapidly in ever increasing circles; whilst the skin and tissues within, over which it had just passed, changed rapidly to the ash gray, and green and bluish hue characteristic of this form of gangrene. This is witnessed most generally in the worst and fatal cases." Constitutional changes during gangrene's active stage were "the derangement of nutrition, secretion, and excretion, and the depression of the nervous and muscular forces, and the perturbations of temperature." These changes were attributed in great measure, if not wholly, to "the absorption of the poisonous matter causing the gangrene, and of the various altered products resulting from the decay of the tissues."[20]

Jones was unable to discern any "uniform periods" in the progress of gangrene cases to either a favorable or fatal termination. His research revealed that the duration of gangrenous infections depended upon "the condition of the system and the constitutional powers at the time of the infection," "the extent to which the constitution is involved by the absorption of the gangrenous matters," "the position, relations, and functions of the diseased parts," "the rapidity and extent to which the disease progresses before being arrested by the powers and processes of nature, or by treatment," "the nature of the local and constitutional treatment," and, above all, "the hygienic condition of the hospital in which the patients are treated." "One or all of these causes," he insisted, "may tend to aggravate the disease and prolong its course." He also believed that the severity of the disease was exacerbated "in a damp, warm, low, malarious atmosphere" and that "natural temperament" exerted an important effect upon the outcome of individual cases. All things being equal, he held, this disorder was "most rapidly managed" and convalescence most rapid in "the nervo-sanguine temperament" while men of "the bilious, nervo-bilious, and bilio-lymphatic temperaments" appeared to suffer most and "to have the most tedious convalescence."[21]

In general Jones relied upon two indicators to predict the outcome of gangrene cases. The first was the patient's complexion. At the height of the infection "the complexion," he noted, "assumes an unhealthy, dusky, leaden hue, the eyes express anxiety, depression, and nervous irritation and exhaustion, the pulse is small, frequent and feeble, and indicates an irritable, enfeebled state of the nervous and muscular systems." "It is possible by these symptoms alone," he believed, "to decide in many cases whether gangrene is present, and whether it is progressing or disappearing." Second, he subscribed to the age-old theory of laudable pus as an indication of the direction of the case, maintaining: "After gangrene has set in, the reappearance of pus should be regarded as a favorable sign, indicating an attempt at organization, and an improvement in the plastic powers of the parts immediately surrounding the altered gangrenous matter."[22]

There was, as far as Jones could tell, no discernible period of crisis in those cases which recovered. Instead there seemed to be gradual and progressive improvement. After the arrest of gangrene the wound presented "a bright red and scarlet, exquisitely sensitive mass of luxuriant granulations, which are highly vascular, and bleed upon the slightest touch. So sensitive is this surface that the most gentle touch will frequently cause the patient, even though he may be a stout, brave soldier, to cry like a child." But the arrest of the infection did not necessarily mean recovery, because as Jones warned: "Many cases terminate fatally, even after the removal of the gangrene, from various causes, as exhaustion of the system by profuse suppuration, the depressing effects of the previous disease, the permanent derangement of the digestion, caused during the active stages of the disease, by bed sores, by pyaemia, and by diarrhoea."[23]

The fortunate soul who survived gangrene and its sequelae was still faced with a lengthy convalescence and the likelihood of some degree of permanent disability. The recovery period was determined by a variety of factors, including "the extent to which the general system has been involved," "the extent of the local injury," "the condition of the wound," and "the surrounding hygienic state."[24] The level of treatment received during this time was especially important. "I have, in many cases which suffered intensely and finally died," Jones grieved, "witnessed a most lamentable indifference and inattention on the part of the nurses and medical attendants to the personal comfort of the patients." He also roundly condemned "inattentive and slovenly surgeons," labeling them a cause of "the most tardy convalescence, and even of death itself." Rapid recovery, he argued, demanded that "the patients should be moved out of the wards into the open air whenever possible"; "the most scrupulous attention should be paid to the condition of the bedding and to the change of position"; and "the patient should be propped up in bed, if possible, for a portion of the day, at least."[25]

The character and degree of disability, Jones held, was "in no manner related to the size or depth of the primary wound" but was determined by "the situation of the gangrene" and "the extent of its ravages." When the infection invaded tissue containing major blood vessels and nerves, for example, "impaired circulation, nutrition, and even complete paralysis" was often the result. Even when there was no serious circulatory or neurological damage, denuded muscles, during the process "of healing by granulation," frequently formed "numerous new attachments, and the symmetry and precision of the muscular movements" was impaired. Thus, as Jones recorded, "withered, discolored, cold, contracted, and paralyzed arms and legs are . . . the results of the local injuries inflicted by hospital gangrene." The overcoming of such disabilities required "great resolution and attention on the part of the patient as well as the physician."[26]

Many of those attacked by gangrene died. In these cases the approach of death was both rapid and terrible. "The edges of the wound," Jones observed, "became hardened and everted, the surface of the wound rises up into a pulpy, ragged, gray and greenish mass. The disease attacks other adjacent structures from day to day, extending its ravages both in length and breadth, and involving aponeuroses, muscles, blood-vessels, nerves, tendons, the periosteum, and bones and joints."[27] Constitutional symptoms also became progressively more grave, and the end was generally announced by "a feeble, rapid pulse, extreme prostration, twitching of the tendons, vomiting, hiccough, involuntary dejections, and ofttimes coma." But it was not uncommon to see dying men "sensible and calm up to the moment of death."[28]

Jones attributed death to any one, or a combination, of a dozen causes. These were the "progressive failure of the powers" under the onslaught of the gangrenous poison, repeated hemorrhage from "exposed and eroded" blood vessels, the "entrance of air" into veins opened by the infection, the "opening of the large joints," the formation of bedsores and the appearance of gangrene in them, the "extensive and rapid disorganization" of sound tissue around the original wound, the "mortification" of internal organs, the invasion of organs essential to life, diarrhea, pyemia, phlebitis, and various sequelae of gangrene, such as "profuse and unhealthy suppuration" from large granulating surfaces, necrosed bones, hectic fever, and the "permanent impairment and debility" of the digestive organs.[29]

In combating hospital gangrene, Jones insisted that "the first essential measure, without which the most enlightened treatment is comparatively valueless, and at best tardy in its action" was to remove the patient from the crowded wards and place him in an isolated room or tent with "the largest possible supply" of fresh air. Jones divided his regimen into constitutional and local measures. The former were designed "to furnish the elements of healthy blood, and of active nutrition, secretion, and repair, to excite and support the vital powers, and to allay nervous irritability." "We have seen," he explained, "that the constitutional symptoms in most cases of hospital gangrene hold a prominent place." Thus "the dejected spirits, the depressed state of the nervous system, the small, accelerated pulse, the feeble, sluggish, capillary circulation, and the depressed state of the extremities" all pointed to "the supporting tonic and stimulating plan of treatment as the rational system."[30]

This plan was twofold, consisting of a highly nutritious diet and combinations of tonics and anodynes after "the morbid secretions of the bowels" had been removed with gentle purgatives or enemas. Jones stressed the paramount importance of diet throughout the course of the gangrene attack, recommending concentrated animal soups, soft-boiled eggs, eggnog, milk punch, a liberal supply of vegetables, and ripe fruit. He also felt that good brandy, whiskey, wine, or porter "administered in moderate quantities" would prove highly beneficial in almost all cases. "I have witnessed," he avowed, "the most decided benefit from the careful but liberal use of alcoholic stimulants in hospital gangrene, and never in a single case had occasion to regret their use." Jones enumerated a wide range of agents and preparations which he had found helpful as tonics and anodynes. These included quinine, sesquichloride of iron, Huxham's tincture of bark (tinctura cinchona composita), chlorate of potassa, a mixture of hydrochloric and nitric acids, Fowler's solution (arsenate of potassa), oil of turpentine, camphor, musk, warm aromatics, spices, and opiates. He prescribed blue mass (calomel) to open the bowels and Seidlitz powder (tartrate of potassa and soda, bicarbonate of soda, and tartaric acid) to keep them open. To his credit he spoke out against the use of bloodletting in gangrene cases, maintaining that it tended to depress further "the enfeebled powers" and inflicted a wound which in turn might become gangrenous.[31]

Local measures were aimed at destroying the poison and diseased tissue and promoting healthy granulation. These things, Jones asserted, could be accomplished best through "the liberal and thorough application of *concentrated fuming nitric acid* to the gangrenous parts."[32] This excruciatingly painful ordeal generally necessitated anesthetization. "During the insensibility of the patient," he instructed, "the surgeon should carefully examine the wound, and first remove all the gangrenous tissues, using the scalpel and scissors, and causing the parts beneath to bleed quite freely. All the sinuses formed under the skin, or between the muscles, or in the cellular or areolar tissue, must be freely laid open, and the dead tissues removed." "The entire wound," he continued, "is then to be carefully wiped out with a sponge or dry lint, and the concentrated acid applied with a brush or mop to the entire surface; and care should be taken that the acid penetrate into all the sinuses and cavities. If any diseased part be untouched or undestroyed by the acid, the disease will recommence and spread from that point." Jones was a firm believer in the beneficial effects of nitric acid. Its failures, he was convinced, were attributable to one or more of the following: failing to apply the acid freely and thoroughly to the infected area, returning the patient to a crowded ward or tent, or neglecting to keep the wound clean after treatment.[33]

Cautery was to be followed by measures aimed at rendering the wound antiseptic through the application of such agents as turpentine, camphorated tincture of opium, tincture of camphor, creosote, and carbolic acid. It was then to be sealed with flax-seed, meal, hop, or charcoal poultices. Jones urged the periodic cleansing of the wound with water and solutions of chlorinated soda, permanganate of potash, nitromuriatic acid, acetic acid, carbolic acid, and pyroligneous acid. "The prompt removal of all detached masses of tissues, and the thorough washing away of all morbid secretions," he advanced, "are most important measures to prevent the recurrence of the disease." He exhibited a further admirably modern position when he insisted that "the person of the gangrene patient should be kept scrupulously clean . . . sponges should be discarded, all rags and dressing should be destroyed as soon as removed from the diseased parts, each patient should be provided with his own wash-bowl and towel, and a nurse should be provided for every five patients."[34]

A strong belief in the important role of contagion in the spread of gangrene made Jones reluctant to endorse amputation as a means of eradicating the infection. "As a general rule," he stated, "no amputation, no matter what be the condition of the wounds, whether gangrenous or healthy, should be performed in the wards of a hospital in which gangrene is prevailing." He labeled such operations "as reprehensible as the careless distribution of healthy and fresh wounds amongst the gangrenous wards." Jones realized, however, that under certain circumstances amputation was necessary: "when a large joint is exposed; when the gangrenous wound is of great size, and the muscles, nerves, and blood-vessels and bones are extensively exposed, and the constitutional powers are undermined by the absorption of the gangrenous matter and the incessant suffering; and when large blood-vessels are destroyed by the destructive action, and there is a danger of death from hemorrhage." Indeed, in some cases, he remarked, "the surgeon gains an advantage by substituting a small defined wound for a large gangrenous surface from which the entire mass of blood may be infected." When amputation was unavoidable, the patient, especially if gangrene was present in the hospital, "should be isolated as far as possible, and every attention paid to proper ventilation, cleanliness, and diet."[35]

One of the most valuable sections of Jones's gangrene study dealt with his views on its prevention. "Abundant supplies of nutritious animal and vegetable food, free ventilation, with the largest possible supply of fresh air to each patient, with scrupulous cleanliness of the wounds, as well as of the person's clothing and bedding, and apartments of the wounded," he asserted, "are the great prophylactic measures against hospital gangrene."[36] This stand is commendable, especially in light of the general lack of knowledge of or concern for preventive medicine in mid-nineteenth-century America.

Jones placed particular emphasis on proper hospital facilities. Hospitals, he believed, should be located "in elevated, well-drained, and well-watered" areas where "the most perfect arrangements" could be made for free ventilation and the removal of all "excrementitious matters." Crowded cities were poor choices. "Thousands of valuable lives," he lamented, "were sacrificed by the suicidal policy instituted upon an immense scale in the earlier periods of the war of using hotels, warehouses, stores, churches, and colleges, in the heart of cities and towns, for military hospitals." There was a considerable diversity of opinion among Confederate surgeons as to the relative merits of tents and wooden hospital buildings. Jones preferred the latter. "Properly constructed wooden hospitals," he commented, "allow of regular cleansing, disinfection, and whitewashing, and afford more regular supplies of fresh air, and of light, as well as greater facilities for the regulation of the temperature and the moisture."[37]

Crowding of the sick and wounded, whether in hospitals or boxcars, was equally deplorable. Crowded hospitals, Jones complained, created a frightening situation where "the simplest diseases assumed malignant characters" and "the foul exhalations of the sick poisoned the wounds of healthy men, and induced erysipelas, pyaemia, and gangrene." He steadfastly maintained that when gangrene appeared in a filthy or crowded hospital "a heavy responsibility rests upon the medical officers." Jones condemned the practice of crowding battle casualties into closely constructed boxcars and transporting them great distances to already crowded general hospitals for treatment, insisting: "The severest epidemics of hospital gangrene have appeared amongst the wounded subjected to these most favorable conditions for the origin and spread of the disease."[38]

Jones also favored the shielding of the newly wounded from gangrene patients. Contemporary medical opinion was unanimous in its acceptance of the necessity of isolating smallpox patients, but physicians had not yet extended this doctrine to other seemingly infectious diseases. Jones went beyond this narrow view, asserting: "As a rule in military practice, the wounded should never be placed in wards with patients suffering from any one of the contagious or infectious diseases, as small-pox, measles, scarlet fever, typhus fever, typhoid fever, pyaemia, or hospital gangrene. And these various diseases should not be indiscriminately mingled together."[39]

The proper management of the wounded in the hospitals was vital to the prevention of gangrene. Protection against crowding was not enough. According each man two thousand cubic feet of air was important, Jones insisted, but so were a number of other measures. It is strange that he felt that the severest cases should be distributed uniformly among the lightest ones. Each ward should be thoroughly evacuated, cleansed, whitewashed, and fumigated with chlorine or sulphurous acid at least every two weeks and more frequently if possible. Coal tar and sulphate of iron, among other similar agents, should be freely used to absorb "noxious gases" and to arrest "decomposition in the faecal and urinary matters in the bed-pans and privies." Straw used for bedding should be frequently changed, the old straw burned, and the bed sacks boiled in water containing permanganate of potassa.

The personal cleanliness of the wounded demanded the most scrupulous attention. Frequent bathing was of paramount importance. In those cases where bathing was impossible Jones recommended the sponging off of the entire body with his own "disinfecting, stimulant, and cleansing lotion" made from hypochloride of soda, tincture of camphor, whiskey, common salt, and water. "This lotion," he boasted, "effectually removes the greasy sweat from the skin, and all filth, and imparts a clean, wholesome smell, which refreshes the patient." The clothing of the wounded and the dressings of their wounds demanded the greatest attention. Soiled clothing, like bed sacks, should be boiled in water containing permanganate of potassa. "The boiling temperature," Jones stressed, "can always be commanded, and should never be neglected, as by this means we coagulate, alter, and destroy the decomposing poisonous matters." Finally he strongly warned against allowing dressing from wounds to collect about the hospital: "The only safe rule for the prevention of hospital gangrene is to burn and destroy all materials which have been used in dressing wounds." "Even when lint and rags have been carefully washed and boiled," he cautioned, "they may still act deleteriously upon the diseased surfaces."[40]

There is much in this report to attack; there is more to praise. On the negative side there is Jones's annoying verbosity, distracting inclusion of extraneous material, and almost inexcusable reliance on numerous outdated sources. On the positive side there is his impressive research, the tremendous amount of empirical knowledge exhibited, and, above all, the modernity of his views as to the role of contagion in the spread of gangrene, the importance of asepsis in treating it, and the necessity of antisepsis in preventing this infection. These strong points are all the more commendable when it is remembered that "the Civil War took place at the very end of the medical 'middle ages'—immediately before bacteriology and aseptic surgery."[41]

Chapter 11
The Balance Sheet

*The desire of my soul, and the ambition
of my entire life, was to preserve, as far as
possible the medical and surgical records of
the Confederate army during this
gigantic struggle.*

Over 600,000 soldiers lost their lives during the Civil War. Untold thousands who later died from disease or injury incurred during the war pushed the death toll incalculably higher. Even more tragic was the fact that the costly biological price this conflict exacted was highly cumulative. "We lost not only these men," Allan Nevins has written, "but their children, and their children's children. . . . We have lost the books they might have written, the scientific discoveries they might have made, the inventions they might have perfected." "Such a loss," he exclaimed, "defies measurement."[1]

Having participated in the bloodshed, the combatants—both Union and Confederate—felt compelled to justify their actions. Indeed the guns had scarcely fallen silent at Appomattox before they began, as Edward Channing put it, "fighting their 'battles o'er again.' "[2] Joseph Jones rallied unhesitatingly to the South's defense anew. Comparative numbers and losses were important features of the renewed sectional struggle. Jones had become interested in Confederate statistics early in the war and, owing to his unique assignment, carefully copied many southern field and hospital reports. He used some of these figures in his reports to Surgeon General Samuel P. Moore, but it was not until after the war that he made full use of them in an attempt to settle the question of Confederate numbers and losses.

This was no easy task. Jones's statistics were incomplete, and the abrupt end of the war, accompanied by the destruction of most southern records, "rendered it difficult, if not impossible, to obtain accurate information." He was compelled, therefore, to rely upon a variety of sources, such as the material in his possession, semiofficial memoirs of Confederate authorities, accounts of "the most trustworthy witnesses," and census figures.[3]

"It is fair to estimate," Jones's findings convinced him, "that the available force, capable of active service in the field did not, during the entire war, exceed *six hundred thousand men.* Of this number not more than *four hundred thousand* were enrolled at any one time as soldiers, and the Confederate States never had, at any one time actively engaged in the field, more than *two hundred thousand men* capable of bearing arms, exclusive of sick, wounded and disabled." The picture for the enemy, Jones asserted, was strikingly different. The North amassed a juggernaut some three to four times larger than the entire southern enrollment. By the time of Lee's surrender there were over one million Union soldiers under arms. "Opposed to this immense army . . . supplied with the best equipment and arms, and with the most abundant rations of food, and flushed with victory and enriched with the spoils of their defenseless enemies," he bemoaned, "the Confederate Government could oppose scarcely one hundred thousand war-torn, and battle-scarred veterans, almost all of whom had at some time been wounded, and who had followed the fortunes of their desperate cause for four years, with scant supplies of clothing, with coarse and scant rations, and almost absolutely without pay."[4]

Turning to Confederate combat losses, Jones (as table 10 shows) calculated that 1,315 southerners were killed, 4,054 were wounded, and 2,772 were taken prisoner during 1861. The intensified hostilities of 1862, the first full year of the war, caused casualties to mount. Battle deaths rose to 18,582; the number of wounded increased to 68,659; and the loss through prisoners totaled

TABLE 10

Confederate Battle Casualties, 1861–1865

Year	Killed	Wounded	Prisoners
1861	1,315	4,054	2,772
1862	18,582	68,659	48,300
1863	11,876	51,313	71,211
1864–1865	22,000	70,000	80,000

48,300. Although 1863 witnessed some of the fiercest fighting of the war, southern battle losses were lower—11,876 killed, 51,313 wounded, and 71,211 captured. Jones's own records only ran through 1863, and the paucity of those available made it impossible "to form an accurate estimate of the Confederate losses from the commencement of the year 1864 to the termination of the struggle near the middle of 1865." Believing that this was "the bloodiest period of the struggle," he felt it fair to set southern casualties at 22,000 killed, 70,000 wounded, and 80,000 captured.[5]

Jones's statistical summary of Confederate numbers and losses, shown in table 11, presents a horrifying picture. "If this calculation, which is given only as an approximation, be correct," Jones remarked, "one-third of all the men actually engaged on the Confederate side were either killed outright upon the field or died of disease and wounds; another third of the entire number were captured and held for indefinite periods, prisoners of war; and of the remaining two hundred thousand, at least half were lost to the service by discharges and desertions," thereby reducing Confederate strength to "scarcely one hundred thousand men" at the time of Lee's surrender. Caught up in the cult of the lost cause, Jones interpreted the decimation of the South's fighting force as exemplary of southern determination and valor, boasting: "The resolution and unsurpassed bravery with which the Confederate leaders conducted this contest, is shown by the fact that during the war, out of 600,000 men in the field, about 500,000 were lost to the service . . . [and] the spirit of the Confederate soldier remained proud and unbroken to the last."[6]

Although Jones published his findings on southern numbers and losses as early as 1869, he was not the first to estimate the Confederacy's cumulative fighting strength at 600,000. In fact this approximation first appeared in the North. In 1867 an un-

TABLE 11

Confederate Numbers and Losses, 1861–1865

Total Confederate forces	600,000
Total deaths from disease and battle	200,000
Taken prisoner	200,000
Discharges from disability and desertions	100,000
Remaining at the end of the war	100,000

identified correspondent for the *New York Tribune* having, in his own words, "carefully analyzed" unspecified but "very nearly complete" returns for the Confederate armies from their organization in the summer of 1861 down to the spring of 1865, wrote: "We judge in all 600,000 different men were in the Confederate ranks during the war."[7]

In all probability Jones never saw this article. If he did he made no mention of it. Yet in the absence of conclusive evidence to the contrary, these two identical estimates, especially since one was northern and the other southern, gave this figure an air of authority, and for a time it was generally accepted in both North and South. For example in the South, General Samuel Cooper, the adjutant and inspector-general of the southern armies, labeled this estimation as "nearly critically correct," and Alexander H. Stephens, the vice president of the Confederacy, popularized it in his history of the war. In the North it was accepted by the editors of the prestigious *American Cyclopaedia*.[8]

Largely because it served as a balm for the agony of defeat, few in the South ever questioned the contention that the southern forces were outnumbered three or four to one. Many in the North, however, never wholeheartedly subscribed to it, and the gradual publication of surviving Confederate records by the U.S. War Department provided them the opportunity to strike. A paper war, often as fervently fought as the actual hostilities, ensued. Joseph Jones, since he was the earliest and one of the most adamant advocates of the southern position, came under steady fire. Criticism ranged from the mild strictures of Colonel William F. Fox to the sweeping contradiction of General Gates P. Thruston. Fox, in his classic *Regimental Losses in the American Civil War*, only briefly commented on Jones's figures. "Most will hold, and with good reasons," he remarked, "that 600,000 is too low an estimate for the total number that served in the Confederate armies. Their military population and sweeping conscriptions indicate more."[9] But Thruston, like Fox a Union officer turned historian, was deeply disturbed by the historical distortion growing out of Jones's statistics. "Dr. Jones' 600,000 estimate," he asserted,

> is engraved upon enduring monuments in the South commemorating the Confederacy, in contrast with the engraved figures of the large official Federal enrolment. The

contrasting figures are printed upon certificates of member-
ship in the Confederate societies. The Southern orators
usually repeat the contrasting numbers at meetings and
dedications in honor of the Confederate soldiers. They are
printed in the Southern school books, and thus a misleading
historical error in figures, as I believe, originally possibly a
just "approximate calculation" of the available force of the
Confederacy has been repeated until its original significance
and meaning have been changed and forgotten.[10]

Jones's most thorough critic was Thomas L. Livermore, one of
the foremost students of Civil War numbers and losses. Livermore's examination of his argument and supporting evidence
revealed what he considered much loose writing and a number of
errors of fact and judgment. These shortcomings, he pointed
out, plagued each category of Jones's statistics: the ratio of
deaths to strength was disproportionately high; the number of
desertions and discharges was too low; the loss in prisoners was
inflated; and the surprisingly small estimate of the Confederate
force remaining at the end of the war was unsupported by fact
(174,223 had surrendered).[11]
    Livermore leveled his strongest criticism at Jones's proof that
the Union armies were three to four times larger than those of the
Confederacy. By the turn of the century when Livermore's work
appeared, southerners and their supporters steadfastly attributed
the downfall of the Confederacy to the supposed great disparity
in numbers and to question this thesis was to its most rabid
advocates tantamount to disparaging the southern war record.
Hoping to avoid a fruitless emotional response, Livermore tact-
fully remarked: "The sustained conflict and terrible loss of four
years of war placed the reputation of Southern valor so high that
exaggerated statements of numbers cannot further exalt in the
estimation of the world. To prove that the estimated ratio of four
to one between the two armies is not founded in fact, does not
diminish that reputation."[12]
    Having dispensed with this false issue, he turned his attention
to the question of comparative numbers. The total Union
strength, 2,898,304, was readily available from War Department
records, but Livermore, like Jones, was forced to rely upon several
indirect approaches to arrive at a reliable estimate for the Confederacy. Of these the estimation of the South's potential fighting

TABLE 12

Union and Confederate Strength according to Thomas L. Livermore

Number of Union enlistments	2,898,304
Available Confederate strength from census of 1860	1,239,000
Confederate enlistments from total average strength of southern regiments	1,227,890–1,406,180
Union strength, reduced to the three-year enlistment	1,556,678
Confederate strength, reduced to the three-year enlistment	1,082,119

force from the census of 1860 and the total average strength of the southern regiments proved the most valuable. The former indicated that as many as 1,239,000 southerners could have borne arms; the latter estimate ranged from 1,227,890 to 1,406,180.[13] But to Livermore merely listing or estimating the number of those who served on each side was an exercise of dubious value since both North and South utilized enlistments of varying duration. Consequently he adopted the three-year enlistment as an acceptable basis for an overall comparison, and in complicated and perhaps controversial computations he placed the Union strength at 1,556, 678 and that of the Confederacy at 1,082,119.[14]

Livermore's figures, shown in table 12, are highly impressive.[15] In comparison Jones's appear inferior and suspect. The question of the relative size of the opposing armies, however, is far from settled. Indeed, despite repeated attack, the contention that the South had no more than 600,000 fighting men and was thereby outnumbered three or four to one on the battlefield has proved remarkably long-lived. Its longevity is largely attributable to the legions of the cult of the lost cause in the South as evidenced in this figure's prominent position in the *Confederate Handbook*, a now outdated compilation of supposed "important data" and "interesting and valuable matter" relating to the war published by a former Confederate officer in 1900. A decade later it was enshrined for posterity in Randolph H. McKim's definitive statement of the southern stand on numbers and losses.[16] At present Livermore's figures hold the field. And yet his computations, according to one of the most widely read textbooks on the Civil War, represent "one of the important exhibits in the testimony rather than a definitive verdict on the whole case."[17]

Numbers are not the important thing. Indeed the time expended debating the relative size of the rival armies might be better spent reflecting on the shocking human misery the participants inflicted on one another. Almost 620,000 lives were lost during this senseless fratricidal struggle, a death toll that easily exceeds the total fatalities of all other American wars. Union deaths have been placed at about 360,000 and those of the Confederacy at 260,000. A sizable number of these fatalities (110,000 Union and 94,000 Confederate) occurred on the battlefield, but the overwhelming majority of them resulted from the ravages of disease.[18] Roughly three out of every five Union and two out of every three Confederate deaths were due to illness. In all there were approximately 10,000,000 cases of sickness during the war (6,000,000 Union and 4,000,000 Confederate). Using Livermore's figures as a basis for comparison, this means that every soldier, northern and southern, fell ill an average of four times.[19] The frequency of wounds was equally distressing. The number of northern wounded is said to have been in the range of from 275,175 to 400,000. Similar figures for the South are not available, but a conservative estimate of at least one-half (137,583–200,000) of the Union totals seems acceptable.[20] Disease, disability, and death therefore were constant companions of the Civil War soldier and exacted a dreadful toll. This is all too clearly borne out in the grim statistic that the Civil War soldier's chances of not returning home were 1 in 4 as compared with 1 in 126 for his comrade in arms during the Korean conflict.[21]

Joseph Jones, as we have seen, developed an early and lasting interest in Confederate medical history, and the collection, classification, and preservation of field and hospital reports became an integral part of his frequent travels throughout the war zone. "The desire of my soul, and the ambition of my entire life," he later wrote, "was to preserve, as far as possible, the medical and surgical records of the Confederate army during this gigantic struggle." The collapse of the Confederacy heightened this ambition.[22]

Jones hoped to compile a definitive medical history of the Confederacy which would "illustrate the patriotic, self-sacrificing and scientific labors" of the southern medical corps.[23] A dearth of sources and a busy professional life prevented him from completing this monumental task. His labors, a number of vignettes, afford at best informative insights into Confederate medical history. Examples are plentiful. During the fifteen months from January 1862 through March 1863 the general hospitals serving the Army of Northern Virginia (exclusive of those in Richmond) reported 113,914 admissions and 5,516 deaths. In the last seven months of this period (September 1862– March 1863) the Richmond hospitals treated 93,852 cases with 3,849 deaths.[24] In each instance combat casualties were of minor importance; the chief cause of disability was disease. This was true throughout the war. The collective experiences of the southern surgeons, Jones pointed out, illustrated "in the most forcible manner the great truth that armies are rendered inefficient and destroyed not so much by actual fighting as by the silent action of disease." Typhoid fever, malaria, diarrhea and dysentery, pneumonia, and the chief children's diseases, such as measles, mumps, and chicken pox, led this biological onslaught. Secondary infections also abounded as seen during the period January 1862– July 1863 when southern surgeons treated 51 cases of pyemia, 11 of gangrene, and 7,403 of erysipelas. The ever-growing numbers of amputations account in large measure for the prevalence of these infections. From June 1, 1862, to February 1, 1864, 1,688 amputations with 1,089 cures and 599 deaths were reported to the surgeon general's office.[25]

Two serious shortcomings, of which Jones was aware, detract significantly from the value of such figures. The most obvious failing is their limited nature. Even more damaging is their questionable level of accuracy as the result of incomplete reporting on the part of the harried southern surgeons. In general these unavoidable defects mar all of Jones's statistics, one notable exception being his figures pertaining to the Charlottesville General Hospital.

This was an important Confederate hospital. Situated in the red clay foothills of the Blue Ridge Mountains in central Virginia, it played a major role in the medical fortunes of the Army of Northern Virginia from July 1861 until the surrender of Charlottesville to General Philip H. Sheridan in early March 1865. Its long unbroken term of service is easily explained by the fact that, despite the frequent battles which raged to the east and west, Charlottesville was virtually untouched by the hostilities and was not seriously endangered until the war was nearly at an end.[26] Accordingly thousands of Confederate casualties from First Manassas (July 21, 1861), Fredericksburg (December 13, 1862), the Wilderness (May 5–7, 1864), Stonewall Jackson's valley campaign (summer of 1862), and the battles around Spotsylvania Courthouse (May 7–10, 1864) were treated here. The record would have been even more impressive had not transportation breakdowns prevented any of the casualties from Second Manassas (August 29–30, 1862) and Chancellorsville (May 1–4, 1863) being sent to Charlottesville.[27]

Founded in July 1861, the Charlottesville General Hospital was under the direction of Dr. James L. Cabell, professor of physiology and surgery in the University of Virginia's school of medicine. His faculty colleague, Dr. John S. Davis, professor of anatomy, materia medica, and botany, served as his chief assistant. The hospital's first facilities were the buildings of the University of Virginia, but the combined effect of burgeoning admissions and opposition from the school's faculty and board of visitors, who viewed the presence of the sick and wounded as "very injurious to the interests of the University," soon forced Cabell to transfer his operation to a number of public buildings, hotels, tents, rude barracks, and private homes.

Joseph Jones visited the hospital only once—in September 1863 while in Virginia to deliver his third report to Surgeon General Samuel P. Moore. He was highly pleased with the "organized system of investigation" he found and the "most valuable assistance" he received from the "intelligent & energetic Surgeons." This hospital, owing both to its proximity to "the grand armies" and "the great battles" and to its "ample accommodations" and "skillful management," Jones believed, "received more than its just proportion of seriously sick & severely wounded." "For these reasons," he asserted, "this was one of the best, if not the very best field for medical observations in the Southern Confederacy."[28] Jones spent most of his time copying the hospital's records which had been "carefully collected & preserved . . . under the intelligent action & supervision of Professors Cabell & Davis," convinced that these figures would furnish "the most reliable data for the determination of many important points in the history of various diseases."[29]

The Charlottesville General Hospital compiled a highly creditable record during the forty-one months (July 1861–February 1865) which Jones's statistics cover. Almost 22,000 casualties, as table 13 shows, were cared for with but 5.2 percent mortality.[30] Expressed in a more forceful manner, this means that out of this large number of cases there was only 1 death in every 19.2 cases

TABLE 13

Medical Statistics for the Charlottesville General Hospital, July 1861–February 1865

	Cases	Deaths
Typhoid fever	1,429	357
Malaria	850	1
Diarrhea and dysentery	2,172	77
Pneumonia	851	250
Measles	1,137	19
Gunshot wounds	5,337	263
Other diseases	9,764	156
TOTALS	21,540	1,123

treated. The leading causes of disability and death, accounting for 54.7 percent (11,766) of the cases and 86.1 percent (967) of the deaths, were typhoid fever, malaria, diarrhea and dysentery, pneumonia, measles, and gunshot wounds. The chief secondary infections—pyemia, erysipelas, tetanus, and gangrene—were also present but were of uncertain importance, attacking 421 patients and claiming few lives. Diseases outnumbered gunshot wounds three to one as both a source of disability and a cause of death. The former was responsible for 16,203 cases and 860 deaths, while 5,337 cases and 263 deaths were attributed to the latter.

Typhoid fever, malaria, and diarrhea and dysentery, as we have seen repeatedly, were the Civil War's great causes of fatalities. Collectively they caused 20.7 percent (4,451) of the cases and 37.8 percent (425) of the deaths in the Charlottesville General Hospital. Typhoid fever was second only to diarrhea and dysentery in terms of total disease-related cases but led all disorders in fatalities. In fact almost one-third (31.8 percent) of all deaths, or nearly 1 in 3, was attributed to this much-feared fever. Fortunately its incidence in both armies, Jones noted, progressively diminished as raw recruits were slowly transformed into seasoned veterans. "Typhoid fever," he observed, "is most liable to attack recruits, and as a general rule, affects the individual but once during life."[31] The history of this disorder in the Charlottesville General Hospital followed this trend beautifully. Typhoid fever caused 1,297 cases and 312 deaths during the period July 1861–August 1863, as compared with 132 cases and 45 deaths during the months September 1863–February 1865. The largest monthly occurrences, moreover, were recorded during the first four months in which the hospital was in operation— July (284), August (74), September (150), and October 1861 (100).

Malaria, a frequent medical problem in the large Civil War armies, accounted for many casualties (850 cases). Yet of this large number of cases, only one terminated fatally. This low death rate can probably be traced to the use of quinine as a specific for malaria.

While the incidence of most major diseases slowly diminished during the war, the morbidity of intestinal disorders steadily increased. True diarrhea and dysentery were unquestionably persistent health hazards in Civil War armies, but since loose bowels are symptomatic of a variety of diseases, there was much misdiagnosis. In addition these disorders were reported to be relatively mild in character. Both of these observations seem germane to the situation in the Charlottesville General Hospital where diarrhea and dysentery, while responsible for 10.1 percent (2,172) of the total casualties, caused few deaths (77).

Respiratory ailments were commonplace in Civil War armies. Aggravated by frequent exposure to cold and inclement weather, they were most prevalent during the cool, wet months of the fall and winter but afflicted soldiers throughout the year. Pneumonia was the most serious respiratory disease, inflicting 851 casualties with 250 deaths. Its 29.4 percent death rate (1 in every 3.4 cases) was the highest for any single disease treated.

Most soldiers came from rural areas. It is not surprising, therefore, that Civil War armies experienced frequent epidemics of measles, smallpox, chicken pox, mumps, and scarlet fever. Many of these disorders were present in the Charlottesville General Hospital, but of them only measles posed a serious problem. It was the third most prevalent disease, behind intestinal disorders and typhoid fever, causing 1,137 cases and 19 deaths.

Bullets were naturally the chief cause of Civil War battle wounds. It has been estimated that they accounted for approximately 250,000 patients and 35,000 deaths in the Union army alone.[32] The overwhelming majority of these casualties were inflicted by the conoidal minie ball. The destructiveness of this bullet was the result of its low velocity which caused it to tumble or flatten on impact, producing a savage, bursting wound on exit. "The shattering, splintering, and splitting of a long bone by the impact of a minie . . . ball," as one southern surgeon graphically put it, "[was] in many instances, both remarkable and frightening."[33] There were 5,337 gunshot wounds recorded in the Charlottesville General Hospital, or approximately one-fourth (24.8 percent) of the total casualties. The wounded here fared quite well, for less than 5 percent (263) of them died, a figure well below the 14 percent wartime average of the Union army.[34]

Far too often, as we have seen, injury on the battlefield and surgery in the hospital were followed by dangerous and frequently fatal secondary infections. The most feared were erysipelas, pyemia, and gangrene. These secondary infections were probably serious hazards in the Charlottesville General Hospital, but their true impact is impossible to assess for two important reasons: none of these conditions were found in the Confederate table of diseases before the middle of 1864 and in many instances when a secondary infection supervened no change was made in diagnosis. It was common for deaths from gangrene, almost always a supervening disease, to appear on the hospital records as due to gunshot wounds.[35]

Erysipelas and pyemia are usually caused by the streptococcal invasion of wounds. They "appeared at an early day" in the Charlottesville General Hospital and "prevailed to a considerable extent," especially among the wounded, crowded into the badly ventilated dormitories and lecture rooms of the University of Virginia. In fact their spread was not arrested until the abandonment of the university buildings and the subsequent placing of the wounded in private quarters. The hospital's records showed only 80 cases of erysipelas and 18 of pyemia. No deaths were recorded from either disease although the latter was frequently fatal. Without doubt, however, the actual incidence of both was much higher and both caused deaths. Jones's examination of individual case records, for example, uncovered almost 20 cases of pyemia among the wounded sent to Charlottesville General Hospital after the battle of First Manassas, all but 2 of them fatal.

Gangrene became one of the Civil War's most serious medical

problems. Jones, as it will be recalled, found what he considered to be the Confederacy's first cases among the records for Stonewall Jackson's wounded men who were treated in the Charlottesville General Hospital following the battle of Port Republic, Virginia (June 8–9, 1862). Thereafter this "disease" progressively increased, although no case was officially recorded until July 1863—more than a year after its initial appearance. Although it is a dangerous disorder no deaths were reported among the 52 gangrene cases appearing in the hospital's statistics. Jones, however, insisted that the surgical wards sustained at least 13 fatalities.

The experiences of Cabell, Davis, and the other surgeons in the Charlottesville General Hospital supported Jones's own findings on the etiology and prevalence of erysipelas, pyemia, and gangrene. Their struggle against secondary infections, he pointed out, clearly indicated that in the early stages of the war these disorders were due almost entirely to "crowding and imperfect ventilation" rather than to any "preexisting condition" of the injured, who were, as a general rule, "well-fed and in high health." Later, as the fortunes of the South waned and the southern soldier was preyed upon by exhaustion, exposure, and the effects of an inadequate diet, supervening diseases were attributable to both "hygienic causes and the preexisting state of the constitution." Crowding patients together, the Charlottesville surgeons discovered, not only "poisoned" the atmosphere but was capable of "rapidly contaminating" the freshly wounded, a point dramatically demonstrated after each major battle with the overcrowding of hospitals and the subsequent soaring of secondary infections. It was soon learned that these disorders were less likely to supervene in small pavillion wards of no more than 20 or 30 patients each.[36]

Arrayed against the ravages of disease and injury in the southern armies was the Confederate medical service. "Well may it be said," Jones reminded, "that to the surgeons of the medical corps is due the credit of maintaining . . . troops in the field."[37] Their tasks were demanding and difficult, requiring, in light of the seemingly insurmountable obstacles which confronted them, a nearly superhuman effort.

The Confederate medical service's problems were legion indeed and seriously threatened its effectiveness. The most basic of these was a chronic and extreme shortage of trained physicians.

Jones believed that only 2,575 men served as surgeons in the southern armies, although a 1916 report of the Association of the Medical Officers of the Army and Navy of the Confederacy placed the total at 3,344. Both figures are appallingly low, especially when one takes into consideration that there were 11,700 physicians to treat the Union sick and wounded.[38] This means that there was approximately 1 doctor for every 133 northern soldiers as compared with 1 for every 324 southerners.[39] There was also a nearly crippling shortage of medical supplies of all types—medicines, instruments, and textbooks. This problem was needlessly exacerbated by the inhumane decision of the North to place medical stores on the contraband list. Even when needed items were available, it will be recalled, the woefully inadequate southern transportation system and the involved Confederate logistics procedures made them virtually inaccessible. Therefore in most cases the southern surgeon was forced to find substitutes or do without. A third major problem, also mentioned earlier, was the constant shifting of hospitals in order to escape the invading Union armies and to treat the sick and wounded in each new sector. These moves not only necessitated the abandonment of many excellent hospital sites as the borders of the Confederacy were steadily pushed inward but also saw the loss of much valuable and irreplaceable equipment and quantities of medical stores. Even worse, perhaps, such forced moves reduced the quality of medical services and made the maintenance of hygiene in the hospitals impossible. The inevitable result was an increase in the disease rate in general and the terrible secondary infections in particular.

Despite such formidable handicaps the southern surgeons kept at their tasks and established an enviable record. "The medical practitioners of the South," as Jones eloquently put it,

> gave their lives and fortunes to their country, without any prospect of military or political fame or preferment. They searched the fields and forests for remedies; they improvised surgical implements from the common instruments of every day life; they marched with the armies, and watched by day and by night in the trenches. The Southern surgeons rescued the wounded on the battle-field, binding up the wounds, and preserving the shattered limbs of their countrymen; the Southern surgeons through four long years op-

posed their skill and untiring energies to the ravages of war and pestilence.

"At all times and under all circumstances," he continued,

> in the rain and sunshine, in the cold winter and burning heat of summer, and the roar of battle, the hissing of bullets and the shriek and crash of shells, the brave hearts, cool heads and strong arms of Southern surgeons were employed but for one purpose—the preservation of the health and lives and the limbs of their countrymen. The Southern surgeons were the first to succor the wounded and the sick, and their ears recorded the last words of love and affection for country and kindred, and their hands closed the eyes of the dying Confederate soldiers.

"It is but just and right," he reasoned, "that a Roll of Honor should be formed of this band of medical heroes."

Yet few historians have singled out the surgeons for praise. Instead the accolades have been bestowed upon what Jones called "the political soldiers" or those who "rose to power and wealth upon the shoulders of the sick and disabled soldiers of the Confederate army by sounding upon all occasions *their war records.*" [40] It is this situation, in part, which has led to the indefensible transformation of the Civil War in America from the needless slaughter that it was into a romantic cause celebre. Not all of the blame lies with the generals: much of it must inevitably rest upon the shoulders of each succeeding generation of Americans since Appomattox. This responsibility is perhaps best understood through a recalling of Allan Nevin's assertion that "every great war has two sides, the glorious and the terrible." Everyone enjoys the former, reveling in the "hundreds of veracious descriptions of . . . pomp and pageantry, [and] innumerable tales of devotion and heroism" but are repulsed by the "sombre remembrance of the butchery, the bereavement, and the long bequest of poverty, exhaustion, and despair." [41] The glorious, while not without a strong appeal, is embarrassingly empty in light of the terrible.

Joseph Jones too was guilty of romanticizing the conflict. He was an ardent secessionist, an unwavering supporter of the war, and in many ways an unreconstructed rebel, deeply revering the lost cause. He may be forgiven to some extent since he was not only a combatant but fought on the losing side. His works, moreover, once stripped of the rhetoric aimed at glorifying the South are a powerful testimonial to the squalor, the stench, and the suffering. Who can read his account of the hell of Andersonville, his examination of the ravages of gangrene in the southern armies, and his vignettes on Confederate medical history without taking a long second look at what has been considered glorious? The color and the drama inevitably give way to a painful awareness of the incredible agony that American inflicted upon American.

Epilogue

Like most southerners after Appomattox Joseph Jones contemplated the future with an uneasiness bordering on fear. His world, the slaveholding South, was gone, never to return. Jones feared that his scientific career had suffered the same fate. For the moment all he could do was to salvage what was left to him. There was no future, he soon learned, in attempting to revive his prewar career at the Medical College of Georgia. New and greener pastures beckoned, first at the University of Nashville and then at the University of Louisiana (later Tulane University). At the Louisiana school he was to build a new life in science, one that was to eclipse his former one in brilliance and achievement.

The Civil War, then, marked the end of an important stage in the life of Joseph Jones: before he had been a budding product of the empirical world of science and the slaveholding South; now that it was over he found himself in a totally different environment—both in science and in the South. For just as Appomattox ushered in a new South, so the work of Louis Pasteur in bacteriology was to revolutionize medical science. The story of the first stage has been told; the remainder has yet to be unfolded.

Notes

Prologue

1. The best recent analysis of scientific interests in the Old South, and the one from which the above synthesis is largely drawn, is Clement Eaton, *The Mind of the Old South*, rev. ed. (Baton Rouge, La., 1967), chap. 11.

2. For the range of scientific interests in the Old South and the achievements of this section's scientists, see T. Cary Johnson, Jr., *Scientific Interests in the Old South*, University of Virginia Institute for Research in the Social Sciences, Publication no. 23 (New York, 1936).

3. Joseph Krafka, Jr., "Joseph Jones, Surgeon C.S.A., "*Journal of the Medical Association of Georgia* 31(1942):353–63; Stanhope Bayne-Jones, "Joseph Jones (1833–1896)," *Bulletin of the Tulane University Medical Faculty* 17(1958):223–30; and Harris D. Riley, "Joseph Jones: Confederate Surgeon," *Journal of the Tennessee State Medical Association* 53(1960):493–504.

Chapter 1

1. E. Merton Coulter, *A Short History of Georgia* (Chapel Hill, N.C., 1933), p. 29.

2. For a detailed history of Liberty County and her people see John B. Mallard, *An Oration, Delivered before the Midway and Newport Library Society . . . March, 1838* (Savannah, Ga., 1838); George White, *Statistics of the State of Georgia* (Savannah, 1849), pp. 369–81; Charles C. Jones, Jr., *The Dead Towns of Georgia*, vol. 4 of *The Collections of the Georgia Historical Society* (Savannah, 1878), pp. 149–51, 172–76; James Stacy, *History of the Midway Congregational Church, Liberty County, Georgia* (Newnan, Ga., 1899); John B. Mallard, "Liberty County, Georgia," *Georgia Historical Quarterly* 2(1918):1–22.

3. "Genealogy of the Jones Family," Charles Colcock Jones Papers, Tulane University, New Orleans (hereafter cited as CCJ-TU); *Savannah Georgian*, March 15, 1839; George White, *Historical Collections of Georgia*, rev. ed. (Baltimore, Md., 1969), pp. 533–37.

4. R. Q. Mallard and Mary Jones, "Rev. Charles Colcock Jones, D.D.," in John S. Wilson, *The Dead of the Synod of Georgia* (Atlanta, Ga., 1869), pp. 185–211; Charles C. Jones to Charles C. Jones, Jr., April 20, 1854, CCJ-TU. Unless otherwise noted biographical information pertaining to Charles Colcock Jones is from these sources.

5. Charles C. Jones to Mary Jones, May 18, September 18, 1830, CCJ-TU.

6. Stacy, *Midway Congregational Church*, pp. 169–70. The best sources for Jones's ministry are his annual reports to the Association for the Religious Instruction of the Negroes in Liberty County. His thirteenth and final one (Savannah, 1848) is of particular importance because of its summary of his activities. Unless otherwise noted material relating to his ministry is drawn from it.

7. Charles C. Jones, *The Religious Instruction of Negroes. A Sermon, Delivered before Association of Planters in Liberty and McIntosh Counties, Georgia*, 4th ed. (Princeton, N.J., 1832).

8. Charles C. Jones to Mary Jones, October 15, 1838, CCJ-TU.

9. Jones, *Thirteenth Annual Report*, pp. 61–62. An historian of the Midway Congregational Church has estimated that during Jones's ministry some 667 slaves joined this church alone. The others made similar gains. In accordance with Jones's wishes the blacks were not set apart in separate churches but, although required to sit in the galleries, were received into and took communion with the white congregations. Stacy, *Midway Congregational Church*, pp. 174–75.

10. *Proceedings of the Meeting in Charleston, S.C., May 13–15, 1845, on the Religious Instruction of the Negroes* (Charleston, 1845). There are frequent requests for Jones's advice on slave religion in CCJ-TU. Jones's published works further enhanced his reputation. He was the compiler of *A Catechism, of Scripture Doctrine and Practice, for Families and Sabbath Schools Designed Also for the Oral Instruction of Colored Persons*, 6th ed. (Princeton, N.J., 1837). This work quickly became well known, even in the North. In addition he wrote a major work on slave religion. Appearing first in 1842, his *Suggestions on the Religious Instruction of the Negroes in the United States* (Savannah, Ga., 1842) went through several editions and was adopted by the Presbyterian Church's Board of Domestic Missions. The annual reports already mentioned were distributed nationally and these also

contributed to his standing as an expert in the field. Random numbers of them can be found in the Joseph Jones Collection, Tulane University, New Orleans, La. (hereafter cited as JJ-TU).

11. New York, 1867. Many of Jones's handwritten sermons and lectures from which this work was prepared are in CCJ-TU. Jones made a final contribution in his campaign to promote the religious instruction of the slaves shortly after the outbreak of the Civil War when he helped organize the Presbyterian Church of the Confederate States of America. As a member of its Domestic Missions Standing Committee he successfully sought the continuation of missionary activities among the Negroes. *Organization of the Presbyterian Church in the Confederate States of America* (Augusta, Ga., [1861?]); Charles C. Jones, *Religious Instruction of the Negroes. An Address Delivered before the General Assembly of the Presbyterian Church, at Augusta, Ga., December 10, 1861* (Richmond, Va., [1862?]); "The Presbyterian Church in Georgia on Secession and Slavery," *Georgia Historical Quarterly* 1(1917): 263–65.

12. Mary Jones to Mary S. Mallard, December 21, 1863, CCJ-TU.

13. Descriptions of the Jones family plantations are drawn primarily from Charles C. Jones, Jr., to Ruth Berrien Jones, May 12, 1888, Charles C. Jones, Jr., Papers, Duke University, Durham (hereafter cited as CCJ, Jr.-Duke); Mary Sharpe Jones and Mary Jones Mallard, *Yankees A'Coming*, ed. Haskell Moore (Tuscaloosa, Ala., 1959); R. Q. Mallard, *Montevideo-Maybank* (Richmond, 1898).

14. Charles C. Jones, Jr., to Charles Colcock and Mary Jones, October 10, 1857, CCJ-TU.

15. "Seventh Census of the United States, 1850. Fourth Series, Agricultural Production, Georgia. Volume Containing the Counties of Irwin to Putnam, June 30, 1850" (Manuscript Returns of the Assistant Marshals, Duke University); "United States Census Returns for C. C. Jones, Liberty County, Ga.," CCJ-TU; "Eighth Census of the United States, 1860. Third Series, Agricultural Production, Georgia. Volume Containing the Counties of Floyd to Murray, June, 1860" (Manuscript Returns of the Assistant Marshals, Duke University).

16. Charles C. Jones to T. J. Shepard, June 2, 1849, CCJ-TU.

17. "Genealogy of the Jones Family," CCJ-TU. For accounts of the lives of Charles C. Jones, Jr., and Mary Sharpe Jones see

Neil S. Penn, "Charles Colcock Jones, Jr., Georgia Archaeologist, Collector, and Historian" (master's thesis, Duke University, 1958); James C. Bonner, "Charles Colcock Jones: The Macaulay of the South," *Georgia Historical Quarterly* 27(1943):324–38; Robert Q. Mallard, "A Biographical Sketch of Mrs. R. Q. Mallard," CCJ-TU. The ensuing description of the Jones youngsters' childhood is, unless otherwise noted, drawn from Charles C. Jones, Jr., to Ruth Berrien Jones, May 12, 1888, CCJ, Jr.-Duke; Mallard, *Montevideo-Maybank*; R. Q. Mallard, *Plantation Life before Emancipation* (Richmond, 1892); Robert M. Myers, ed., *The Children of Pride: A True Story of Georgia and the Civil War* (New Haven, Conn., 1972).

18. Mary S. Mallard to Mary Jones, October 16, 1860, CCJ-TU.

19. Joseph Jones to Charles C. Jones, August 13, 1853, JJ-TU.

20. Myers, *Children of Pride*, p. 10.

21. Charles C. Jones, Jr., *Address Delivered at Midway Meeting House in Liberty County, Georgia, On the Second Wednesday in March 1889* (Augusta, Ga., 1889), pp. 14–15.

22. Myers, *Children of Pride*, p. 10.

23. Mallard, *Montevideo-Maybank*, p. 15.

24. Mallard, *Plantation Life before Emancipation*, p. 28.

25. Charles C. Jones, Jr., to Ruth Berrien Jones, May 12, 1888, CCJ, Jr.-Duke.

Chapter 2

1. Alexander Mackay, *The Western World, or Travels in the United States in 1846–47*, 3 vols. (London, 1849), 2:200.

2. All references to South Carolina College, unless otherwise noted, are from Daniel W. Hollis, *University of South Carolina*, 2 vols. (Columbia, S.C., 1951–56),1; M. LaBorde, *History of the South Carolina College, from Its Incorporation December 19, 1809, to November 25, 1857* (Columbia, S.C., 1859); Edgar W. Knight, *A Documentary History of Education in the South before 1860*, 5 vols. (Chapel Hill, N.C., 1949–53), 3.

3. Charles C. Jones, Jr., to Ruth Berrien Jones, May 12, 1888, CCJ, Jr.-Duke; Charles C. Jones to Col. William Maxwell, December 23, 1848, CCJ-TU; Charles C. Jones to T. J. Shepard, February 1, 1849, CCJ-TU.

4. Knight, *Documentary History of Education in the South*, 3: 340–41.

5. LaBorde, *History of the South Carolina College*, pp. 273–77.

6. Quoted in Hollis, *University of South Carolina*, 1:156.

7. Joseph Jones to Mary Sharpe Jones, December 24, 1849, CCJ-TU.

8. Ibid.

9. Clement Eaton, *The Mind of the Old South*, rev. ed. (Baton Rouge, La., 1967), p. 275.

10. Hollis, *University of South Carolina*, 1:254.

11. Charles C. Jones to Joseph Jones, August 30, 1850, JJ-TU.

12. Grace King, *New Orleans, the Place and the People* (New York, 1895), pp. 382–83.

13. "Copy, for Joseph, Maybank, Liberty County, Ga., July 26th 1850," JJ-TU.

14. Charles C. Jones, Jr., to Charles C. and Mary Jones, August 13, 1850, CCJ-TU; Mary Jones to sister, August 14, 1850, CCJ-TU; Charles C. Jones to Joseph Jones, September 12, 1850, CCJ-TU.

15. Charles C. Jones, Jr., to Charles C. Jones, August 9, 1850, ibid. Details pertaining to Princeton are from Thomas J. Wertenbaker, *Princeton, 1746–1896* (Princeton, N.J., 1946).

16. Charles C. Jones, Jr., to Charles C. Jones, August 9, 1850, CCJ-TU; Joseph Jones to Charles C. and Mary Jones, August 31, 1850, CCJ-TU; Charles C. Jones to Joseph Jones, August 20, 1850, JJ-TU.

17. Wertenbaker, *Princeton*, pp. 185, 245.

18. Joseph Jones to Charles C. and Mary Jones, August 31, 1850, JJ-TU.

19. John R. Williams, ed., *Academic Honors in Princeton University, 1748–1902* (Princeton, N.J., 1902), p. 56; Charles C. Jones to Joseph Jones, March 9, 1852, JJ-TU; Mary Jones to Laura E. Maxwell, March 22, 1852, CCJ-TU.

20. Charles C. Jones to Joseph Jones, March 9, 1852, JJ-TU. The best survey of this controversy is William F. Stanton's *The Leopard's Spots: Scientific Attitudes toward Race in America, 1815–59* (Chicago, 1960).

21. Later, as a medical student, Jones wrote: "If I had my collegiate course to go over again I would devote most of my time to those sciences, which would render one practically useful to his fellow men, instead of pouring over branches, which are in many respects, only mere accomplishments." Joseph Jones to Charles C. Jones, February 10, 1854, JJ-TU.

22. Wertenbaker, *Princeton*, p. 227.

23. *General Catalog of Princeton University, 1746–1906* (Philadelphia, 1908), p. 186; Mary Jones to Charles C. Jones, July 15, 1853, CCJ-TU; Mary Jones to sister, September 13, 1853, CCJ-TU; Joseph Jones, *Medical and Surgical Memoirs*, 3 vols. in 4 (New Orleans, La., 1876–90), 2:71.

24. For a detailed history of the University of Pennsylvania's medical department and nineteenth-century American medical education see Joseph Carson, *A History of the Medical Department of the University of Pennsylvania, from Its Foundation in 1765* (Philadelphia, 1869); George W. Corner, *Two Centuries of Medicine: A History of the School of Medicine, University of Pennsylvania* (Philadelphia, 1965); William F. Norwood, *Medical Education in the United States before the Civil War* (Philadelphia, 1944). According to Corner a majority of the students were generally from south of the Mason-Dixon line.

25. John A. Wyeth, *With Sabre and Scalpel: The Autobiography of a Soldier and Surgeon* (New York, 1914), p. 327.

26. Mary Jones to sister, September 13, 1853, CCJ-TU; Mary Jones to Charles C. Jones, Jr., September 14, 1853, Charles C. Jones, Jr., Papers, University of Georgia, Athens (hereafter cited as CCJ, Jr.-Ga.).

27. Corner, *Two Centuries of Medicine*, pp. 103–5.

28. Ibid., 83–84; Joseph Jones to Charles C. Jones, January 23, 1853 [1854], JJ-TU.

29. "Medical Students and Their Habits," *Nashville Journal of Medicine and Surgery* 17(1859):179–81.

30. Joseph Jones to Mary Jones, November 24, 1853, January 20, 1854, JJ-TU; Joseph Jones to Charles C. Jones, December 30, 1853, JJ-TU.

31. Quoted in Corner, *Two Centuries of Medicine*, p. 95.

32. Joseph Jones to Charles C. Jones, Jr., November 1, 1853, CCJ, Jr.-Ga.; Joseph Jones to Mary Jones, November 24, 1853, January 10, 1855, January 21, 1856, JJ-TU; Joseph Jones to Charles C. Jones, February 10, 1854, February 7, 1855, January 1, 1855 [1856], April 30, 1856, CCJ, Jr.-Ga.; Charles C. Jones to Joseph Jones, October 18, December 21, 1854, CCJ, Jr.-Ga.; Mary Holmes to Mary Jones, May 15, 1856, CCJ-TU.

33. Corner, *Two Centuries of Medicine*, pp. 76–77; Joseph Jones to Charles C. Jones, January 23, 1853 [1854], JJ-TU.

34. Henry B. Shafer, *The American Medical Profession, 1783*

to 1850, Columbia University Studies in the Social Sciences, Publication no. 417 (New York, 1936), pp. 65–66.

35. Joseph Jones to Mary Jones, November 24, 1853, JJ-TU.

36. Joseph Jones to Charles C. Jones, January 23, 1853 [1854], JJ-TU; Charles C. Jones, Jr., to Mary Jones, April 10, 1854, CCJ-TU; Charles C. Jones, Jr., to Charles C. and Mary Jones, April 24, 1854, CCJ-TU; Charles C. Jones to Charles C. Jones, Jr., April 20, 1854, CCJ, Jr.-Ga.; Jones, *Memoirs*, 1:71, 272; 2: 699–701, 886. Joseph Jones was convinced that victory over disease would be achieved not through treating the symptoms but in stamping out its cause. "Experience has taught," he wrote at the beginning of his medical training, "that it is in vain for the physician to attempt to check those violent Epidemics, which sweep over, & almost depopulate whole Continents, when they are in full career. He should study the first causes of these Epidemics & remove & control these causes before they have begun their work." Joseph Jones to Mary Jones, November 24, 1853, JJ-TU.

37. Charles C. Jones to Charles C. Jones, Jr., September 11, 1854, CCJ, Jr.-Ga.; Mary Jones to Charles C. Jones, Jr., September 14, 1854, CCJ, Jr.-Ga.

38. Charles C. Jones to Joseph Jones, October 18, December 21, 1854, JJ-TU; Joseph Jones to Charles C. and Mary Jones, January 9, 1855, CCJ-TU; Joseph Jones, "Abstract of Experiments upon the Physical Influences Exerted by Living, Organic and Inorganic Membranes upon Chemical Substances, in Solution, Passing through Them by Endosmose," *American Journal of the Medical Sciences*, n.s. 19(1855):555-60. This same issue carried a second article by Jones—"Observations upon the Kidney and Its Excretions in Different Animals" (pp. 295–336). Nothing in the various Jones collections clarifies its history.

39. William B. Carpenter, *Human Physiology*, ed. Francis G. Smith (Philadelphia, 1856), pp. 139–42; Joseph Jones to Charles C. Jones, December 21, 1855, JJ-TU.

40. Joseph Leidy to Charles C. Jones, November 17, 1854, CCJ-TU; Joseph Jones to Charles C. and Mary Jones, January 1, 1855, JJ-TU.

41. Charles C. Jones to Mary Sharpe Jones, September 27, 1855, CCJ-TU; Joseph Jones to Mary Jones, January 21, 1856, JJ-TU; Jones, *Memoirs*, 1:510, 516, 564–77; 2:201, 1311–17.

42. Joseph Jones to Charles C. Jones, November 28, 1855, JJ-

TU. This study was published, but not until after Joseph's graduation from medical school; see Joseph Jones, "Digestion of Albumen and Flesh, and the Comparative Anatomy and Physiology of the Pancreas," *Medical Examiner*, n.s. 12(1856):257–76.

43. Joseph Jones, "Physical, Chemical, and Physiological Investigations upon the Vital Phenomena, Structure, and Offices of the Solids and Fluids of Animals," *American Journal of the Medical Sciences*, n.s. 32(1856):12–63.

44. Joseph Jones to Charles C. Jones, March 11, 1856, JJ-TU; Joseph Jones to Charles C. and Mary Jones, March 29, 1856, JJ-TU; Charles C. Jones to Joseph Jones, March 31, 1856, JJ-TU; Mary Jones to sister, March 31, 1856, CCJ-TU.

45. Joseph Jones to Charles C. Jones, December 21, 1855, JJ-TU; Joseph Jones to Mary Jones, January 21, 1856, JJ-TU.

46. Joseph Jones to Charles C. Jones, March 11, 1856, JJ-TU; Joseph Henry to Joseph Jones, March 20, 1856, Joseph Jones Collection, Louisiana State University, Baton Rouge (hereafter cited as JJ-LSU).

47. Joseph Jones to Joseph Henry, March 25, 1856, JJ-LSU.

48. Joseph Henry to Joseph Jones, March 26, 1856, JJ-LSU.

49. Joseph Jones to Charles C. and Mary Jones, March 29, 1856, JJ-TU.

50. Charles C. Jones to Joseph Jones, March 29, 1856, JJ-TU. Joseph, somewhat reluctantly, accepted this offer of aid, asking for $100 on April 30. His father responded a week later with a check for $130. Joseph Jones to Charles C. Jones, April 30, 1856, JJ-TU. Charles C. Jones to Joseph Jones, May 7, 1856, JJ-TU.

51. Joseph Jones to Joseph Henry, March 31, 1856, JJ-LSU.

52. Joseph Henry to Joseph Jones, April 2, 1856, JJ-LSU.

53. Joseph Jones to Joseph Henry, April 17, 22, 1856, JJ-LSU.

54. Joseph Henry to Joseph Jones, April 19, 1856, JJ-LSU.

55. Joseph Jones to Joseph Henry, April 22, 1856, JJ-LSU.

56. Joseph Henry to Joseph Jones, April 24, 1856, JJ-LSU.

57. Joseph Jones to Joseph Henry, May 7, 1856, JJ-LSU.

58. Joseph Henry to Joseph Jones, May 9, 1856, JJ-LSU.

59. Joseph Jones to Joseph Henry, May 10, 1856, JJ-LSU; Joseph Jones to Charles C. Jones, May 14, 1856, JJ-TU.

60. Joseph Henry to Joseph Jones, May 13, 1856, JJ-LSU.

61. Ibid., May 5, June 7, 20, 1856; Spencer F. Baird to Joseph Jones, June 6, 19, July 15, 1856, JJ-LSU; Mary Jones to Charles C. Jones, Jr., June 25, 1856, CCJ, Jr.-Ga.

62. Joseph Jones, "Investigations, Chemical and Physiological, Relative to Certain American Vertebrata," *Smithsonian Contributions to Knowledge* 7(1856).

Chapter 3

1. Joseph Jones to Charles C. Jones, May 14, 1856, JJ-TU.

2. For a history of the Savannah Medical College see "Faculty Minutes of the Savannah Medical College, 1853–1862," Georgia Historical Society, Savannah (hereafter cited as "Faculty Minutes").

3. Mary Sharpe Jones to Joseph Jones, December 21, 1853, CCJ-TU; Dr. C. W. West to Charles C. Jones, January 14, 1856, JJ-TU.

4. Charles C. Jones to Joseph Jones, January 31, 1855 [1856], JJ-TU.

5. "Faculty Minutes," April 2, 1856; Dr. J. G. Howard to Joseph Jones, April 10, 1856, JJ-TU; Joseph Jones to Dr. J. G. Howard, April 23, 1856, JJ-TU; Joseph Jones to Charles C. Jones, April 30, 1856, JJ-TU.

6. Charles C. Jones to Joseph Jones, May 5, 7, 1856, JJ-TU.

7. Charles C. Jones to Joseph Jones, May 5, 1856, JJ-TU.

8. "Faculty Minutes," May 19, 1856; Joseph Jones to Charles C. Jones, May 14, 1856, JJ-TU.

9. Mary Jones to Charles C. Jones, Jr., July 10, 1856, CCJ, Jr.-Ga.; Mary Sharpe Jones to Charles C. Jones, Jr., September 25, 1856, CCJ, Jr.-Ga.

10. Charles C. Jones, Jr., to Mary Jones, July 12, 1856, CCJ-TU.

11. Charles Mackay, *Life and Liberty in America; or, Sketches of a Tour in the United States and Canada in 1857–8* (New York, 1859), pp. 209–10.

12. Mary Sharpe Jones to Susan M. Cumming, September 13, 1856, CCJ-TU; Charles C. Jones to Charles C. Jones, Jr., October 2, 1856, CCJ, Jr.-Ga.

13. This and other reactions that are equally favorable are contained in Mary Jones to Charles C. Jones, October 22, 1856, JJ-LSU.

14. Charles C. Jones to Mary Jones, October 23, 1856, CCJ-TU.

15. Joseph Jones to Charles C. and Mary Jones, November 3, 1856, JJ-TU.

16. Charles C. Jones to Mary Jones, October 23, 1856, CCJ-TU; Joseph Jones to Charles C. and Mary Jones, January 10, 1856 [1857], JJ-TU.

17. Charles C. Jones, Jr., to Charles C. and Mary Jones, January 24, 1857, CCJ-TU.

18. Joseph Jones to Charles C. Jones, October 5, 1857, JJ-TU.

19. Henry H. Jones to Charles C. Jones, July 1, 1857, CCJ-TU.

20. Joseph Jones to Charles C. Jones, July 6, 1857, JJ-TU.

21. Ibid., January 10, October 15, 1857.

22. For a sampling of the many references to this research see Joseph Jones to Charles C. and Mary Jones, January 6, 1857, JJ-TU; Joseph Jones to Charles C. Jones, July 13, September 8, October 5, 15, 1857, JJ-TU; Charles C. Jones, Jr., to Charles C. and Mary Jones, November 6, 1857, CCJ, Jr.-Ga.; Joseph Jones to Caroline Davis, June 22, 1859, JJ-TU; Jones, *Memoirs*, 2:5, 140–48, 469–73, 530, 705–8, 767–87, 799–827; Joseph Jones, "Outline of Investigations into the Nature, Causes and Prevention of Endemic and Epidemic Diseases, and More Especially Malarial Fever . . . ," in *Transactions of the International Medical Congress*, ed. John B. Hamilton, 9th sess. (1887), 4:495 (hereafter cited as Jones, "Outline of Investigations"); Joseph Jones, "Black Vomit of Yellow Fever," *New Orleans Medical and Surgical Journal*, n.s. 4(1876):159.

23. Joseph Jones to Charles C. Jones, October 15, 1857, CCJ-TU. For a brief background of the nature of American medical research in the nineteenth century see Richard H. Shryock, "Trends in American Medical Research during the Nineteenth Century," *Proceedings of the American Philosophical Society* 91 (1947):58–63.

24. Joseph Jones to Charles C. Jones, July 13, August 14, 1857, JJ-TU; Charles C. Jones, Jr., to Joseph Jones, July 26, 1857, JJ-TU; Charles C. Jones to Joseph Jones, August 10, 1857, CCJ-TU.

25. Charles C. Jones to Joseph Jones, August 10, 1857, CCJ-TU.

26. "Faculty Minutes," September 8, 1857.

27. Joseph Jones to Charles C. Jones, October 7, 1857, JJ-TU; Charles C. Jones to Joseph Jones, October 12, 1857, JJ-TU.

28. "Faculty Minutes," October 15, 17, 1857.

29. S. W. M., review of "Investigations, Chemical and Physiological, Relative to Certain American Vertebrata" by Joseph

Jones, in *Smithsonian Contributions to Knowledge: North American Medico-Chirurgical Review* 5(1857):697–99.

30. Charles C. Jones to Joseph Jones, September 1, 1857, JJ-TU. Jones's favorable review appeared in the *Charleston Medical Journal and Review* 12(1857):654. It was, indeed, kinder to him, but it would be stretching the truth to say that it offset the critical one. In reality, this was a one-page generally complimentary critique of all of his publications.

31. S. D. Gross to Joseph Jones, September 2, 1857, JJ-TU; Joseph Jones to Charles C. Jones, September 8, 1857, JJ-TU.

32. E. Merton Coulter, *College Life in the Old South* (New York, 1928), pp. 299–300. This is the standard work on the University of Georgia and the one on which the ensuing sketch is based.

33. Ibid., pp. 85–87.

34. Joseph Jones to Charles C. Jones, January 27, 1858, JJ-TU.

35. Ibid., March 1, 1857.

36. Charles C. Jones to Joseph Jones, March 5, 1858, JJ-TU.

37. Joseph Jones to Charles C. and Mary Jones, March 3, 1858, JJ-TU. The careers of the LeConte brothers are discussed in Johnson, *Scientific Interests in the Old South*.

38. Henry F. Campbell to Joseph Jones, March 5, 1858, JJ-TU; Joseph Jones to Charles C. and Mary Jones, March 13, 1858, JJ-TU.

39. Charles C. Jones to Joseph Jones, March 11, 18, 1858, JJ-TU.

40. Joseph Jones to Charles C. Jones, March 24, 1858, JJ-TU.

41. Charles C. Jones, Jr., to Charles C. and Mary Jones, April 3, 1858, CCJ-TU.

42. Juriah Harriss, "Appointment of Professor Joseph Jones," *Savannah Journal of Medicine* 1(1858):71–72; see also "Medical College of Georgia—Appointment of Professor Joseph Jones," *Southern Medical and Surgical Journal,* n.s. 14(1848):282–83; "Medical College of Georgia," *Medical News and Library* 6 (1858):78.

43. Joseph Jones to Charles C. and Mary Jones, April 22, 1858, JJ-TU.

44. Charles C. Jones to Joseph and Charles C. Jones, Jr., April 2, 1852, JJ-TU.

45. Charles C. Jones to Joseph Jones, April 27, 1858, JJ-TU.

46. Joseph Jones to Charles C. Jones, October 25, 1858, JJ-TU.

47. Ibid., April 26, 1858; William F. Mitchell to Charles C.

Jones, April 27, 1858, JJ-TU; Charles C. Jones to Joseph Jones, May 4, 1858, JJ-TU; Joseph Jones to Charles C. Jones, October 25, December 9, 25, 1858, February 8, 1859, JJ-TU.

48. Henry F. Campbell to Joseph Jones, March 5, 1858, JJ-TU.

49. Joseph Jones, "Cases of Diabetes Mellitus," *Southern Medical and Surgical Journal*, n.s. 14(1858):292–315.

50. Joseph Jones, "Observations on Malarial Fever," *Southern Medical and Surgical Journal*, n.s. 14(1858):363–98, 435–39, 506–38, 579–601, 651–76, 723–43; 15(1859):74–100, 147–72, 219–45. Campbell was especially enthused with Jones's findings on malaria and drew heavily on them in a report to the American Medical Association. He discussed Jones's results alongside those of well-known national and international physiologists. Henry F. Campbell, "Report on the Nervous System in Febrile Diseases, and the Classification of Fevers by the Nervous System," *Transactions of the American Medical Association* 11(1858):549–720.

51. Jones, "Observations on Malarial Fever," pp. 579–601.

52. Ibid., pp. 363–77.

53. Charles C. Jones, Jr., to Charles C. and Mary Jones, April 3, September 11, 1858, CCJ-TU; Charles C. Jones to Charles C. Jones, Jr., September 2, 1858, CCJ, Jr.-Ga.

54. Fredrika Bremer, *The Homes of the New World: Impressions of America*, trans. Mary Howitt, 3 vols. in 1 (London, 1853), 1:380–81.

55. "Medical Colleges of the United States," *American Medical Times* 1(1860):255.

56. William F. Norwood, *Medical Education in the United States before the Civil War* (Philadelphia, 1944), p. 279.

57. Joseph Jones to Charles C. Jones, September 16, 1858, JJ-TU; Joseph Jones to Mary Jones, November 1, 1858, JJ-TU.

58. Joseph Jones to Charles C. Jones, December 9, 1858, JJ-TU; see also *Thirtieth Annual Announcement of the Medical College of Georgia* (Augusta, Ga., 1861), p. 6.

59. Joseph Jones to Caroline Davis, February 25, 1859, JJ-TU.

60. Joseph Jones to Charles C. Jones, February 19, 1859, JJ-TU.

61. Joseph Jones to Charles C. Jones, May 10, 1859, JJ-TU.

62. Joseph Jones to Charles C. and Mary Jones, April 23, 1858, JJ-TU.

63. Joseph Jones to Caroline Davis, April 21, 1859, JJ-TU. At a second meeting, held in Milledgeville the following November, the proposal was scrapped. Jones again represented the Medical College of Georgia. Joseph Jones to Charles C. and Mary Jones, November 8, 1859, JJ-TU.

64. Joseph Jones to Charles C. and Mary Jones, April 23, 1859, JJ-TU.

65. Joseph Jones to Mary Jones, May 3, 1859, JJ-TU.

66. Joseph Jones to Charles C. and Mary Jones, April 23, 1859, JJ-TU.

67. *Transactions of the American Medical Association* 11 (1858):31, 35. A good short account of mid-nineteenth century medical education and its problems is William F. Norwood, "American Medical Education from the Revolutionary War to the Civil War," *Journal of Medical Education* 32(1957):433–48. For the goals of the A.M.A. see *Proceedings of the National Convention, Held in New York, May, 1846, and in Philadelphia, May, 1847* (Philadelphia, 1847), pp. 15–16.

68. Joseph Jones to Mary Jones, May 3, 1859, JJ-TU. Jones and Campbell represented the Medical College of Georgia at this meeting. For its proceedings see "Medical Teachers' Convention," *Cincinnati Lancet and Observer*, n.s. 2(1859):445–49.

69. Jones, "Outline of Investigations," p. 497. Jones's thesis, if this study actually had one, was that "malarial poison destroyed the blood corpuscles more rapidly than other febrile poison and diminished the phosphates of the blood." Joseph Jones, "Mollites Ossium," *Transactions of the American Medical Association* 20(1869):375.

70. *Transactions of the American Medical Association* 12 (1859):29–31.

71. Quoted in Robert Q. Mallard to Mary S. Mallard, May 18, 1859, CCJ-TU.

72. Joseph Jones to Caroline Davis, June 11, 26, August 2, 26, 1859, JJ-TU. The break came in early July when Jones visited his fiancee for a week or more. Joseph Jones to Caroline Davis, June 22, 1859, JJ-TU; Joseph Jones to Mary Jones, July 15, 1859, JJ-TU.

73. Joseph Jones to Caroline Davis, September 11, 1859, JJ-TU. Joseph Jones, "General View of the Therapeutic Application of Electricity, being an Outline of Lectures Delivered upon This Subject before the Class of 1859 and 1860, in the

Medical College of Georgia, at Augusta," *Southern Medical and Surgical Journal*, n.s. 11(1860):9–17.

74. Joseph Jones to Caroline Davis, August 4, 1859, JJ-TU.

75. Ibid.

76. Joseph Jones, *Suggestions on Medical Education. Introductory Lecture to the Course of 1859–'60, in the Medical College of Georgia* (Augusta, Ga., 1860).

77. Joseph Jones to Charles C. Jones, December 6, 1859, JJ-TU. Each student lost cost the school at least $105, the price of a course of lectures, plus the matriculation and graduation fees. *Thirtieth Annual Announcement of the Medical College of Georgia.*

78. Joseph Jones to Mary Jones, September 24, 1859, JJ-TU; Charles C. Jones to Joseph Jones, October 3, 1859, JJ-TU; Charles C. Jones, Jr., to Charles C. Jones, October 6, 1859, CCJ, Jr.-Ga. The value of summer medical schools was another question that the AMA was far from agreement on (see for example "The Medical Association—Breakers Ahead," *Nashville Medical Monthly* 2(1860):509–11). This being the case, Jones was very much concerned with the image that he projected to the older schools, especially the University of Pennsylvania. For many years he entertained thoughts of returning there eventually to teach. Had it not been for the Civil War there may have been a possibility of this. His benefactor there, Samuel Jackson, wrote him in 1857: "My strength is improving and I shall be able to undertake another course in the University but the end is not far distant. I should like to hold on a little longer that you might have a fair chance in a competition for the vacant chair." Samuel Jackson to Joseph Jones, September 21, 1857, JJ-TU.

79. Joseph Jones to Caroline Davis, February 25, 1859, JJ-TU. Caroline Davis was also descended from a prominent Southern family; see Joseph B. Cumming, *A Sketch of the Descendants of David Cumming and Memoirs of the War between the States,* ed. Mary G. S. Cumming (n.p., 1925), p. 13.

80. Joseph Jones to Caroline Davis, March 13, 1859, JJ-TU.

81. Ibid., April 13, 1859.

82. Ibid., June 5, 1859.

83. Joseph Jones to Charles C. Jones, February 19, 1859, JJ-TU.

84. Joseph Jones to Caroline Davis, October 26, 1859, JJ-TU. Jones had no way of knowing that his family's apparent immunity to malaria on Colonel's Island was not due to acclimati-

zation but to the salt water marshes which did not support the malaria-bearing *Anopheles* mosquito.

85. Joseph Jones to Charles C. Jones, October 4, 6, December 6, 1859, JJ-TU; Caroline Jones to Charles C. Jones, December 29, 1859, JJ-TU.

Chapter 4

1. Joseph Jones to Charles C. Jones, November 6, 1860, JJ-TU; "Return of Southern Medical Students from Northern Colleges," *Southern Medical and Surgical Journal*, n.s. 16(1860):73–76.

2. Joseph Jones to Charles C. Jones, February 22, March 24, 1860, JJ-TU; *Joseph Jones' Laboratory for Practical Instruction in Medical Physics, Chemistry and Pharmacy, Toxicology, Experimental Physiology, and Comparative Anatomy* (Augusta, Ga., 1860). Jones also found time to pursue his study of southern diseases. Jones, *Memoirs*, 1:303, 391–92, 516.

3. Erwin H. Ackerknecht, *A Short History of Medicine*, rev. ed. (New York, 1968), pp. 120–21, 172. For Jones's research involving the clinical thermometer see his *Memoirs*, 1:71, 272; 2:699–701, 886. His use of the clinical thermometer and microscope is even more praiseworthy when it is pointed out that the medical department of the Union Army did not even have a microscope until 1863, and the whole army had no more than twenty clinical thermometers. Adams further contends that Jones was the only Confederate surgeon to use the clinical thermometer. George W. Adams, *Doctors in Blue: The Medical History of the Union Army in the Civil War* (New York, 1952), p. 51; George W. Adams, "Confederate Medicine," *Journal of Southern History* 6 (1940):156.

4. "Private Instruction in Chemistry, &c.," *Southern Medical and Surgical Journal*, n.s. 16(1860):311.

5. "News and Miscellany," *Medical and Surgical Reporter*, n.s. 3(1860):510.

6. Daniel Lee, "A Useful Museum and Laboratory," *Southern Field and Fireside* 1(1860):313. Lee's life is fully explored in E. Merton Coulter's *Daniel Lee, Agriculturalist: His Life North and South* (Athens, Ga., 1972).

7. Joseph Jones to Charles C. Jones, March 24, April 30, November 6, 1860, JJ-TU.

8. Howell Cobb, *Organization of the Cotton Power* (Macon, Ga.,

1858); Weymouth T. Jordan, *Rebels in the Making: Planters' Conventions and Southern Propaganda* (Tuscaloosa, Ala., 1958), pp. 104–21; *Weekly Georgia Telegraph* (Macon), June 15, 1860; *Georgia Journal and Messenger* (Macon), June 20, 1860.

9. Joseph Jones to Charles C. Jones, April 30, August 7, 1860, JJ-TU; Joseph Jones to Charles C. and Mary Jones, June 30, 1860, JJ-TU.

10. Joseph Jones to Caroline Jones, May 25, 1860, JJ-TU.

11. Joseph Jones to Charles C. Jones, April 30, 1860, JJ-TU.

12. "Cotton Planters Convention—Analysis of Fertilizers," *Daily Chronicle & Sentinel* (Augusta), May 16, 1860. In an effort to make his analyses as fair as possible Jones had his brother send him a second set of samples of the fertilizers tested from Savannah. Still some of the vendors took issue with his evaluation of their report and attacked his report. "Mapes' Superphosphate," *Daily Chronicle & Sentinel* (Augusta), November 7, 1860.

13. Joseph Jones to Caroline Jones, May 25, 1860, JJ-TU; Joseph Jones to Charles C. and Mary Jones, June 30, 1860, JJ-TU; Joseph Jones to Charles C. Jones, August 7, November 6, 1860, JJ-TU; Charles C. Jones, Jr., to Charles C. and Mary Jones, July 18, September 9, 1860, CCJ-TU. In his research Jones studied the effects of poisons and electricity on animals in relation to his broader study of southern diseases. Jones, *Memoirs*, 1:320–21, 391–92, 513–16, 524; Joseph Jones, "Poisonous Effects of Cyanide of Potassium," *New Orleans Medical and Surgical Journal*, n.s. 4(1877):780–81.

14. J. H. Douglas, review of volume 12 of the *Transactions of the American Medical Association* (Philadelphia, 1859), in *American Medical Monthly* 13(1860):138. For Jones's study see Joseph Jones, "Observations on Some of the Physical, Chemical, Physiological and Pathological Phenomena of Malarial Fever," *Transactions of the American Medical Association* 12(1859):209–627.

15. Review of volume 12 of the *Transactions of the American Medical Association* (Philadelphia, 1859), in the *Nashville Journal of Medicine and Surgery* 18(1860):237–38.

16. Review of volume 12 of the *Transactions of the American Medical Association* (Philadelphia, 1859), in the *Charleston Medical Journal and Review* 15(1860):366.

17. "Editorial Department," *Louisville Medical Journal* 1 (1860):63–64.

18. Review . . . , *Charleston Medical Journal and Review*, p. 366.

Jones apparently did not see these critical reviews. If he did it is strange that there is no record of his usual charge of a personal attack. A number of the reviewers felt that the extraordinary length of Jones's study proved that the A.M.A. needed to scrutinize more closely the material it published in its *Transactions*, a view many in the medical profession had held for some time. A typical expression of this feeling is the review of volume 12 in the *Maryland and Virginia Medical Journal,* n.s. 1(1860):77.

19. Joseph Jones to Charles C. Jones, August 7, 1860, JJ-TU; Joseph Jones, "Report to the 'Cotton Planters' Convention, of Georgia,' on the Marls and Shell Limestone of Georgia," *Daily Telegraph* (Macon), August 9–10, 1860; Joseph Jones, "Report to the Cotton Planters' Convention of Georgia, upon the Relative Amounts of Phosphate of Lime, Contained in the Marls and Shell Limestone of Georgia, and Various Commercial Manures," ibid., August 30, 1860. The latter article was reprinted in the *Southern Field and Fireside* 2(1860):110.

20. Daniel Lee, "Marls of Burke County, Georgia," *Southern Field and Fireside* 2(1860):102; see also "The Cotton Planters' Convention and Its First Annual Fair," *Daily Chronicle & Sentinel* (Augusta), September 18, 1860.

21. Charles C. Jones, Jr., to Charles C. and Mary Jones, September 9, 1860, CCJ-TU.

22. Mary Jones to Joseph Jones, [September, 1860], JJ-LSU. Jones did find time, however, to become an elder in the Presbyterian Church. Joseph Jones to Charles C. Jones, July 5, August 7, November 6, 1860, JJ-TU; Mary Jones to Joseph and Caroline Jones, November 15, 1860, JJ-LSU.

23. Joseph Jones, *First Report to the Cotton Planters' Convention of Georgia on the Agricultural Resources of Georgia* (Augusta, Ga., 1860).

24. "Prof. Jones' Agricultural Report," *Southern Cultivator* 18(1860):388.

25. Joseph Jones to Charles C. Jones, November 6, 1860, JJ-TU. Only seventy students enrolled at the Medical College of Georgia for the 1860–1861 session.

26. Charles C. Jones to Charles C. Jones, Jr., November 19, 1860, CCJ-TU.

27. [Cotton Planters' Convention], *Memorial. To the Honorable, the Senate and House of Representatives of the State of Georgia in General Assembly Met* [Macon, Ga., 1860], p. 11. Augusta's

Daily Chronicle & Sentinel (December 16, 1860) strongly endorsed the memorial and commended the Cotton Planters' Convention for nominating Jones for the position of state chemist. "A more competent, laborious, skillful, painstaking man," the editor asserted, "cannot probably be found in the State."

28. Joseph Jones to Charles C. Jones, November 6, 1860, JJ-TU.

29. Daniel Lee, review of *First Report to the Cotton Planters' Convention of Georgia, on the Agricultural Resources of Georgia*, in *Southern Field and Fireside* 2(1860):190.

30. Daniel Lee, "Marl & Lime as Sources of Fertility," ibid., p. 198.

31. Lee, review of *First Report*, p. 190.

32. Joseph Jones, *Report to the Cotton Planters' Convention of Georgia on Baker & Jarvis' Island Guano and Other Matters of Interest to Planters* (Savannah, Ga., 1860), pp. 7–9.

33. Daniel Lee, "Phosphatic Guanos," *Southern Field and Fireside* 2(1860):214.

34. "Prof. Jones' Report Defended," *Southern Cultivator* 18 (1860):373–74.

35. "Prof. Jones and Dr. Lee," *Southern Cultivator* 19(1861): 98–100.

36. A. B. Tucker, "A Review of a Report to the Cotton Planters' Convention. By Jos. Jones, M.D., &c.," *Savannah Journal of Medicine* 3(1861):353–57.

37. L. D. Ford, "Professor Joseph Jones, in the *Savannah Journal of Medicine*," ibid., pp. 421–27. As Ford points out there was some foreign notice of Jones's works, especially in England where he claimed that they received "friendly notice at the hands of Richard Owen, Benjamin Ward Richardson, Edmund A. Parkes and William Aitken." His studies apparently never reached Germany. Jones, *Memoirs*, 2:702.

38. Joseph Jones to Charles C. Jones, November 6, 1860, JJ-TU.

39. Charles C. Jones, Jr., to Charles C. and Mary Jones, November 7, 1860, CCJ, Jr.-Ga.

40. Mary Jones to Joseph and Caroline Jones, November 15, 1860, JJ-LSU.

41. Mary Jones to Charles C. Jones, Jr., November 15, 1860, CCJ, Jr.-Ga.

42. "First Annual Fair of the Cotton Planters' Convention of

the State of Georgia," *American Cotton Planter and Soil of the South*, n.s. 4(1860):533–35; Jordan, *Rebels in the Making: Planters' Conventions and Southern Propaganda* (Tuscaloosa, Ala., 1959), pp. 116–21.

43. Joseph Jones, *Agricultural Resources of Georgia. Address before the Cotton Planters' Convention of Georgia at Macon, December 13, 1860* (Augusta, Ga., 1861).

44. *Daily Chronicle & Sentinel* (Augusta), December 21, 1860; "Prof. Jones' Speech," *Daily Telegraph* (Macon), December 14, 1860. Copies of the address were printed and sold for $2.00. Mary Jones to Joseph and Caroline Jones, January 1, 1861, JJ-LSU.

45. Joseph Jones to Mary Jones, December 25, 1860, JJ-TU; "The Bill," *Daily Chronicle & Sentinel* (Augusta), December 16, 1860.

46. Mary Jones to Charles C. Jones, Jr., January 3, 1861, CCJ, Jr.-Ga.; J. V. Jones to Joseph Jones, January 12, 1861, JJ-LSU; H. H. Waters to James V. Jones, January 1, 1861, JJ-LSU; T. J. Smith to Joseph Jones, January 22, 1861, JJ-LSU; H. H. Waters to Thomas W. Fleming, Thomas Mallard, and others, March 26, 1861, CCJ-TU.

47. Joseph Jones to Caroline Jones, December 12, 1860, JJ-TU. At the June 1861 meeting of the Cotton Planters' Convention a resolution was adopted authorizing the payment of one thousand dollars in Confederate bonds to Jones "not as an act of compensation, but as a testimonial of our appreciation of invaluable services rendered in his department of science to cotton planters of the South." *Daily Constitutionalist* (Augusta), June 18, 1861. This was the closest to compensation that Jones came.

48. Charles C. and Mary Jones to Joseph and Caroline Jones, December 18, 1860, JJ-TU.

49. Jones, *Memoirs*, 1:317–18, 394–96, 514–15; Jones, "Poisonous Effects of Cyanide of Potassium," pp. 781–82.

50. Joseph Jones to Charles C. Jones, January 17, 1861, JJ-TU.

51. For a more detailed account of the Southern medical profession in the sectional conflict see John Duffy, "A Note on Ante-Bellum Southern Nationalism and Medical Practice," *Journal of Southern History* 34(1968):266–76.

52. Ralph A. Wooster, *The Secession Conventions of the South* (Princeton, N.J., 1962), pp. 80–100.

Chapter 5

1. Joseph Jones to Charles C. Jones, February 5, 1861, JJ-TU.
2. Mary Jones to Joseph and Caroline Jones, January 1, 1861, JJ-LSU.
3. Joseph Jones to Caroline Jones, April 6, 1861, JJ-TU; see also Charles C. Jones to Charles C. Jones, Jr., April 2, 1861, CCJ, Jr.-Ga.; Joseph Jones to Charles C. Jones, April 4, 1861, JJ-TU.
4. Charles C. Jones to Charles C. Jones, Jr., May 9, 1861, CCJ, Jr.-Ga.
5. Caroline Jones to Mary Jones, May 10, 1861, JJ-TU.
6. Joseph Jones to Charles C. and Mary Jones, June 6, 1861, JJ-TU; Charles C. Jones to Charles C. Jones, Jr., May 9, 1861, CCJ, Jr.-Ga. For a history of this unit see Charles C. Jones, *Historical Address, Delivered to the Liberty Independent Troop, upon Its Anniversary, February 22, 1856* (Savannah, Ga., 1856).
7. Charles C. Jones to Charles C. Jones, Jr., May 9, 1861, CCJ, Jr.-Ga.
8. Ibid., May 30, 1861; Joseph Jones to Charles C. and Mary Jones, June 6, 1861, JJ-TU.
9. The major part of the lengthy correspondence relating this sad chapter in Jones family history is to be found in Robert M. Myers, ed., *The Children of Pride* (New Haven, Conn., 1972), pp. 701–16; in addition see Charles C. Jones, Jr., to Joseph Jones, June 25, 1861, JJ-TU; Caroline Jones to Joseph Jones, June 28, 1861, JJ-TU; Joseph Jones to Caroline Jones, June 28, July 6, 7, 1861, JJ-TU.
10. Joseph Jones to Charles C. and Mary Jones, June 6, 1861, JJ-TU.
11. Joseph Jones to Charles C. Jones, July 31, 1861, JJ-TU. Jones also found some time to advance his study of southern diseases, especially the effects of various poisons on animals and birds. Jones, *Memoirs*, 1:291–319, 511–14, 525; Jones, "Poisonous Effects of Cyanide of Potassium," *New Orleans Journal of the Medical Sciences*, n.s. 4(1877):781–82; Jones, "Experiments upon the Action of Carbonic Acid Gas upon Animals," JJ-TU.
12. Joseph Jones, "Sulphate of Quinia Administered in Small Doses during Health, the Best Means of Preventing Chill and Fever, and Bilious Fever in Those Exposed to the Unhealthy Climate of the Rich Low-Lands and Swamps of the Southern Confederacy," *Southern Medical and Surgical Journal*, n.s. 17 (1861):593–614. Jones later enlarged this article to encompass

his wartime investigations and appended it to one of his reports to Surgeon General Samuel P. Moore. After the war he published the revised study; see Joseph Jones, "Quinine as a Prophylactic against Malarial Fever: Being an Appendix to the Third Report on Typhoid and Malarial Fevers, Delivered to the Surgeon General of the Late C.S.A. August 1864," *Nashville Journal of Medicine and Surgery,* n.s. 2(1867):441–72.

13. Joseph Jones, "Indigenous Remedies of the Southern Confederacy Which May Be Employed in the Treatment of Malarial Fever," *Southern Medical and Surgical Journal,* n.s. 17(1861): 673–718, 753–87. This study was reprinted in several other southern medical journals. After the war Jones also enlarged and republished it; see Joseph Jones, "Indigenous Remedies of the Southern States, Which May Be Employed as Substitutes for Sulphate of Quinine in the Treatment of Malarial Fever," *St. Louis Medical Reporter* 3(1868):261–75, 293–312, 389–98.

14. Joseph Jones to Charles C. Jones, July 31, 1861, JJ-TU.

15. Caroline Jones to Mary Jones, May 10, 1861, JJ-TU; Caroline Jones to Charles C. and Mary Jones, September 14, 1861, JJ-TU.

16. Charles C. Jones, Jr., to Charles C. Jones, October 7, 1861, CCJ, Jr.-Ga.

17. Charles C. Jones to Charles C. Jones, Jr., October 9, 1861, CCJ, Jr.-Ga.

18. Joseph Jones to Caroline Jones, October 8, 1861, JJ-TU.

19. Caroline Jones to Charles C. and Mary Jones, September 14, 1861, JJ-TU; Mary Jones to Charles C. Jones, Jr., June 18, 1861, CCJ, Jr.-Ga.

20. Joseph Jones to Caroline Jones, October 23, 1861, JJ-TU; Charles C. Jones, Jr., to Charles C. and Mary Jones, September 7, 1861, CCJ, Jr.-Ga.

21. As late as June 1861 the school's official organ asserted that classes would reconvene on the first Monday in November. According to Jones, however, no classes were held after the spring of 1861. "Editorial and Miscellaneous," *Southern Medical and Surgical Journal,* n.s. 17(1861):511–12; Joseph Jones to L. A. Dugas, March 28, 1862, JJ-LSU; see also T. Conn Bryan, *Confederate Georgia* (Athens, Ga., 1953), pp. 216, 221.

22. Joseph Jones to Caroline Jones, October 11, 1861, JJ-TU; Charles C. Jones to Charles C. Jones, Jr., December 20, 1861, CCJ, Jr.-Ga.

23. Joseph Jones to Charles C. Jones, October 2, 1861, JJ-TU; Charles C. Jones, Jr., to Charles C. Jones, October 7, 1861, CCJ, Jr.-Ga. Charles C. Jones, Jr., joined the Chatham Artillery as soon as his term as Mayor of Savannah was completed in late October 1861. Charles C. Jones to Charles C. Jones, Jr., October 7, 1861, CCJ, Jr.-Ga.

24. Joseph Jones to Caroline Jones, October 8, 13, 1861, JJ-TU.

25. Mary Jones to Caroline Jones, November 6, 1861, JJ-TU.

26. Joseph Jones to Caroline Jones, October 8, 1861, JJ-TU.

27. Ibid., October 16, 1861.

28. See especially his letter of October 16, cited in the preceding note. Unless otherwise noted the ensuing account of life in the Liberty Independent Troop is based on the contents of this letter.

29. Charles C. Jones to Mrs. Eliza G. Robarts, November 4, 1861, CCJ-TU.

30. Joseph Jones to Caroline Jones, October 18, 1861, JJ-TU.

31. Ibid., October 16, 1861; see also Mary Jones to Mary S. Mallard, October 17, 1861, CCJ-TU; Charles C. Jones to Mary S. Mallard, October 26, 1861, CCJ-TU.

32. Joseph Jones to Caroline Jones, October 23, 1861, JJ-TU; see also Joseph Jones to Charles C. Jones, November 7, 1861, JJ-TU.

33. Joseph Jones to Caroline Jones, October 31, November 17, 1861, JJ-TU. Jones later estimated that he traveled over 2,000 miles on horseback as surgeon of the Liberty Independent Troop. Joseph Jones, "Investigations on Typhoid Fever CSA 1861–1865," JJ-TU.

34. Mary Jones to Caroline Jones, November 6, 1861, JJ-TU.

35. Caroline Jones to Joseph Jones, November 18, 1861, JJ-TU.

36. Joseph Jones to Caroline Jones, October 23, 1861, JJ-TU. Charles C. Jones to Eliza G. Robarts, November 4, 1861, CCJ-TU; Mary S. Mallard to Mary Jones, November 4, 1861, CCJ-TU.

37. Jones, "Investigations on Typhoid Fever."

38. Joseph Jones, "Diseases Treated amongst the Liberty Independent Troop & amongst the Whites & Blacks in the South-Eastern Portion of Liberty County, Georgia during 6 months, October to April 1862," in Jones, "Investigations on Typhoid

Fever." Unless otherwise noted the statistics pertaining to the Liberty Independent Troop are from this table.

39. Jones, *Agricultural Resources of Georgia, Address before the Cotton Planters' Convention of Georgia at Macon, December 13, 1860* (Augusta, Ga., 1861), pp. 4–7.

40. Mallard, "Liberty County, Georgia," pp. 13–15.

41. Jones, "Investigations on Typhoid Fever." For a detailed history of Sunbury see Charles C. Jones, Jr., *The Dead Towns of Georgia*, vol. 4 of the *Collections of the Georgia Historical Society* (Savannah, Ga., 1878), pp. 141–223.

42. Joseph Jones to Caroline Jones, November 7, 1861. In this letter Jones points out that the citizens of Liberty County demanded protection. "It is thought impolitic," he wrote, "to leave several thousand negroes without the presence & protection of the whites."

43. Jones, "Investigations on Typhoid Fever." Jones realized that the fresh water swamps of the Riceboro area were unhealthy but for the wrong reason. He blamed the "offensive vapors" they gave off, failing to realize that they were ideal breeding places for the malaria-bearing *Anopheles* mosquito.

44. Unless otherwise noted all background material in this study relating to Civil War medicine is drawn from Adams, *Doctors in Blue: The Medical History of the Union Army in the Civil War* (New York, 1952); Horace H. Cunningham, *Doctors in Gray: The Confederate Medical Service* (Baton Rouge, La., 1968).

45. Jones, "Investigations on Typhoid Fever."

46. Jones, *Agricultural Resources of Georgia*, p. 6.

47. Quoted in Cunningham, *Doctors in Gray*, pp. 185–86.

48. Jones, "Investigations on Typhoid Fever."

49. Horace Montgomery, *Howell Cobb's Confederate Career* (Tuscaloosa, Ala., 1959), p. 35.

50. Jones, "Investigations on Typhoid Fever."

51. Joseph Jones to Caroline Jones, October 23, 1861, JJ-TU.

52. Ibid., December 15, 1861.

53. Ibid., January 6, 1862; Jones, *Memoirs*, 1:298, 521; Joseph Jones to L. A. Dugas, March 28, 1862, JJ-LSU.

54. Joseph Jones to Caroline Jones, November 4, 1861, JJ-TU.

55. Ibid., October 18, 1861.

56. Ibid., November 4, 1861.

57. Ibid., November 6, 1861.

58. Joseph Jones to Charles C. Jones, November 8, 9, 1861, JJ-TU.

59. Joseph Jones to Caroline Jones, November 17, 21, 1861, JJ-TU; Mary Jones to Joseph Jones, November 18, 1861, JJ-TU; Charles C. Jones to Joseph Jones, November 30, 1861, JJ-TU; Charles C. Jones to R. Q. Mallard, November 30, 1861, CCJ-TU; Mary Jones to Charles C. Jones, December 4, 1861, CCJ-TU; Charles C. Jones to Mary Jones, December 5, 9, 11, 1861, CCJ-TU.

60. Joseph Jones to Caroline Jones, December 7, 1861, JJ-TU.

61. Charles C. Jones to Charles C. Jones, Jr., December 25, 1861, CCJ, Jr.-Ga.; Joseph Jones to Caroline Jones, December 26, 1861, JJ-TU.

62. Joseph Jones to Caroline Jones, December 31, 1861, JJ-TU.

63. Ibid.; see also Mary S. Mallard to Caroline Jones, January 8, 1862, JJ-TU; Mary Jones to Charles C. Jones, Jr., January 9, 1862, CCJ, Jr.-Ga.; Charles C. Jones to Charles C. Jones, Jr., January 29, 1862, CCJ, Jr.-Ga.; Charles C. Jones, Jr., to Charles C. Jones, February 21, 1862, CCJ, Jr.-Ga.; Charles C. Jones, Jr., to Mary Jones, March 14, 1862, CCJ, Jr.-Ga.

64. Charles C. Jones to Joseph Jones, September 11, 1861, JJ-TU; Joseph Jones to Caroline Jones, October 8, 1861, JJ-TU; J. V. Jones to Joseph Jones, October 18, 26, 1861, JJ-TU; Charles C. Jones, Jr., to Charles C. Jones, November 25, 1861, CCJ-TU. The exact arrangements which Charles C. Jones, Jr., made in Burke County are not clear. He did, however, purchase in October 1862, a 1,412 acre plantation, "Buck-Head," there for $14,120. Charles C. Jones, Jr., to Charles C. Jones, October 16, 1862, CCJ, Jr.-Ga.

65. Charles C. Jones, "Diary, 1862," pp. 17–18, 64–67, CCJ-TU.

66. Ibid., p. 72; Charles C. Jones, "Diary, 1863," p. 5, CCJ-TU; "Removals out of Liberty 1861–1862 & 1863," CCJ-TU.

67. Mary Jones to Charles C. Jones, Jr., March 27, 1862, CCJ, Jr.-Ga.

68. Joseph Jones to L. A. Dugas, March 28, 1862, JJ-LSU.

69. Joseph Jones to Pierce B. Wilson, March 27, 1862, JJ-LSU; Joseph Jones to L. A. Dugas, March 25, 28, 1862, JJ-LSU.

70. Joseph Jones to Caroline Jones, November 7, 1861, JJ-TU.

71. Joseph Jones to Charles C. Jones, November 9, 1861, JJ-TU.

72. Joseph Jones to Caroline Jones, October 8, 1861, JJ-TU.

Chapter 6

1. Mary Jones to Charles C. Jones, Jr., March 27, April 16, 1862, CCJ, Jr.-Ga.; Charles C. Jones to Charles C. Jones, Jr., April 21, 1862, CCJ, Jr.-Ga.; Joseph Jones to Caroline Jones, April 21, 1862, JJ-TU.

2. Joseph Jones to Caroline Jones, November 7, 1861, JJ-TU.

3. Unless otherwise noted the account of Jones's role in combating this Union threat to coastal Liberty County is based on Joseph Jones to Caroline Jones, April 28, 1862, JJ-TU; Charles C. Jones to Charles C. Jones, Jr., April 28, 1862, CCJ, Jr.-Ga.

4. Joseph Jones to Caroline Jones, November 7, 1861, JJ-TU. For accounts of the splitting of the Liberty Independent Troop see Jones, "Investigations on Typhoid Fever CSA 1861–1865," JJ-TU; Joseph Jones to Caroline Jones, April 21, 1862, JJ-TU; Charles C. Jones to Charles C. Jones, Jr., April 21, 1862, CCJ, Jr.-Ga.

5. Charles C. Jones, Jr., to Charles C. Jones, April 28, 1862, CCJ, Jr.-Ga.

6. Caroline Jones to Mary Jones, May 3, 1862, JJ-TU.

7. Joseph Jones to Caroline Jones, December 18, 1861, JJ-TU; see also ibid., November 7, 1861; Caroline Jones to Joseph Jones, November 12, 1861, JJ-TU; Joseph Milligan to Caroline Jones, November 13, 1861, JJ-TU.

8. Joseph Jones to Caroline Jones, December 18, 1861, JJ-TU.

9. Charles C. Jones to Joseph Jones, June 6, 1862, JJ-TU.

10. Joseph Jones to Charles C. Jones, June 3, 1862, JJ-TU; see also Mary S. Mallard to Charles C. Jones, August 26, 1862, CCJ-TU; Joseph Jones, "Experiments Illustrating the Direct Action of Hydrocyanic Acid upon the Medulla Oblongata," *Medical Record* 2(1867):457–59; Joseph Jones, "Experiments with the Poison of the American Copperhead," *Medical Record* 3(1868): 289–92; Jones, "Poisonous Effects of Cyanide of Potassium," *New Orleans Medical and Surgical Journal,* n.s. 4(1877):779–80; Jones, *Memoirs,* 1:297–99, 521–22.

11. Charles C. Jones to Joseph Jones, June 14, 1862, JJ-TU; Charles C. Jones to Caroline Jones, August [?], 1862, JJ-TU; Joseph Jones, "Investigations upon the Nature, Causes, and Treatment of Hospital Gangrene as It Prevailed in the Confederate Armies, 1861–1865," pp. 146–67, JJ-TU (hereafter cited as Jones, "Investigations—Gangrene"). This study was published

after the war by the United States Sanitary Commission; see Frank H. Hamilton, ed., *Surgical Memoirs of the War of the Rebellion*, 2 vols. (New York, 1870–71), 2:143–570. Citings are from this.

12. Joseph Jones to Charles C. and Mary Jones, July 8, 1862, JJ-TU. Jones was concerned about the soldiers' spiritual as well as physical welfare and presented them with a Testament and religious tracts, remarking that he hoped to continue this practice as long as he remained with the army. Ibid., January 20, 1863.

13. Caroline Jones to Charles C. Jones, June 17, 1862, CCJ-TU; Mary Jones to Caroline Jones, June 21, 1862, JJ-TU.

14. Joseph Jones to Charles C. and Mary Jones, July 8, 1862, JJ-TU.

15. Ibid.

16. Charles C. Jones to Joseph Jones, July 21, 1862, JJ-TU.

17. Richmond, 1863, p. 12. Jones's wartime research revealed a 91 percent death rate for traumatic tetanus in the Confederate army as compared with 92 percent for the Union army. Jones, *Memoirs*, 1:384.

18. Jones, *Memoirs*, 1:142–55.

19. Ibid., 669–98; 2:723–39.

20. Ibid., 2:753–61; Joseph Jones, "Relations of Pneumonia and Malarial Fever: With Practical Observations upon the Antiperiodic or Abortive Method of Treating Pneumonia," *Southern Medical and Surgical Journal*, series 3, 1(1866):243–58.

21. Jones, "Investigations—Gangrene," pp. 147–48.

22. Joseph Jones to Charles C. and Mary Jones, July 14, 1862, CCJ, Jr.-Ga.; Jones, "Investigations on Typhoid Fever."

23. Charles C. Jones, Jr., to Charles C. and Mary Jones, July 14, 1862, CCJ, Jr.-Ga.; Charles C. Jones, Jr., to Charles C. Jones, October 1, 1862, CCJ, Jr.-Ga.

24. Caroline Jones to Charles C. and Mary Jones, September 8, 1862, JJ-TU; see also Charles C. Jones to Joseph Jones, October 4, 1862, JJ-TU.

25. Charles C. Jones to Joseph Jones, September 11, 1862, JJ-TU.

26. Charles C. Jones, "Diary, 1862," pp. 63–64, CCJ-TU.

27. Joseph Jones to Charles C. Jones, December 5, 1862, JJ-TU; Charles C. Jones, Jr., to Charles C. Jones, December 12, 1862, CCJ, Jr.-Ga.

28. Joseph Jones to Charles C. Jones, December 5, 1862, JJ-TU.

29. Adjt. & Inspct. Genl's. Office, Richmond, Va., December 22d, 1862, Special Orders No. 299, in Louis Manigault, "Journal of Louis Manigault," microfilm copy in JJ-TU (hereafter cited as Manigault, "Journal").

30. Joseph Jones to Charles C. and Mary Jones, January 20, 1863, JJ-TU.

31. Charles C. Jones to Joseph Jones, December 19, 1862, JJ-TU.

32. Charles C. Jones, Jr., to Charles C. Jones, February 10, 1863, CCJ, Jr.-Ga.

33. Joseph Jones to Samuel P. Moore, February 9, 1863 in Jones, *Memoirs*, 1:vi–vii. This report was lost in the fire which destroyed much of Richmond, including the surgeon general's office, upon the South's evacuation of the city in March 1865. But to Jones's credit its most important parts were published as the lead article in the first number of the *Confederate States Medical & Surgical Journal* in January 1864 as "Traumatic Tetanus," pp. 1–5.

34. Samuel P. Moore to Joseph Jones, February 17, 1863 in Jones, *Memoirs*, 1:vii.

35. Joseph and Caroline Jones to Mary Jones, March 11, 1863, JJ-TU; Joseph Jones to Mary Jones, March 14, 1863, JJ-TU; Joseph Jones, "Detached Cavalry Commands Serving Chiefly between the Altamaha and Ogeechee Rivers on the Coast of Georgia," JJ-TU.

36. Jones, "Detached Cavalry Commands . . . on the Georgia Coast." Jones verified these conclusions by means of subsequent examinations of the records of these commands. JJ-TU.

37. Charles C. Jones to Charles C. Jones, Jr., March 4, 1863, CCJ, Jr.-Ga.; Joseph Jones to Charles C. Jones, February 18, 1863, JJ-TU; Joseph Jones to Caroline Jones, March 3, 6, 1863, JJ-TU.

38. The war ended before Jones had time to finish his observations on this disease. He still thought his findings were important enough to include in his *Memoirs;* see 1:411–38, 454–56, 484–85, 501–53; see also Joseph Jones, "Observations upon Cerebro-Spinal Meningitis as it Appeared Amongst the Soldiers of the Confederate States Army during the Civil War of 1861–1865," JJ-TU.

39. Joseph Jones to Charles C. Jones, December 5, 1862, JJ-TU.

40. Mary Jones to Charles C. Jones, Jr., March 16–17, 1863, CCJ, Jr.-Ga.

41. Joseph Jones to Mary Jones, April 7, 1863, JJ-TU. In remembrance Joseph Jones compiled a brief volume on his father's life and death for the other members of the family. Joseph Jones to Mary Jones, June 27, 1863, JJ-TU. A copy is in JJ-TU.

42. Joseph Jones to Mary Jones, April 7, 1863, JJ-TU.

43. Joseph Jones to Mary Jones, April 7, 1863, JJ-TU; Jones, "Investigations on Typhoid Fever."

44. Charles C. Jones, Jr., to Mary Jones, April 12, 1863, CCJ, Jr.-Ga.; Mary Jones to Charles C. Jones, Jr., April 14, 1863, CCJ, Jr.-Ga.; Joseph Jones to Mary Jones, April 17, 1863, JJ-TU. Jones had exacted a similar promise from the surgeons of the detached cavalry commands serving on the Georgia coast. In neither case was the response significant. Examples can be found in JJ-TU.

45. Joseph Jones to Mary Jones, April 29, June 27, 1863, JJ-TU; Charles C. Jones, Jr., to Mary Jones, May 28, 1863, CCJ, Jr.-Ga.; Mary Jones to Charles C. Jones, Jr., July 3, 1863, CCJ, Jr.-Ga.

46. Joseph Jones to Samuel P. Moore, June 28, 1863 in Jones, *Memoirs*, 1:vii–ix; Joseph Jones to Samuel P. Moore, June 30, 1863, JJ-TU. For Jones's fullest argument that typhus did not occur in the Confederate armies, see Joseph Jones, "Investigations upon the Diseases of the Federal Prisoners Confined to Camp Sumter, Andersonville, Ga.," pp. 600–601 (hereafter cited as Jones, "Investigations—Andersonville"). This report consists of three large, handwritten volumes; volumes 1 and 3 are in JJ-TU and volume 2 is in JJ-LSU. This study was later published by the United States Sanitary Commission in the first volume of its *Sanitary Memoirs of the War of the Rebellion*, 2 vols. (New York, 1867–1869); see Austin Flint, ed., *Contributions Relating to the Causation and Prevention of Diseases, and to Camp Diseases, Together with a Report of the Diseases, etc., Among the Prisoners at Andersonville, Ga.* (New York, 1867), pp. 470–655. Citings are from this printed version. The leading Union surgeons agreed that many cases diagnosed as typhus were probably typhoid fever but believed that some cases of true typhus did occur. U.S. Surgeon General's Office, *Medical and Surgical History of the War of*

the Rebellion, 3 vols. in 6 (Washington, D.C., 1870–1888), vol. 1, pt. 3:323–24 (hereafter cited as *MSH*).

47. Samuel P. Moore to Joseph Jones, July 15, 1863 in Jones, *Memoirs*, 1:ix; Joseph Jones to Samuel P. Moore, October 16, 1863, JJ-TU; Joseph Jones to J. Julian Chisolm, November 7, 1863, ibid.

48. Joseph Jones to Caroline Jones, August 7, 1863, JJ-TU; Joseph Jones to Mary Jones, October 7, 1863, JJ-TU.

49. Joseph Jones to Mary Jones, October 7, 1863, JJ-TU.

50. Joseph Jones to Caroline Jones, August 7, 1863, JJ-TU.

51. Joseph Jones to Mary Jones, October 7, 1863, JJ-TU; Jones, "Investigations—Gangrene," pp. 149–50.

52. Alfred H. Bill, *The Beleaguered City: Richmond, 1861–1865* (New York, 1946), p. 186.

53. Joseph Jones to Caroline Jones, August 13, 1863, JJ-TU.

54. Emory M. Thomas, *The Confederate State of Richmond: A Biography of the Capital* (Austin, Tex., 1971), p. 57.

55. Joseph Jones to Caroline Jones, August 13, 1863, JJ-TU.

56. Joseph Jones to Mary Jones, October 7, 1863, JJ-TU.

57. Joseph Jones to Mary S. Mallard, August 26, 1863, CCJ-TU.

58. Joseph Jones to Mary Jones, October 7, 1863, JJ-TU.

59. Ibid. A copy of these orders, dated September 3, can be found in Manigault, "Journal."

60. Joseph Jones to Mary Jones, October 7, 1863, JJ-TU.

61. Joseph Jones, "Outline of the Results of an Examination of the Statistics & Records of Charlottesville General Hospital, Va.," pp. 15–18, JJ-TU (hereafter cited as Jones, "Outline of the Results of an Examination—Charlottesville").

62. Joseph Jones to Samuel P. Moore, October 16, 1863 in Jones, *Memoirs*, 2:739–40.

63. Joseph Jones to Mary Jones, October 7, 1863, JJ-TU.

64. Joseph Jones to Caroline Jones, September 9, 1863, JJ-TU.

65. Ibid.; Joseph Jones to Mary Jones, October 7, 1863, JJ-TU; Jones, "Investigations—Gangrene," pp. 149–50.

66. Joseph Jones to Mary Jones, October 7, 1863, JJ-TU.

Chapter 7

1. Joseph Jones to Samuel P. Moore, October 16, 1863 in Jones, *Memoirs*, 2:739–40; see also Joseph Jones to Mary Jones, October 7, 1863, JJ-TU.

2. Joseph Jones to Samuel P. Moore, October 16, 1863; Joseph Jones to Caroline Jones, October 13, 15, 18, 1863, JJ-TU; Joseph Jones to Louis Manigault, October 20, 1863 in Manigault, "Journal"; Jones, *Memoirs*, 2:744–53, 787–91. The controversy over the specificity of disease forms was not conclusively settled until the rise of the age of bacteriology in the latter part of the nineteenth century. Erwin H. Ackerknecht, *A Short History of Medicine*, rev. ed. (New York, 1968), p. 183.

3. Jones, "Investigations—Gangrene," pp. 151–53.

4. Joseph Jones to Mary Jones, November 19, 1863, JJ-TU.

5. Caroline Jones to Mary Jones, November 6, 16, 1863, JJ-TU.

6. Mary Jones to Caroline Jones, October 24, 1863, JJ-LSU; Joseph Jones to J. Julian Chisolm, November 7, 1863, JJ-TU; Joseph Jones to Louis Manigault, January 11, February 2, 1864 in Manigault, "Journal"; Louis Manigault to Joseph Jones, October 14, 1863, January 12, 26, 1864 in Manigault, "Journal"; Charles C. Jones, Jr., to Col. C. J. Colcock, January 20, 1864, JJ-TU; Mary Jones to Mary S. Mallard, February 5, 1864, CCJ-TU; Jones, "Investigations on Typhoid Fever"; Joseph Jones, "Medical and Surgical Notes on the Confederate Operations in and Around Pensacola Florida 1861–1865," JJ-TU.

7. Joseph Jones to J. M. Johnston, March 1, 1864 in Manigault, "Journal"; Louis Manigault to Joseph Jones, March 3, 1864 in Manigault, "Journal"; Joseph Jones to J. Julian Chisolm, November 7, 1863, JJ-TU; Joseph Jones to Mary Jones, November 19, 30, 1863, April 18, 1864, JJ-TU; Mary Jones to Caroline Jones, November 20, 1863, JJ-TU; Mary Jones to Joseph Jones, April 2, 1864, JJ-TU.

8. Joseph Jones to Samuel P. Moore, October 16, 1863, JJ-TU; Louis Manigault to Joseph Jones, October 1, 1863 in Manigault, "Journal"; Joseph Jones to Charles Manigault, November [7?], 1863 in Manigault, "Journal." It was only after considerable difficulty that Jones was able to persuade the Confederate government to pay Manigault and his other assistants. Joseph Jones to Samuel P. Moore, October 16, 1863, JJ-TU; Joseph Jones to William H. Prioleau, October 19, 1863, JJ-TU.

9. Mary S. Mallard to Mary Jones, May 27, 1864, CCJ-TU.

10. Joseph Jones to Louis Manigault, June 28, 1864 in Manigault, "Journal"; Mary S. Mallard to Mary Jones, July 1, 1864, CCJ-TU.

11. Joseph Jones, "Outline of the Military and Medical Operations of the Army of Tennessee and Mississippi under the Command of General Joseph E. Johnston from Dalton to Atlanta, Georgia," pp. 65–67, JJ-TU.

12. Joseph Jones to Caroline Jones, June 30, 1864, JJ-TU.

13. Joseph Jones, "The Medical History of the Confederate Army and Navy," *Southern Historical Society Papers* 20(1892): 133.

14. Joseph Jones, "Defence of Atlanta, Georgia by General J. B. Hood, July 18th–September 1864," pp. 70–71, JJ-TU.

15. James O. Breeden, "A Medical History of the Later Stages of the Atlanta Campaign," *Journal of Southern History* 35(1969): 31–59. Copyright 1969 by the Southern Historical Association.

16. Louis Manigault, "Visit to Charleston, So. Ca." in Manigault, "Journal."

17. Joseph Jones to Mrs. S. M. Maxwell, July 30, 1864, CCJ-TU; Jones, *Memoirs*, 1:ix–x.

18. Joseph Jones to Samuel P. Moore, August 6, 1864, JJ-LSU; see also Manigault, "Visit to Charleston, So. Ca." in Manigault, "Journal." Jones appended to this report a revised and enlarged version of his article published at the beginning of the war on the value of small doses of quinine as a prophylactic against malaria. The revised study did not change the original thesis but did enrich the account with additional material drawn from his wartime research.

19. Jones, *Memoirs*, 1:x.

20. Much has been written about Andersonville. The best recent account is Ovid L. Futch's *History of Andersonville Prison* (Gainesville, Fla., 1968).

21. Jones, "Investigations—Andersonville," pp. 471–72.

22. Samuel P. Moore to Surgeon Isaiah H. White, August 6, 1864, JJ-TU.

23. Jones, "Investigations—Andersonville," p. 472; "Requisition from Surgeon Joseph Jones, Augusta, Ga., upon Surgeon Chisolm, August 6, 1864" in Manigault, "Journal"; Joseph Jones to Surgeon J. J. Chisolm, August 15, 1864 in Manigault "Journal"; "Invoices of Medicines, &c., August 18, 1864," JJ-LSU; Joseph Jones, *Outline of Observations on Hospital Gangrene as It Manifested Itself in the Confederate Armies, during the American Civil War, 1861–1865* (New Orleans, La., 1869), p. 3.

24. Jones, "Investigations—Andersonville," p. 472n.

25. Joseph Jones to Caroline Jones, October 13, 1863, JJ-TU.

26. Caroline Jones to Mary Jones, November 6, 1863, JJ-TU.

27. Mary Jones to Mary S. Mallard, August 22, 1864, CCJ-TU; Mary Jones to Laura E. Buttolph, September 3, 1864, CCJ-TU; Mary Jones to Susan M. Cumming, September 29, 1864, CCJ-TU.

28. Louis Manigault to Maria E. White, October 22–23, 1864 in Manigault, "Journal."

29. Jones, "Investigations—Andersonville," pp. 472–73.

30. Ibid.

31. Joseph Jones to Samuel P. Moore, October 19, 1864 in Manigault, "Journal."

32. Louis Manigault to Mrs. Louis Manigault, September 18, 1864 in Manigault, "Journal."

33. Joseph Jones to Mary Jones, September 22, 1864, JJ-TU.

34. Ibid.

35. Jones, "Investigations—Andersonville," p. 479.

36. Quoted in Futch, *History of Andersonville Prison*, p. 110.

37. Louis Manigault to Maria E. White, October 22–23, 1864 in Manigault, "Journal."

38. Joseph Jones to Lewis D. Ford, October 19, 1864, JJ-TU.

39. Joseph Jones to Samuel P. Moore, October 19, 1864 in Manigault, "Journal."

40. Jones, "Investigations—Gangrene," p. 154; Joseph Jones, "Modification of Yellow Fever by Preceding Diseased States of the System," *Atlanta Medical and Surgical Journal,* n.s. 11 (1873):157–61; Joseph Jones, *Original Investigations on the Natural History (Symptoms and Pathology) of Yellow Fever. 1854–1894* (Chicago, 1894), p. 41.

41. Joseph Jones to Caroline Jones, October 1, 16, 1864, JJ-TU; Louis Manigault to Joseph Jones, October 1, 10, 1864 in Manigault, "Journal"; Joseph Jones to Lewis D. Ford, October 19, 1864, JJ-TU; Jones, "Investigations—Andersonville," pp. 476–77. There is an extensive correspondence in JJ-TU as a result of Jones's efforts to enlist the assistance of the surgeons of the Army of Tennessee in his study of gangrene.

42. A copy of this circular can be found in JJ-TU; see also Joseph Jones, "Inquiries upon Hospital Gangrene, Addressed to the Medical Officers of the Confederate Army," *Nashville Journal of Medicine and Surgery,* n.s. 1(1866):241–51. Jones was so impressed with several of the responses he received that he arranged

for their publication after the war in the *Nashville Journal of Medicine and Surgery*. One surgeon, an admirer of Jones, who did not receive a questionnaire wrote offering his experiences. "I hope and believe," he concluded, "that yr. labors will enhance yr. reputation, already exalted, and contribute largely to the progress of our science and the welfare of mankind." William B. Norcross to Joseph Jones, January 31, 1865, JJ-LSU.

43. Jones, "Investigations—Andersonville," pp. 476–77; see also Charles C. Jones, Jr., *General Sherman's March from Atlanta to the Coast* (Augusta, Ga., 1884).

44. Jacob D. Cox, *The March to the Sea: Franklin and Nashville* (New York, 1882), p. 40.

45. Mark M. Boatner III, *The Civil War Dictionary* (New York, 1959), p. 459.

46. Joseph Jones to Charles C. Jones, Jr., December 16, 1864, JJ-TU; see also Joseph Jones to Mary Jones, February 1, 1865, JJ-TU.

47. Mary Jones to Gen. James H. Wilson, August 1, 1865, CCJ-TU; see also Mary Sharpe Jones and Mary Jones Mallard, *Yankees A' Coming*, ed. Haskell Moore (Tuscaloosa, Ala., 1959), pp. 33–84.

48. Caroline Jones to Mary Jones, February 14, 1865, CCJ-TU.

49. Joseph Jones to Mary Jones, February 1, 1865, JJ-TU; Caroline Jones to Mary Jones, February 14, 1865, CCJ-TU.

Chapter 8

1. Joseph Jones to Mary Jones, February 1, 1865, JJ-TU. Facts pertaining to the conclusion of the war are based on the account of James G. Randall and David Donald in *The Civil War and Reconstruction*, 2d ed., rev. (Lexington, Mass., 1969).

2. Jones, "Investigations—Andersonville," p. 477; Mary Jones to Susan M. Cumming, March 25, 1865, CCJ-TU; "Travel Notes of Mary Jones, Mar. 31–Apr. 13, 1865," CCJ-TU; Mary Jones to Charles C. Jones, Jr., April 6, 1865, CCJ, Jr.-Ga.; Mary Jones to Joseph Jones, May 2, 1865, JJ-LSU.

3. Caroline Jones to Mary Jones, April 30, 1865, CCJ-TU; Jones, "Investigations—Andersonville," p. 477.

4. Jones, "Investigations—Andersonville," p. 477. The immediate postwar period also saw the birth of Jones's third child,

Charles Colcock. Mary S. Mallard to Joseph Jones, August 10, 1865, CCJ-TU.

5. Ovid L. Futch, *History of Andersonville Prison*, (Gainesville, Fla., 1968), p. 117.

6. Ella Lonn, *Foreigners in the Confederacy* (Chapel Hill, N.C., 1940), p. 275.

7. Jones, "Investigations—Andersonville," pp. 477–78.

8. Joseph Jones, "The Treatment of Prisoners during the War between the States," *Southern Historical Society Papers* 1(1876): 171–74.

9. Norton P. Chipman, *The Horrors of Andersonville Rebel Prison* (San Francisco, Calif., 1891), p. 85.

10. Jones, "Investigations—Andersonville," p. 478.

11. Joseph Jones to Caroline Jones, September 30, 1865, JJ-TU.

12. Ibid., October 3, 1865.

13. Jones, "Investigations—Andersonville," pp. 478–81.

14. Joseph Jones to Caroline Jones, October 3, 1865, JJ-TU.

15. Ibid., October 7, 1865. Jones's lost reports were never found. In 1867 he wrote Manigault: "I was truly grieved, to find after careful search in Richmond and Washington, that the volume which you had copied with such care & accuracy, & illustrated so handsomely, was destroyed by fire." Joseph Jones to Louis Manigault, July 12, 1867 in Manigault, "Journal."

16. For Jones's testimony and for the abstract of his report see U.S. House of Representatives, *Trial of Henry Wirz*, Exec. Doc. no. 23, 40th Cong., 2d Sess. (Washington, D.C., 1868), pp. 618–42. At a later date this abstract was printed and included in the *Official Records;* see U.S. War Department, *The War of the Rebellion: A Compilation of the Official Records of the Union and Confederate Armies*, 70 vols. in 128 (Washington, D.C., 1880–1901), ser. 2, 8:588–632.

17. Joseph Jones to Caroline Jones, October 8, 1865, JJ-TU.

18. Norton P. Chipman, *The Tragedy of Andersonville*, 2d ed., rev. (San Francisco, Calif., 1911), pp. 80–81.

19. *Trial of Henry Wirz*, pp. 640–42.

20. Jones, "The Treatment of Prisoners," p. 174.

21. *Trial of Henry Wirz*, pp. 760–61.

22. Joseph Jones to Caroline Jones, October 8, 1865, JJ-TU.

23. *Daily Constitutionalist* (Augusta, Ga.), August 18, 1866.

24. James O. Breeden, "Joseph Jones, a Major Source for

Nineteenth Century Southern Medical History," *Bulletin of the Tulane University Medical Faculty* 26(1967):41–48.

25. Allan Nevins, "The Glorious and the Terrible," *Saturday Review* 44(September 2, 1961):9.

26. Joseph Jones, "Causes Which Impaired the Strength of the Confederate Army," JJ-TU.

Chapter 9

1. The material in this chapter recently appeared in a slightly different form in the *Bulletin of the History of Medicine;* see "Andersonville—A Southern Surgeon's Story," 47(1973):317–43. The best account of the confusion of voices over Andersonville is Ovid L. Futch's *History of Andersonville Prison* (Gainesville, Fla., 1968), pp. 133–42.

2. Jones, "Investigations—Andersonville," pp. 477–80.

3. Ibid., pp. 470–82. That more editing was not done is surprising, for this manuscript exhibited all of Jones's shortcomings as a writer. The deleted chapter on hospital gangrene was later included in the United States Sanitary Commission's *Surgical Memoirs of the War of the Rebellion.* The material has been restored in this study in order to present a complete picture of the Andersonville prisoners' health problems.

4. Ibid., pp. 483–500, 520.

5. Ibid., p. 500.

6. Ibid., pp. 494–95.

7. Ibid., p. 500.

8. Ibid., p. 502. Jones did not see Andersonville at its worst. The prison population had been reduced to 15,000 by the time of his arrival with the removal of half of the prisoners to Millen, Savannah, Charleston and other points "in anticipation of an advance by General Sherman's forces from Atlanta, with the design of liberating their captive brethren" (p. 507).

9. Ibid., pp. 503–7.

10. Ibid., pp. 521–22.

11. Ibid., p. 511.

12. Ibid., p. 504.

13. Ibid., pp. 506–7.

14. Ibid., p. 516.

15. Ibid., pp. 519–22.

16. Ibid., p. 523.

17. Ibid., pp. 512–13.

18. Ibid., p. 521. Paroled prisoners served not just as hospital attendants but were used throughout the prison. Several hundred of them were employed as clerks, carpenters, cooks, and druggists. They benefited immensely from their privileged position. "These men who had the liberty of the entire post," Jones noted, "were well clothed, and presented a stout, healthy appearance, and as a general rule appeared to be in better circumstances, and to enjoy much more robust health than the Confederate troops guarding the prisoners" (p. 518).

19. Ibid., pp. 525–30. Jones was a careless statistician, and his figures contain a number of annoying errors. It is hoped that these have been located and corrected. The U.S. Surgeon General's Office concurred in Jones's contention that these figures were too low. See *MSH*, vol. 1, pt. 2, pp. 28–29.

20. Jones, "Investigations—Andersonville," pp. 554–62.

21. Ibid., pp. 532, 563.

22. Ibid., pp. 567–68.

23. Ibid., p. 564.

24. Ibid., pp. 582–95.

25. Ibid., p. 601.

26. Ibid., pp. 600–601.

27. Ibid., pp. 563–64.

28. Ibid., pp. 614–15. There are many references to the results of vaccination at Andersonville in U.S. House of Representatives, *Trial of Henry Wirz*, Exec. Doc. no. 23, 40th Cong., 2d Sess. (Washington, D.C., 1868), pp. 618–42.

29. Jones, "Investigations—Andersonville," p. 654.

30. Ibid., pp. 615–22. Jones's research on spurious vaccination served as the basis for two articles after the war; see Joseph Jones, "Spurious Vaccination," *Southern Medical and Surgical Journal*, series 3, 1(1866):165–80; Joseph Jones, "Researches on 'Spurious Vaccination,' or the Abnormal Phenomena Accompanying and Following Vaccination in the Confederate Army, during the Recent American Civil War, 1861–1865," *Nashville Journal of Medicine and Surgery*, n.s. 2(1867):1–31, 81–120, 161–221.

31. Jones, "Investigations—Andersonville," p. 644.

32. Ibid., p. 514.

33. Ibid., pp. 620–22.

34. Ibid., pp. 523, 644–45.

35. Ibid., pp. 625–26. As bad as the ravages of scurvy were at Andersonville Jones believed that the situation could have been

far worse, pointing to the "efforts made by the medical staff and by the officers in charge of the commissary department to furnish the prisoners with such vegetables as could under the circumstances be commanded in a sparsely settled country" (p. 627).

36. Ibid., pp. 627–28.

37. Ibid., p. 647. Members of the United States Sanitary Commission who visited Andersonville at the close of the war supported Jones's claim about the edibility of Southern cornbread. Observing huge piles of it decaying in the stockade and prison, they attributed any starvation among the prisoners to a peculiarity of the northern appetite "since it is well known that Southern soldiers and negroes thrive on such fare." Quoted in Byron Stimson, "Scurvy in the Civil War—A Medical Report," *Civil War Times Illustrated* 5(1966):23. While such a diet might have prevented starvation it would not have prevented scurvy, for cornbread is totally deficient in vitamin C.

38. Jones, "Investigations—Andersonville," pp. 629, 647–48.

39. Ibid., pp. 629–41.

40. Ibid., p. 520.

41. Jones, "Investigations—Gangrene," pp. 532–33.

42. Ibid., pp. 521–23. The paucity of statistics was due largely to the fact that gangrene did not appear on the Southern list of diseases until July 1864; it never appeared on the Union one.

43. Jones, "Investigations—Andersonville," pp. 520, 653.

44. Ibid., p. 649.

45. Ibid., pp. 534–35.

46. Ibid., pp. 533–34. Jones's report ended with fourteen general conclusions, but these have been incorporated in the text of this chapter and to list them would be repetitious.

47. Ibid., p. 516.

Chapter 10

1. Jones, "Investigations—Gangrene," pp. 146–55.

2. Ibid., p. 502. A similar fate befell many southern surgeons and nurses. "A number of cases," Jones remarked, "have come under my notice where nurses and surgeons have accidentally wounded their hands in dressing gangrenous wounds" (p. 259).

3. Ibid., pp. 286–88.

4. Ibid., p. 238.

5. Ibid., p. 507.

6. Ibid., pp. 173, 384–85. For a copy of the Confederate table

of diseases used until the middle of 1864 see Confederate States of America, *Regulations for the Medical Department of the Confederate States Army* (Richmond, Va., 1861). A copy of the revised version can be found in JJ-TU. As implied earlier, gangrene never appeared in the Union nomenclature. *MSH*, vol. 1, pt. 1, pp. xii–xx.

7. Jones, "Outline of the Results of an Examination—Charlottesville," pp. 25–33. Union surgeons observed the gangrenous infection of wounds as early as 1861, but gangrene excited little interest until late 1862 when epidemics flared up in the army hospitals at Frederick, Maryland, and Philadelphia. The Union surgeons soon learned to control the infection through the liberal use of bromine. See *MSH*, vol. 2, pt. 3, pp. 825–29, 850.

8. Jones, "Investigations—Gangrene," pp. 385–87.

9. John Ashhurst, Jr., review of Frank H. Hamilton, ed., *Surgical Memoirs of the War of the Rebellion*, in *American Journal of the Medical Sciences*, n.s. 62(1871):456. To Jones's credit he admirably summarized this report in a sixty-page pamphlet entitled *Outline of Observations on Hospital Gangrene as It Manifested Itself in the Confederate Armies, during the American Civil War, 1861–1865* (New Orleans, La., 1869).

10. Jones, "Investigations—Gangrene," p. 146.

11. Ibid., p. 209.

12. Ibid., pp. 186–89.

13. Ibid., pp. 228–46.

14. Ibid., pp. 452–67.

15. Ibid., pp. 465–67.

16. Ibid., pp. 497–507.

17. Ibid., pp. 265–66; see also Joseph Jones, "Observations upon Gangrenous Inflammation, Based upon Microscopical Examinations of the Disintegrating Matters of the Hospital Gangrene," *Medical Record* 3(1868):218–20. Jones's claim of having discovered the typhoid bacillus rested on his having observed microorganisms in the intestinal canal, in mesenteric and Peyer's glands, and in urine of typhoid patients during the war. See Jones, *Memoirs*, 2:152–61.

18. Jones, "Investigations—Gangrene," p. 348.

19. Ibid., pp. 246–47.

20. Ibid., pp. 246–47, 256–57.

21. Ibid., pp. 372–73, 465.

22. Ibid., p. 263; Jones, *Outline of Observations on Hospital Gan-*

grene, p. 15; Jones, "Observations upon Gangrenous Inflammation," p. 219.

23. Jones, "Investigations—Gangrene," p. 260.
24. Jones, *Outline of Observations on Hospital Gangrene*, p. 36.
25. Jones, "Investigations—Gangrene," p. 379.
26. Ibid., pp. 379–84.
27. Ibid., p. 261.
28. Ibid., p. 387.
29. Ibid., pp. 387–451.
30. Ibid., p. 556.
31. Ibid., pp. 556–60; Jones, *Outline of Observations on Hospital Gangrene*, p. 57. As the threat of gangrene increased in the Confederate armies Jones gave up his practice of drawing blood for his experiments. He subsequently limited his examinations to blood collected during hemorrhages and amputations, imploring Confederate surgeons to save blood for him in porcelain receptacles he provided for this specific purpose. Joseph Jones, "Investigations upon the Changes of the Blood in Hospital (Moist) Gangrene," *Richmond and Louisville Medical Journal* 6(1868):225–26.
32. Jones, *Outline of Observations on Hospital Gangrene*, p. 58.
33. Jones, "Investigations—Gangrene," p. 561.
34. Ibid., pp. 562–63. Although he makes no reference to it in this study, in his Andersonville manuscript Jones called attention to the fact that maggots cleaned gangrenous wounds, writing: "I have frequently seen neglected wounds amongst the Confederate soldiers filled with maggots . . . and as far as my experience extends, these worms destroy only the dead tissues, and do not injure specially the well parts." "I have even heard surgeons affirm," he added, "that a gangrenous wound which has been thoroughly cleansed by maggots heals more rapidly than if it had been left to itself." Jones, "Investigations—Andersonville," p. 521.
35. Jones, "Investigations—Gangrene," pp. 562–63.
36. Ibid., p. 548.
37. Ibid., pp. 549–51.
38. Ibid., pp. 548–51.
39. Ibid., p. 550. Both sides tended to establish special hospitals for specific diseases during the course of the war. George W. Adams, *Doctors in Blue: The Medical History of the Union Army*

in the Civil War (New York, 1952), p. 171; H. H. Cunningham, *Doctors in Gray: The Confederate Medical Service* (Baton Rouge, La., 1958), pp. 196, 215.

40. Jones, "Investigations—Gangrene," pp. 551–53.
41. Adams, *Doctors in Blue*, p. 228.

Chapter 11

1. Allan Nevins, "The Glorious and the Terrible," *Saturday Review* 44(September 2,1961):46–47.

2. Edward Channing, *A History of the United States*, 6 vols. (New York, 1905–25), 6:430.

3. Joseph Jones, "Observations upon the Losses of the Confederate Armies from Battle, Wounds and Disease, during the American Civil War of 1861–1865, with Investigations upon the Number and Character of the Diseases Supervening upon Gun-Shot Wounds," *Richmond and Louisville Medical Journal* 8(1869): 340. This was a four-part article; the complete citing is 8(1869): 339–58, 451–80; 9(1870):257–75, 635–57.

4. Ibid., 8:470–74.
5. Ibid., 8:341–46.
6. Ibid., 8:470–73.
7. *New York Tribune*, June 26, 1867.
8. "Confederate Losses during the War—Correspondence between Dr. Joseph Jones and General Cooper," *Southern Historical Society Papers* 7(1879):290; Alexander H. Stephens, *A Constitutional View of the Late War between the States*, 2 vols. (Philadelphia, 1870), 2:630; George Ripley and Charles A. Dana, eds., *The American Cyclopaedia*, 16 vols. (New York, 1883), 5:232.

9. William F. Fox, *Regimental Losses in the American Civil War, 1861–65*, 4th ed. (Albany, N.Y., 1898), p. 552.

10. Quoted in Thomas L. Livermore, "The Numbers in the Confederate Army, 1861–1865," *Proceedings of the Massachusetts Historical Society*, ser. 2, 18(1903–04):435.

11. Ibid., pp. 434–35; Thomas L. Livermore, *Numbers and Losses in the Civil War in America, 1861–65* (New York, 1901), pp. 2–9.

12. Livermore, *Numbers and Losses*, pp. 2–3.

13. Ibid., pp. 23–40. Livermore later cited the number of Confederate survivors listed in the census of 1890 as additional proof of his contention that the South had more than a million fight-

ing men. Livermore, "The Numbers in the Confederate Army,"
pp. 441–42.

14. Livermore, *Numbers and Losses*, pp. 50–63.

15. Ibid., p. 63.

16. Robert C. Wood, *Confederate Handbook: A Compilation of Important Data and Other Interesting and Valuable Matter Relating to the War between the States, 1861–1865* (New Orleans, La., 1900), p. 24; Randolph H. McKim, *The Numerical Strength of the Confederate Army* (New York, 1912), pp. 20–27.

17. James G. Randall and David Donald, *The Civil War and Reconstruction*, 2d ed., rev. (Lexington, Mass., 1969), p. 530.

18. Estimates of Civil War deaths vary greatly. Those cited here are found in Randall and Donald, *Civil War and Reconstruction*, p. 531. For conflicting estimates see Paul E. Steiner, *Disease in the Civil War* (Springfield, Ill., 1968), p. 8; George W. Adams, *Doctors in Blue: The Medical History of the Union Army in the Civil War* (New York, 1952), p. 3; H. H. Cunningham, *Doctors in Gray: The Confederate Medical Service* (Baton Rouge, La., 1958), pp. 3–8.

19. Stewart Brooks, *Civil War Medicine* (Springfield, Ill., 1966), pp. 6, 106; Adams, *Doctors in Blue*, p. 3. Jones held that every southern soldier became ill an average of six times. Jones, "Medical History of the Confederate Army and Navy," p. 115.

20. The extremes of this estimate were set by Randall and Donald (*Civil War and Reconstruction*, p. 531) and Adams (*Doctors in Blue*, p. 3).

21. Brooks, *Civil War Medicine*, p. 6.

22. Jones, "Medical History of the Confederate Army and Navy," p. 136.

23. Ibid. Jones was approached about, or at least seriously considered, participating in the preparation of a medical history of the war. Asserting that "no US Surgeon north or west" enjoyed a higher reputation than Jones, Charles A. Lee, the apparent editor, pointed out: "*The work must cover the whole ground,* & I can promise that not a sentence will be published, relating to the Southern armies, but what meets with Dr. Jones' approval" (Charles A. Lee to [?], October 1, 1865, JJ-LSU).

24. Jones, "Observations upon the Losses of the Confederate Armies," pp. 652–53.

25. Ibid., pp. 348–52.

26. Biographical information pertaining to this hospital is based on its best existing history: Chalmers R. Gemmill, "The Charlottesville General Hospital, 1861–1865," *Magazine of Albemarle County History* 22(1963–64):91–160.

27. Jones, "Observations upon the Losses of the Confederate Armies," pp. 262–67.

28. Ibid., p. 262.

29. Jones, "Outline of the Results of an Examination—Charlottesville." Jones completed his statistics for this hospital's wartime years in a mid-October 1865 interview with Davis with whom he maintained a correspondence following the war. Jones's figures are complete except for a three-month break from August through October 1864. The records from which he compiled his statistics are preserved in the National Archives; see "Register of Patients, General Hospital, Charlottesville, Virginia," Record Group 109, chap. 6, vols. 214–16.

30. "Cases and Deaths from Some of the Principal Diseases and Gun-Shot Wounds, and Supervening Diseases, Pyaemia, Hospital Gangrene, etc., in the General Hospital, Charlottesville, Va., 1861–1865," in Jones, "Observations upon the Losses of the Confederate Armies," opposite p. 272.

31. Jones, "Observations upon the Losses of the Confederate Armies," p. 272.

32. Adams, *Doctors in Blue*, p. 113.

33. Cunningham, *Doctors in Gray*, p. 220.

34. Adams, *Doctors in Blue*, p. 113.

35. Jones, "Observations upon the Losses of the Confederate Armies," p. 268. It was not until the beginning of May 1863 that supervening diseases were noted in the records of the Charlottesville General Hospital. "Register of Patients, General Hospital, Charlottesville, Virginia," vol. 215.

36. Jones, "Observations upon the Losses of the Confederate Armies," pp. 268–75.

37. Jones, "Medical History of the Confederate Army and Navy," p. 115.

38. Ibid., pp. 117–19; Richard B. Stark, "Surgeons and Surgical Care of the Confederate States Army," *Virginia Medical Monthly* 87(1960):231; Cunningham, *Doctors in Gray*, pp. 36–37; Adams, *Doctors in Blue*, pp. 9, 47.

39. These statistics are based on the figures of Livermore and

the report of the Association of the Medical Officers of the Army and Navy of the Confederacy.

40. Jones, "Medical History of the Confederate Army and Navy," pp. 113–14.

41. Nevins, "The Glorious and the Terrible," p. 9.

A Note On Sources

Many sources went into the preparation of this study. While it is based almost exclusively on primary material, numerous secondary sources were profitably consulted. The purpose of this brief note is to call to the reader's attention the most important material made use of in each category.

A. Primary Sources

Primary sources consulted fall into two categories—manuscript and printed. The former is by far the more important, for five indispensable manuscript collections yielded the bulk of the information contained in this volume. These were the Joseph Jones collections at Tulane University in New Orleans and at Louisiana State University at Baton Rouge, the Charles Colcock Jones Papers at Tulane University, and the Charles Colcock Jones, Jr., collections at the University of Georgia in Athens and at Duke University in Durham.

The two sizable collections of Joseph Jones's papers provided the nucleus for this study. The one at Tulane University was the single most important source consulted. Spanning Jones's life, it consists of fourteen hundred pieces of correspondence and more than twelve hundred manuscript and printed items. A wealth of material is contained here. The letters are wondrously informative, shedding a great deal of light not only upon Jones's life but upon the world in which he lived as well. The manuscript and printed material is equally indispensable. Especially valuable were a number of notebooks containing many of Jones's class, lecture, and research notes; copies, frequently in manuscript form, of his publications; many of the Confederate statistics he copied for use in his reports to the surgeon general; manuscript fragments of these reports (including several beautiful hand-drawn colored plates); the manuscript copy of his gangrene report and volumes 1 and 3 of his Andersonville investigations (volume 2 is at Louisiana State University); medical records he collected after the war to write his medical and surgical history of the Confederate army and navy; several manuscript chapters of this work; numerous pamphlets and newspaper clippings that Jones, an inveterate collector, preserved; a microfilm copy of the very valuable journal of Louis Manigault, his wartime secretary; and many fine photographs.

Louisiana State University's collection of Joseph Jones memorabilia is not nearly so extensive. It does, however, contain many important items. This collection is especially rich in material pertaining to Jones's school days and early years as a professional. Many of his class and lecture notes and the entire correspondence with Joseph Henry, the Smithsonian's director, concerning his 1856 article for the institution's *Contributions to Knowledge* are located here. Other items of importance in this collection are the manuscript second volume of Jones's Andersonville investigations and numerous compilations of his Confederate statistics.

The Charles Colcock Jones Papers at Tulane University are ostensibly a collection of the papers of Joseph Jones's father, but in reality they are much more. Consisting of more than five thousand items, this collection contains much valuable material, not just on the career of Charles Colcock Jones but also on Jones's family history. It proved especially useful in recreating Joseph Jones's background, childhood, adolescence, and early manhood. The major part of this collection is a lively correspondence between Charles Colcock Jones and the various members of his immediate and extended families. So impressive are these letters that Robert Manson Myers has edited and published the most informative of them from the Civil War era in *Children of Pride* (New Haven, Conn., 1972), a monumental documentary study of the Jones family between 1854 and 1868.

Of the two collections of the Charles Colcock Jones, Jr., papers, the one at the University of Georgia was the more valuable in the preparation of this study. The collection contains more than three thousand items, mostly of correspondence, pertaining to the career of Charles Colcock Jones, Jr., a noted lawyer and historian. Yet many important insights into the life of Joseph Jones have been gleaned from these letters. Many of those written during the era of the Civil War have been included in Myers' *Children of Pride*. Duke University's collection of Charles Colcock Jones, Jr.'s papers, while helpful, proved less valuable. Consisting primarily of a number of letterpress books, it is largely concerned with the post–Civil War period, a time beyond the scope of this work.

A considerable amount of printed primary material pertaining to Joseph Jones's life exists and was consulted with profit. Jones himself was the author of much of it. A prolific writer, he published over one hundred books and articles during his life. Many of these were either written during or deal to some extent with his Old South career. It would serve no significant purpose to list all of Jones's works that were used, for they have been fully documented at the appropriate places in the text. One, however, does seem sufficiently crucial to the success of this work to single out for special notice; this is his three-volume *Medical and Surgical Memoirs* (New Orleans, La., 1876–1890). Although irritatingly prolix, discursive, and repetitious, this is a major source for the study of Jones's life, containing both biographical material and lengthy discussions of his scientific endeavors and accomplishments.

Publications by various members of the Jones family also provided much valuable information. Charles Colcock Jones's writings on his ministry among the slaves, especially his *Thirteenth Annual Report of the Association for the Religious Instruction of the Religious Instruction of the Negroes in Liberty County* (Savannah, Ga., 1848), were of great importance in analyzing his career. His *Historical Address, Delivered to the Liberty Independent Troop, upon Its Anniversary, February 22, 1856* (Savannah, Ga., 1856) is of interest for the historical background it lays.

Among Charles Colcock Jones, Jr.'s publications, two played important roles in the preparation of this study. These were his *Dead Towns of Georgia* (Savannah, Ga., 1878) and his *Address Delivered at Midway Meeting House in Liberty County, Georgia, on the Second Wednesday in March 1889 on the Occasion of the Relaying of the Corner Stone of a Monument to be Erected in Honor of the Founders of Midway Church and Congregation* (Augusta, Ga., 1889).

Mary Jones, Joseph Jones's mother, collaborated with others in two valuable works. First, she and Robert Quarterman Mallard, her son-in-law, contributed a highly informative chapter on Charles Colcock Jones to John S. Wilson's *The Dead of the Synod of Georgia* (Atlanta, Ga., 1869). Second, Mary Jones and her daughter, Mary Sharpe Jones Mallard, kept a diary during the Union invasion of coastal Georgia during the fall and winter of 1864–1865. The original diary from which the perceptive volume, *Yankees A'Coming* (Tuscaloosa, Ala., 1959), was prepared by

Haskell Moore is preserved in the Charles Colcock Jones Papers at Tulane University.

Finally, Robert Quarterman Mallard, the husband of Mary Sharpe Jones, published two very useful accounts of his childhood in Liberty County with reminiscences of the Jones family: *Plantation Life before Emancipation* (Richmond, Va., 1892) and *Montevideo-Maybank: Some Memoirs of a Southern Christian Household in the Olden Times; or, the Family Life of the Rev. Charles Colcock Jones, D.D., of Liberty County, Ga.* (Richmond, Va., 1898).

Two official and two semiofficial government publications of a primary nature were extensively consulted. The official government publications are the three-volume *Medical and Surgical History of the War of the Rebellion* (Washington, D.C., 1870–1888) prepared under the auspices of the U.S. Surgeon General's Office and the U.S. House of Representatives' *Trial of Henry Wirz* (Washington, D.C., 1868). Of even greater importance were the United States Sanitary Commission's *Sanitary Memoirs of the War of the Rebellion* (New York, 1867–1869) and *Surgical Memoirs of the War of the Rebellion* (New York, 1870–1871). These works sponsored by the semiofficial U.S. Sanitary Commission, each consisting of two volumes, contain Jones's investigations on Andersonville and gangrene respectively.

Various newspapers also furnished important primary material. Those most extensively consulted were the *Daily Chronicle & Sentinel* and the *Daily Constitutionalist* in Augusta and the *Daily Telegraph*, the *Weekly Georgia Telegraph*, and the *Georgia Journal and Messenger* in Macon.

B. Secondary Sources

Secondary sources were consulted to furnish background information, to verify events and developments discussed in the primary material, and to give greater depth and historical perspective to the major points raised in this study. Considering the important role they played, it seems proper that some attention be given to the major secondary sources used in the preparation of this study.

Jones's unique background, as the son of a large planter who was also a leading minister to the slaves, necessitated an examination both of the slave system and of religion in the Old South. Among the many studies examined, those that proved especially valuable included Ulrich B. Phillips's *Life and Labor in the Old South* (Boston, Mass., 1929); Kenneth M. Stampp's *The Peculiar Institution: Slavery in the Ante Bellum South* (New York, 1956); Ralph B. Flanders's *Plantation Slavery in Georgia* (Chapel Hill, N.C., 1933); James Stacy's *History of the Midway Congregational Church, Liberty County, Georgia* (Newnan, Ga., 1899); Carter G. Woodson's *History of the Negro Church*, 2d ed. (Washington, D.C., 1921); Ernest T. Thompson's two-volume *Presbyterians in the South* (Richmond, Va., 1963); and Andrew E. Murray's *Presbyterians and the Negro—A History* (Philadelphia, 1966).

Several studies facilitated the placing of Jones's nineteenth-century education in its proper perspective. The first volume of Daniel W. Hollis's two-volume *University of South Carolina* (Columbia, S.C., 1951–1956) and Thomas J. Wertenbaker's *Princeton, 1746–1896* (Princeton, N.J., 1946) were indispensable aids in the area of his undergraduate education. His professional training in medicine was illumined by William F. Norwood's classic *Medical Education in the United States before the Civil War* (Philadelphia, 1944) and George W. Corner's *Two Centuries of Medicine: A History of the School of Medicine, University of Pennsylvania* (Philadelphia, 1965).

The best brief account of the medical world which Jones entered after his graduation from the University of Pennsylvania in 1856 is provided by Erwin H. Ackerknecht in his *Short History of Medicine*, rev. ed. (New York, 1968). A definitive history of medicine in the American scene has yet to be written, but existing studies that proved useful were Francis R. Packard's two-volume *History of Medicine in the United States* (New York, 1931); Henry B. Shafer's *American Medical Profession, 1783 to 1850* (New York, 1936); Richard H. Shryock's *Medicine and Society in America: 1660–1860* (Ithaca, N.Y., 1962); Joseph F. Kett's *Formation of the American Medical Profession: The Role of Institutions, 1780–1860* (New Haven, Conn., 1968); and William G. Rothstein's *American Physicians in the 19th Century: From Sects to Science* (Baltimore, Md., 1972). There is no full-scale study devoted exclusively to the southern medical profession, which, while sharing many of the same principles and problems with its counterpart in the North, was in several fundamental ways a separate entity. Valuable insights can be obtained from Richard H. Shryock's old but still unsurpassed article "Medical Practice in the Old South" which appeared in

the *South Atlantic Quarterly* in 1940 and John Duffy's brief introduction to states' rights medicine in the Old South, "A Note on
Ante-Bellum Southern Nationalism and Medical Practice,"
which appeared in the *Journal of Southern History* in 1968.

Joseph Jones was more than a physician; he was also one of the
antebellum South's true scientists. It is difficult to separate
physical and biological scientists during much of the nineteenth
century, a condition well illustrated by the fact that many of the
nation's leading scientists were trained as physicians. Still several
studies that focus on the scientific world of the early nineteenth
century were consulted with good results. The best general study
is George H. Daniels's *American Science in the Age of Jackson*
(New York, 1968). T. Cary Johnson, Jr.'s old and patronizing
Scientific Interests in the Old South (New York, 1936) is good for
identifying the South's scientific community. A shorter but more
balanced southern study is Clement Eaton's chapter on the
scientific mind in his *Mind of the Old South*, rev. ed. (Baton
Rouge, La., 1967).

The choice of sources on the Civil War is almost limitless. The
one relied upon in this study is the widely consulted work of
James G. Randall and David Donald, *The Civil War and Reconstruction*, 2d ed., rev. (Lexington, Mass., 1969). T. Conn Bryan's
Confederate Georgia (Athens, Ga., 1953) was a valuable supplement for developments in Jones's home state. The late Allan
Nevin's essay "The Glorious and the Terrible" which appeared
in *Saturday Review* in 1961 was of inestimable value in helping
the author set a tone for the interpretation of Jones's Civil War
investigations. Ovid L. Futch's *History of Andersonville Prison*
(Gainesville, Fla., 1968) is an excellent introduction to conditions
at this large southern prison. The springboard for any study of
Civil War numbers and losses is Thomas L. Livermore's *Numbers
and Losses in the Civil War in America, 1861–65* (New York,
1901). The best statement of the southern position is Randolph
McKim's *Numerical Strength of the Confederate Army* (New York,
1912).

There is no comprehensive account of the medical history of
the Civil War to which Joseph Jones was such an important con-
tributor. Each side, however, has received considerable attention.
George W. Adams's *Doctors in Blue: The Medical History of the
Union Army in the Civil War* (New York, 1952) is superb. Horace
H. Cunningham's *Doctors in Gray: The Confederate Medical Ser-*

vice (Baton Rouge, La., 1958), while not on a par with Adams's volume, is a good source of information about medicine in the Confederacy—and one that gives a good deal of attention to the accomplishments of Joseph Jones. Other useful studies are Stewart Brooks's *Civil War Medicine* (Springfield, Ill., 1966) and Paul E. Steiner's *Diseases in the Civil War: Natural Biological Warfare in 1861–1865* (Springfield, Ill., 1968).

Index

Albemarle County, Va., 144

Altamaha River, 131

American Cyclopaedia: and Civil War numbers and losses, 218

American Journal of the Medical Sciences, 28, 36

American Medical Association: 1859 annual meeting of, 58–61; *Transactions* of, 60–61, 72–74, 249 n.18; mentioned, 23

American Medical Monthly, 72

Amputation. *See* surgery

Andersonville prison: investigations at, 156–60; preparation of report on, 162; confiscation and use of report on, in Wirz trial, 169–76; report on, 178–98; medical topography, 179; conditions in the stockade, 180–83; management of the sick, 183–85; medical statistics, 186; health of the Confederate garrison, 187; principal diseases, 188–96; proposals for reform, 196; exoneration of Confederate authorities, 196–98; mentioned, 145, 199, 230, 271 nn. 31, 34

Anopheles mosquito. *See* Fevers— Malaria

Appomattox Court House, Va.: surrender at, 168; mentioned, 215, 229, 231

Arcadia plantation: description of, 6–7; during the Civil War, 114, 117, 120

Army (Confederate): principal diseases of, 107–10, 224–26; decline of health of, 177, 203–4; effect of ration on health of, 192, 203; Jones preserves the statistics of, 142, 143, 148, 149, 151, 155, 162, 176, 215; combat statistics of, 215–21; medical statistics of, 103–10, 153–54, 223–27; defeat of, 168. *See also* Army of Northern Virginia and Army of Tennessee

Army (Union): Jones's antipathy toward, 116, 135, 164; health of casualties from, 139; depredations of, in Liberty County, 163–66; size of, 215–21

Army Medical Board (for the military districts of South Carolina and Georgia), 128, 129

Army Medical Museum, 171–72

Army of Northern Virginia: Jones's investigations in the hospitals of, 138–44; defeat of, 154; insights into the medical history of, 222

Army of Tennessee: Jones's investigations in the hospitals of, 151, 160–62; during the Atlanta campaign, 150–54, 201; defeat of, 168; mentioned, 145, 163, 198, 204, 264 n.41

Arnold, Richard D.: at Savannah Medical College, 37; friend and benefactor of Jones, 40, 42, 43; mentioned, 93

Association for the Religious Instruction of Negroes in Liberty County, Georgia, 3, 4

Association of the Medical Officers of the Army and Navy of the Confederacy, 228

Athens, Ga.: description of, 46– 47; mentioned, 42, 43, 50, 51, 52, 58, 64, 148

Atlanta, Ga.: campaign for, 150– 54; mentioned, 58, 148, 162, 163, 197, 201

Atlanta campaign, medical history of. *See* Army of Tennessee

Augusta, Ga.: description of, 56; headquarters for Jones's Civil War investigations, 137; threat of invasion of, by Sherman, 166; Jones returns to, at the end of the Civil War, 176; mentioned, 43, 48, 51, 57, 64, 67, 69, 91, 92, 94, 97, 98, 112, 114, 117, 121, 122, 132,

*This book has been composed in Monotype
Cochin named for Nicholas Cochin,
the 18th-century French type cutter
and copperplate engraver. Versions
of Cochin have been produced by the
Peignot Foundry in France (1912),
Lanston Monotype in America (1921),
and English Monotype (1927). The
American version by Sol Hess is
the one used here for the text.*

*Composition & printing by
Heritage Printers, Inc.*

Design by Jonathan Greene

W. HOLD. N

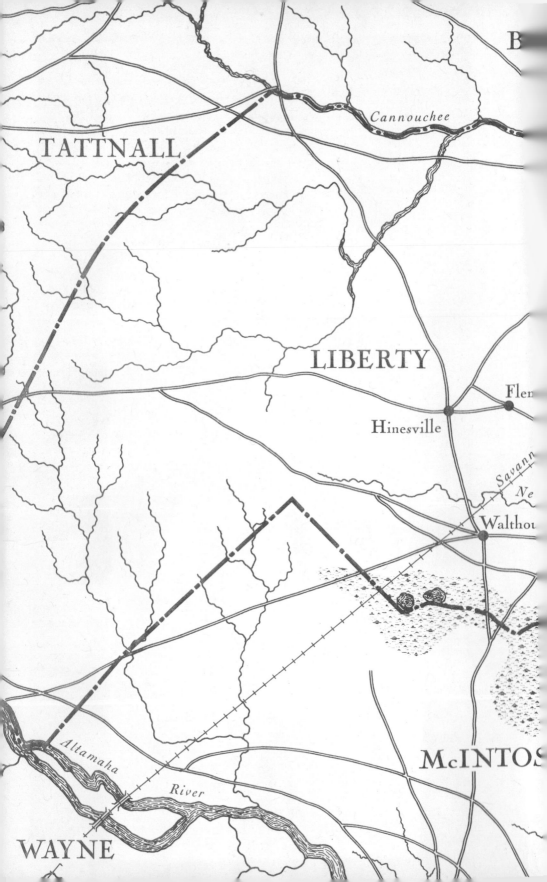